Z
1808
N4   Price,
P74   The Guiana Maroons...

76-841

DATE DUE   JUL   2000

		JUN	2004
		JUL 09	
		JUL X X 2015	

DUE DATE
11/30/09

THE GUIANA MAROONS

JOHNS HOPKINS STUDIES IN ATLANTIC HISTORY AND CULTURE
Richard Price and Franklin W. Knight, General Editors

THE GUIANA MAROONS

A HISTORICAL AND BIBLIOGRAPHICAL INTRODUCTION

Richard Price

THE JOHNS HOPKINS UNIVERSITY PRESS
Baltimore and London

Manufactured in the United States of America

The Johns Hopkins University Press, Baltimore, Maryland 21218
The Johns Hopkins Press Ltd., London

Library of Congress Catalog Card Number 76-8498
ISBN 0-8018-1840-0

Library of Congress Cataloging in Publication data
will be found on the last printed page of this book.

*For Sranan, the new nation,
in the hope that each of its population groups
may freely choose its own destiny*

CONTENTS

PART THREE

A BIBLIOGRAPHY OF THE GUIANA MAROONS, 1667-1975

TABLES

FIGURES

PREFACE

The past few years have seen greatly increased interest, by scholars and the public alike, in maroon societies—those remarkable communities formed by rebel slaves throughout the Americas. This book is intended as a general introduction to the maroons of Suriname, the largest surviving maroon populations in the Hemisphere. It is written in the hope that these courageous and dignified peoples, now striving so hard to adjust to changing political realities, may be more completely understood, both within Suriname and abroad.

The book covers more than three centuries of Suriname history, from the founding of a permanent colony in 1651 to the achievement of independence in 1975. It is divided into three parts. The first provides a historical framework within which to approach the study of the Suriname maroons; the second constitutes an extended bibliographical essay on the literature written about maroons in the Guianas; and the final section lists the more than 1350 relevant references. As discussed in the introduction to Part Three, the list itself was compiled over a five-year period; Part Two was drafted during the summer of 1974; and Part One was written during 1975, though it draws on materials that have been in preparation for several years. Sidney W. Mintz made a very helpful reading of the first two parts. Sally Price has contributed to many phases of this project over the years, sharing fully her knowledge of Bush Negro societies. As with our other publications, we hope that this book in some small way may serve as a token of our gratitude to, and solidarity with, the Saramaka people, whose guests we have so often been.

THE GUIANA MAROONS

 PART ONE

A HISTORICAL FRAMEWORK

Part One attempts to provide a general framework within which to approach the study of Suriname's maroon societies. The first section presents a brief bird's-eye view of these societies, intended for the reader approaching them for the first time.[1] The remaining four sections constitute an extended argument for the relevance of a historical perspective to the understanding of these maroon cultures and societies. Much of the data cited comes from research still in progress, and the findings cannot be considered definitive. Yet it is hoped that these preliminary incursions into colonial history will stimulate debate among other specialists, and result some day in greater understanding of the ways that maroons, deep in the forests of Suriname, created some of the most extraordinary cultures and societies in the Hemisphere.

OVERVIEW

For more than four centuries, maroon societies—communities created by runaway slaves—were a widespread concomitant of plantation life in the Americas. Ranging from tiny bands that survived less than a year to powerful states having thousands of members and surviving for generations or even centuries, these communities still form semi-independent enclaves in several parts of the Hemisphere, remaining fiercely proud of their maroon origins and, in some cases at least, faithful to unique cultural traditions which were forged during the earliest days of Afro-American history.

Increasingly, scholars are recognizing that maroons and their communities hold a special significance for students of slave societies. For while maroons represented, from one perspective, the antithesis of all that slavery stood for,

---

1. This section draws heavily on my earlier, more extensive overview of maroon societies in the Americas (Price 1973), to which the reader is directed for general bibliographical references.

they were at the same time everywhere an embarrassingly visible part of these systems. Just as the very nature of plantation slavery implied violence and resistance, the wilderness setting of early New World plantations made *marronage* and the existence of organized maroon communities a ubiquitous reality. Throughout Afro-America, such communities stood out as a heroic challenge to white authority, and as the living proof of "the existence of a slave consciousness that refused to be limited by the whites' conception and manipulation of it" (Parris 1972:1; see also Mintz 1971).

It was marronage on the grand scale, with individual fugitives banding together to create independent communities of their own, that struck most directly at the foundations of the plantation system, presenting military and economic threats which often taxed the colonists to their very limits. In a remarkable number of cases throughout the Americas, the whites were forced to bring themselves to sue their former slaves for peace. Typically, such treaties—which we know of from Brazil, Colombia, Cuba, Ecuador, Española, Jamaica, and Mexico, as well as Suriname—offered maroon communities their freedom, recognized their territorial integrity, and made some provision for meeting their economic needs, demanding in return an agreement to end all hostilities toward the plantations, to return all future runaways and, often, to aid the whites in hunting them down. Of course, many maroon communities never reached this stage, being crushed by massive force of arms; and even when treaties were proposed they were sometimes refused or quickly violated. Nevertheless, new maroon communities seemed to appear almost as quickly as the old ones could be exterminated, and they remained what one author called "the chronic plague" of plantation societies right up to final Emancipation, after which they were in most cases gradually absorbed into the surrounding rural population.

For some 300 years, the Guianas have been the classic setting for maroon communities. Though local maroons in French and British Guiana were wiped out by the end of the eighteenth century, the maroons of Suriname, known as "Bush Negroes," have long been the Hemisphere's largest maroon population. Except perhaps for Haiti, these have been the most highly developed independent societies and cultures in the history of Afro-America. Unlike the countless maroon communities elsewhere, which were brought to their knees by an overpowering force of arms, or those which, by gradual assimilation into the general population, are disappearing as sociocultural entities, the Bush Negro tribes are still in many respects vigorous and flourishing societies, though it is less easy today than it was a decade ago to call them "states within a state."[2]

---

2. A note on terminology may be appropriate here. The English word "maroon," like the French *marron*, derives from Spanish *cimarrón*. As used in the New World,

The ancestors of the Bush Negro tribes escaped from the plantations of coastal Suriname between the mid-seventeenth and late eighteenth centuries. The three initial groups, after more than a half century of brutal guerrilla warfare against colonial and European troops, signed peace treaties with the government in the 1760s. The late eighteenth century witnessed new hostilities, culminating in the formation of three more tribes. For the next hundred years these societies were allowed to develop more or less in isolation, yet they always remained dependent on coastal society for certain manufactured items, from cloth and pots to axes and guns. During the wars, such goods had been obtained by raiding plantations; following the treaties, the government instead supplied them as periodic "tribute," allowing in addition brief trading trips to the coast; during the last hundred years, Bush Negroes have engaged heavily in logging and coastal wage labor. Today, depopulation due to the emigration of men to the coast has become a serious problem, Christian missions have brought education and medical care to some remote areas, and there are even some scores of Bush Negroes living, working, and continuing their education in the Netherlands. Nevertheless, of all the maroon societies in the Americas, those of the Bush Negroes have been most successful in forging their own destinies. And even in 1975, it would not be hard for a casual visitor in some Bush Negro villages to imagine himself a full continent and several centuries away.

Today, there are six Bush Negro tribes: the Djuka and Saramaka (each 15,000 to 20,000 people), the Matawai, Aluku, and Paramaka (each closer to

---

cimarrón originally referred to domestic cattle which had taken to the hills in Hispaniola (Parry and Sherlock 1965:14) and soon after to Indian slaves who had escaped from the Spaniards as well (Franco 1968:92). By the end of the 1530s, it was already beginning to refer primarily to Afro-American runaways (Franco 1968:93; see also Guillot 1961:38), and had strong connotations of "fierceness," of being "wild" and "unbroken" (Friederici 1960:191-92). During the seventeenth and early eighteenth centuries the Dutch in Suriname generally used the terms *marron* or *weglooper* (runaway). But the official recognition of the free maroon societies brought into common use the term *Boschneger* (Bush Negro). In the draft treaty of 1749 and in subsequent documents, *marron* and *weglooper* tended to be used for illegal runaways, and *Boschneger* for those whose freedom had been confirmed by the treaties. This may help explain the strong Saramaka resistance during the 1960s to attempts by coastal Creole black nationalists to change official usage from *Boschneger* to *Boslandcreool* (in an attempt to identify Bush Negroes for political purposes with the Creoles). Saramaka elders told me forcefully that they were not "Creoles," and that "Bush Negroes" had fought and won their freedom, in contrast to Creoles, who simply "took the whip" until the Dutch crown saw fit to emancipate them (see also Simons 1960a and 1960b). And it is worth noting that the various Bush Negro political, youth, and cultural organizations that have sprung up in the last decade choose *Bosneger* as their rallying term (e.g., the Algemene Bosneger Jongeren Organisatie, the Vereniging voor Bosnegers Kunst en Cultuur, the Progressieve Bosnegers Partij). In this book, I use "Bush Negro" and "Suriname maroon" interchangeably—the first out of respect for an "internal" perspective, the second in a bow to scholarly convention. Both terms, it seems to me, have earned the right to represent a heritage of heroism and dignity.

2,000), and the Kwinti (fewer than 500).[3] Tribal territories are shown in the sketch map (Fig. 1), though it must be added that increasingly large numbers of Bush Negroes are now living in and around Paramaribo.[4] These societies, though formed under broadly similar historical and ecological conditions, nevertheless display significant variations in everything from language, diet, and dress to patterns of marriage, residence, and migratory wage labor. From a cultural point of view, the greatest differences were traditionally between the Saramaka, Matawai, and Kwinti, on the one hand, and the Djuka, Aluku, and Paramaka, on the other. However, the differential development of Suriname's interior by government and mining interests is complicating this picture today.

To generalize broadly: Villages, which average one hundred to two hundred residents, consist of a core of matrilineally related kinsmen plus some spouses and descendants of lineage men. Matriliny dominates descent ideology, with "matriclans" and "matrilineages" (the precise nature of which varies from tribe to tribe) forming the basic units of the formal social structure. Since the colonial government signed treaties with the Djuka, Saramaka, and Matawai in the mid-eighteenth century, and placed the Aluku, Paramaka, and Kwinti in "protectorate" relationships under these treaty tribes during the nineteenth century, a loose framework of indirect rule has obtained. Each tribe, except the tiny Kwinti, has a government-approved Paramount Chief (*gaamá, granman*)—who from an internal tribal perspective might traditionally have been better glossed as "king"—a series of headmen (*kabitêni*), and other public officials. Traditionally, the role of these officials in political and social control was exercised in a context replete with oracles, spirit possession, and other forms of divination, though today the government is increasingly asserting its presumed right to intervene directly in the affairs of the tribes, and some of the sacred base of the tribal officials' power is being eroded. In general, Bush Negroes enjoy an extremely rich ritual life, and the

---

3. Today, because of its colonial connotations, the term "tribe" is increasingly avoided by many anthropologists. In this book I use it selectively and in a technical sense, to imply a combination of segmentary organization, territorial control, and the strong interpenetration of principles of kinship and locality with economic, political, and religious life (see Sahlins 1968). When referring to the early agglomerations of runaways in the forest, I more often use such terms as "band," "group" or "community"; in reference to the eighteenth-century posttreaty period, when sociopolitical institutions were still very much in flux, I tend—following contemporary usage—to use "nation" or "people"; and for the last century and a half, during which these societies display the technical features outlined above, I use "tribe." Today, this latter term is becoming less and less accurate as a label, as Suriname becomes a nation in its own right and as the "tribal" institutions of the past 150 years are in rapid change. Soon, in some contexts at least, it may be more accurate to speak of the six Bush Negro "ethnic groups." And the day may not be too far off when together they may best be viewed as a single ethnic group within Suriname's pluralistic social matrix.

4. For example, Green estimates this proportion to be as high as 50 to 60 percent of the total Matawai population (1974:7).

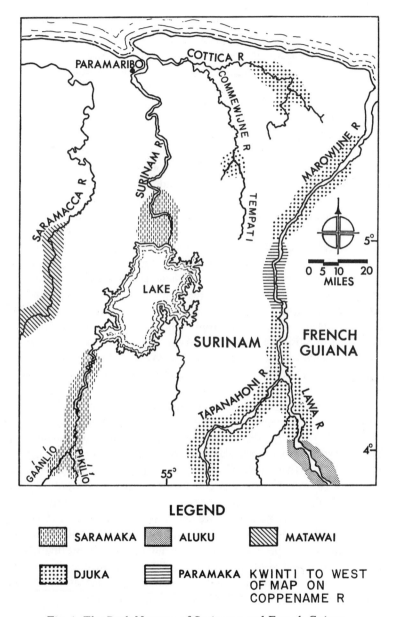

LEGEND

SARAMAKA	ALUKU	MATAWAI
DJUKA	PARAMAKA	KWINTI TO WEST OF MAP ON COPPENAME R

Fig. 1. The Bush Negroes of Suriname and French Guiana.

NOTE: This map is schematic only. Among the details not shown are a Kwinti enclave in Matawai territory, several mixed villages of Matawais, Saramakas, and Djukas on the Lower Saramacca River, and villages of Sara Kreek Djukas, displaced by the artificial lake, just north of the dam.

complex series of shrines and cults serve as foci for groups of residentially dispersed kinsmen. Their economy has long been based on a combination of periodic male wage labor on the coast and swidden horticulture and hunting and fishing; material culture includes both selected coastal imports and a wide variety of products fashioned by local techniques. Unusually skillful artists, performers, and orators, Bush Negroes in general exhibit a strongly aesthetic approach to life.

Today, Bush Negro societies are facing severe pressures for sociocultural change. While it may once have been easy for them to maintain a world view rooted in isolationism and in a belief in their superiority over both whites and coastal blacks, the recent rise in the standard of living on the coast, and a growing sense of their political powerlessness in the national arena have made them increasingly aware that their societies have, in some respects at least, been left behind. The construction by Alcoa and the Suriname government of a giant hydroelectric project, which flooded almost half of Saramaka tribal territory in the 1960s, was only the most dramatic of many recent events to demonstrate to Bush Negroes their ultimate powerlessness. And the continued sadness and poverty of the planned towns that shelter some 4000 refugees from the dam is a constant reminder of these events and their implications. Having now become involved, almost in spite of themselves, in the party politics of Suriname, and finding themselves dependent on the decisions of corporations based thousands of miles away, Bush Negroes are fast realizing that their traditional isolationist strategy holds little promise for the future.

Indeed, as this book goes to press, the government of the newly independent nation of Suriname is in the initial stages of implementing a "development plan" that calls for the forced consolidation of the Bush Negro populations into several massive new planned towns in the interior, where they will, presumably, have their level of civilization "raised" as they become more fully integrated into the emerging new nation. That the extraordinary sociocultural achievements of the Bush Negroes, created under conditions of such adversity, should be vulnerable to this development plan seems no less appalling because we have already seen the dreary scenario played out in other parts of the world. But in this case, at least, the outcome is still not finally sealed, and we can hope that political, economic, and even academic pressures may bring about a reconsideration, and an ultimate plan that affords all Bush Negroes genuine freedom of choice in determining their future.

HISTORICAL DEMOGRAPHY OF THE
PLANTATION COLONY OF SURINAME

Although there were a number of earlier, abortive attempts at colonization, the first large-scale, permanent settlement in what is now Suriname was made in 1651 by one-hundred pioneers sent out by Lord Willoughby from Barbados. (For population trends summarized in this paragraph, see Fig. 2.) The English colony reached its peak by the beginning of 1665, when it had forty to fifty profitable sugar estates, a white population of about 1500, and a slave force made up of some 3000 Africans and 400 American Indians (Byam 1667:199; Warren 1667:17; Voorhoeve and Lichtveld 1975:3). However, during the next year, an epidemic ravaged the colony, and 200 of the settlers left with some of their slaves; at about the same time, some 200 Portuguese Jewish refugees arrived from Brazil via Holland and Cayenne with many of their own slaves and took up residence as planters, joining a much smaller group of Sephardim, some of whom had been there since before the establishment of Willoughby's settlement (Byam 1667; van Dantzig 1968:77; Nassy 1788, I:11-12; Rens 1953:25, 29; van der Straaten 1973; van Sijpesteijn 1854:4, 7; Voorhoeve and Lichtveld 1975:2). In early 1667, the colony was captured by the Zeelander Abraham Crijnssen and, several months later, was formally ceded to the Dutch as part of the Treaty of Breda. However, later that year an English fleet (apparently unaware of the treaty) invaded, sacked, and ruined most of the major estates (Nassy 1788, I:26). During the next twelve years, almost all the remaining English settlers (about 1000 people) left Suriname, taking with them more than 2000 African slaves, who represented all but a handful of those imported prior to 1667 (Voorhoeve and Lichtveld 1975:2-3).[5] During the half century following the Dutch acquisition of Suriname, a new and remarkably diverse European population established roots, and by 1715 they numbered some 2000—Dutch, French, Portuguese Jews, Germans, Scandinavians, and others. Meanwhile, importations from Africa had boosted the slave population to about 22,000. Between 1715 and 1735, increased numbers of imports from Africa brought the black population to some 50,000, the size it was to maintain, with little variation, until the end of the slave trade in the early nineteenth century.[6]

---

5. The British were prohibited from removing slaves imported after the Treaty of Breda.

6. There remains in my mind some doubt about the precise date at which the slave force reached this figure. Standard accounts (e.g., Benjamins and Snelleman 1914-17:665; van Lier 1971:27) are based on a single documentary source dating from 1785 that gives the 1738 slave population as 51,096. However, data based on slave import figures—which were low during the early and mid-1730s—suggest either that the 50,000 figure may have been reached by the 1720s or that it may not have been achieved until after the compensatory high level of imports of the late 1730s and early and mid-1740s (see below). Final settlement of the question of the role of "interlopers" in the Dutch trade—considered insignificant by Postma (1970) but estimated as having one-third to one-half of the trade by others (see Emmer 1972:740)—may be necessary before the shape of the proposed growth curve can be considered definitive. Nevertheless, I have recently found independent evidence that supports the positing of a relatively small slave force in 1700 that grew substantially during the next quarter century. Not only did Suriname's sugar production more than double during this period (see Nassy 1788, II:88-90), but the changing ratios of slave population to sugar production in Jamaica and Barbados over the course of the late seventeenth and early eighteenth centuries (Dunn 1972: 203; Sheridan 1973:487) indicate curves almost identical to that in Fig. 1.

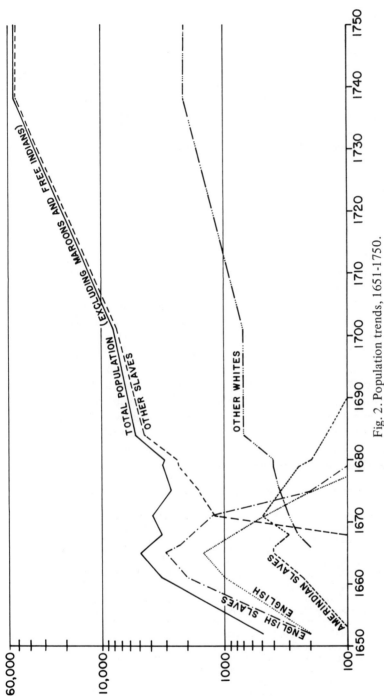

Fig. 2. Population trends, 1651-1750.

NOTE: Published estimates of prenineteenth-century population figures for Suriname are often discrepant and tend to use original sources only selectively. My data are by no means a definitive rendering, though I have tried to trace as many of the figures as possible back to their original sources. It should be mentioned that most contemporary figures or estimates are for a single year and often for a single population group, so that different and often haphazard criteria for counting are involved. Moreover, many figures are biased or interested—based on records for head taxes, war or insurance losses, and so forth. To juxtapose such figures on a single graph should not be taken as more than an indication of major trends.

SOURCES INCLUDE: Benjamins and Snelleman 1914-17:613; 665; van der Linde 1966:42, 50; Rens 1953:79; Voorhoeve and Lichtveld 1975: 2-3; Warren 1667:17.

A closer look at the growth of the slave population will help disclose some of the characteristics that lent Suriname slave society its distinctive shape. The key data are summarized in Table 1.

The most striking feature of Suriname's demographic history is the extraordinary cost of its slave system in human lives. Between 1668 and 1823, some 300,000 to 325,000 African slaves were imported into the colony; yet at the end of this period the total black population of Suriname was only about 50,000.[7] The North American colonies are believed to have imported a not dissimilar number of slaves (427,000), during a comparable period; yet in 1825 the United States had a black population of some 2 million! Even Jamaica and Saint-Domingue, perhaps the two sugar colonies most notorious for their rapid consumption of human lives, did not compare to Suriname in this regard; Jamaica imported some 748,000 slaves and had a black population in 1830 of 357,000, while Saint-Domingue imported 864,000 to achieve a population of 480,000 on the eve of the Revolution (population figures from Curtin 1969:78-79, 268; Craton 1975:275). As one observer noted for Suriname,

> In order to increase production, the slaves are driven to the breaking point. If they collapse under the burden, [they] . . . buy others . . . . In this manner, we have seen some plantations swallow as many as *four slave complements* in a period of twenty-five years [Simons 1934:300, his italics].

In terms of its wastage of human life, then, Suriname appears to have the dubious distinction of standing near one extreme among the major plantation colonies of the New World.

The large discrepancy between deaths and births of Suriname slaves, coupled with the very high rate of importation, produced a slave population with an unusually high proportion of Africans at almost every period in its history. Indeed, during the sixty years following the Dutch takeover of 1667, the number of Africans imported *in each ten-year period* amounted to between 110 percent and 220 percent of the total slave population at the beginning of that same decade (see Table 1, above).

Throughout the first one hundred years of the colony's history, more than 90 percent of the slave population was African-born. Even more striking, at any time until the mid-eighteenth century, over half the slave population consisted of Africans who had arrived in Suriname within the previous decade; and well into that century, over one-third of the slaves had left Africa

---

7. My total import figures are comprised of 1600 imports from 1668-70; 146,000 from 1671-1750; 100,000 to 125,000 (using a figure of 4 to 5 percent net annual decrease) from 1751-1800; 30,000 from 1801-13; and 25,000 from 1814-23 (cf. van Lier 1971:124-25).

Table 1. Black Population Growth 1671-1750

	Black Population 1st Year of Decade	Average Annual Increase	As a %	Average Annual Slave Imports	As a %	Average Annual Net Decrease	As a %	Suriname-born Slaves, 1st Year of Decade	As a %
1671-80	1,200[a]	160	13	246	20.5	90		40	3
1681-90	2,800	230	8	434	15.5	210	7.5	90	3
1691-1700	5,100[b]	240	5	638	12.5	380		250	5
1701-10	7,500	1100	15	1650	22	500		600	8
1711-20	18,000[c]	1100	6.1	2340	13	1210	6.7	1000	6
1721-30	29,000[c]	1100	3.7	3190	11	1940		1950	7
1731-40	40,000[c]	1000	2.5	3600	9	2680		3850	10
1741-50	50,000	0	0	2500	5	2500	5	5000	10

[a]This figure excludes those slaves owned by the English, removed from the colony by 1680 (see Fig. 2).

[b]Extrapolated from 1681 and 1701 figures. Imports during the 1680s would have been at a higher rate, if one accepts the statement of Oudschans Dentz (1938:106) that in one three-year period, 1683-85, ten ships with 4327 slaves arrived in Suriname.

[c]Extrapolated from 1701 and 1740 figures. I have chosen this rough extrapolation because a number of facts that would be necessary for a more exact model are missing for this period. These are, then, average figures, and are not intended to be exact for any particular subperiod. It appears, for example, that in the waning years of the West India Company monopoly (the early and mid-1730s) total imports may have averaged only about 2000 per year (using the figures in Hartsinck 1770:740, augmented by 5 percent—see Postma 1970:104-5, 181), and that in the period 1738-47—encompassing some of the best years of the Dutch trade (Emmer 1972:741)—West India Company shipments were supplemented by an annual average of about 2250 slaves brought in by private traders (Hartsinck 1770:740, with average-slaves-per-shipment figure taken from Postma 1970:151). The unresolved question of the role of interlopers (see n. 6, above) further clouds this picture. Similarly, though I indicate a constant slave population of 50,000 for the second half of the eighteenth century, this figure at times may actually have reached as high as 58,000 and as low as 45,000 (Benjamins and Snelleman 1914-17:665; Nassy 1788, II:40). Such fluctuations, however important, do not seem crucial for the purposes of this study.

NOTE: This table represents a model of Suriname's slave demography through time, and is based on historical sources as well as inferences from demographic data from elsewhere in the Caribbean. Figures for average annual net decrease were arrived at (1) for 1671-1700, with the aid of Craton's discussion of Jamaica in its early years (see, in particular, 1975:268 and n. 45); (2) for 1701-40, with the aid of Curtin's 1673-1703 Jamaica data (1969:58-59); and (3) for 1740 onward, using several Suriname estimates, including those summarized by van Lier (1971:169). The relevance of the Jamaica data inheres in the similarity of the demographic characteristics of the early slave populations in those two societies, and in the great similarity of the growth curve for the slave population in Jamaica between 1673 and 1703 (when it went from 9500 to 45,000) and that for Suriname between 1701 and 1735 (when it went from 7500 to about 47,000). The 6.7 percent figure is an *average* estimate for the 1701-40 period; the real value probably went from close to 9 percent at the beginning to about 5 percent at the end. It is worth noting that part of the reason that Suriname's annual net decrease figures are elevated compared to those of most other colonies is the prevalence of marronage, which probably accounted for 10 to 15 percent of the annual net decreases. At every period, the figures for average annual slave imports, derived from those for annual population increase and annual net decrease, fit well within my expectations based on independent data on actual sample cargos shipped to Suriname.

The figures on Suriname-born slaves (the two right-hand columns) derive from a model based in part on the birth rates in Craton's Jamaica data (1975:284), and estimates of age-specific mortality rates for Suriname. (Note that in Jamaica, the native-born population grew to 10 percent of the slave force soon after the end of the thirty-year buildup to 45,000 slaves.)

11

Table 2. "Africanness" of Suriname Population 1690-1770

	Left Africa within Past 5 Years	Left Africa within Past 10 Years	Born in Africa	Total Black Population
1690	1,714 (35%)	3,030 (62%)	4,636 (95%)	4,870
1710	6,518 (39%)	11,550 (64%)	15,990 (95%)	16,900
1730	12,640 (32%)	22,400 (56%)	35,240 (91%)	38,900
1740	14,220 (28%)	25,200 (50%)	45,000 (90%)	50,000
1770	10,000 (20%)	17,500 (35%)	35,000 (70%)	50,000

NOTE: In the absence of data that would permit the construction of reliable mortality curves for cohorts of slaves through time, I utilize two straight-line extrapolations, for purposes of illustration. For the first column, mortality by year n was estimated at 35 percent for slaves imported in year n-5, 28% for those in year n-4 ... 7 percent for those in year n-1. For the second column, mortality was estimated at 50 percent for slaves imported in year n-10, 45 percent in year n-9 ... 5 percent in year n-1. The 1770 "African-born" figure is an estimate based on applying a birth rate of 1.4 (see Craton 175:284) to the earlier figures.

within the previous five years (see Table 2). (For rough comparison, one might note that in the North American colonies, native-born blacks already outnumbered Africans by 1680, and that a century later Africans made up only 20 percent of the black population—Fogel and Engerman 1974:23.) On the plantations in Suriname, the population's closeness to Africa must have been even more striking than the figures in Table 2 would suggest, for it was general policy to keep Creole slaves in the capital, and to send new imports immediately to the hinterland (Wolbers 1861:123; Buschkens 1973:54). It follows from this that the plantation population was not only overwhelmingly African, but that it also must have been disproportionately male, and disproportionately adult. Until 1735, more than 70 percent of the total imports to Suriname were male, and children constituted under 7 percent (see Postma 1970:104, 179-80); even after the planters began more seriously to encourage breeding as a replacement strategy in the period after 1735, the proportion of female imports did not rise above 40 percent, nor that of children above 22 percent (*ibid.*).

All slave populations in the Americas shared—at least in their early periods—several notable demographic features: high proportions of men to women, adults to children, young adults to the elderly, and Africans to Creoles. The statistics that I have presented above, however rough in an absolute sense, should serve at least to suggest that the slave population of Suriname retained these "skewed" or "aberrant" characteristics much more strongly, and for a much longer time, than almost any other colony in the Hemisphere. And I shall argue, in a later section, that these demographic features played a major role in influencing the ultimate shape of Suriname's maroon societies as well.

Table 3. African Provenience of Dutch Slaves

	1640s-1700	1701-1725	1726-1735	1736-1795
Windward Coast	–	–	4%	49%
Gold Coast	2%	17%	29%	26%
Slave Coast	64%	50%	33%	1%
Loango/Angola	34%	33%	33%	24%

NOTE: For present purposes, these four areas are defined as follows: The "Windward Coast," which stretches from just south of the Gambia all the way to Assini, corresponds to the coastal regions of the modern states of Guinea-Bissau, Guinea, Sierra Leone, Liberia, and Ivory Coast (and thereby encompasses Curtin's [1969] "Sierra Leone," and "Windward Coast" areas). My "Gold Coast" is roughly coterminous with modern Ghana, stretching from Assini in the west to the Volta in the east. My "Slave Coast" corresponds to the coastal regions of present-day Togo and Dahomey. My "Loango/Angola" stretches from Cape Lopez south to the Orange River (corresponding to Curtin's "Central Africa" region), with the Dutch trade focused on the area between Cape Lopez and the mouth of the Congo.

As for the African provenience of Suriname slaves at different periods, our knowledge is still far from complete. Yet the latest findings suggest substantial revisions of the standard accounts in terms of the relative importance of various geographic regions and in terms of traditional assessments of relative tribal homogeneity (see Price 1975).

From the founding of the colony until about 1735, the Dutch West India Company virtually monopolized the Dutch slave trade and was almost the sole supplier of slaves to Suriname. Even during the initial English period of Suriname's colonization, the slaves—almost all of whom, except for the maroons, were later removed from Suriname—had been supplied largely by the Dutch West India Company. (Curtin notes that "up to 1663, the slave trade to Barbados was practically a Dutch monopoly" [1969; cf. also Bridenbaugh and Bridenbaugh 1972:245, 248]; and the Dutch eagerly supplied the English planters in Suriname as well, directly from Africa [Rens 1953:79], and possibly via their slave depots at Curaçao also [van Dantzig 1968:77].) After 1735, when the so-called Period of Free Trade got under way (Postma 1970:44-45), the trade to Suriname diversified, but it is still possible, on the basis of archival records examined recently by historians, to present a preliminary summary of the African ports of origin for the slaves—a summary that is probably most reliable for the pre-1735 period. Table 3 offers a rough summary of the ports of origin for slaves shipped by the Dutch between the 1640s and 1795 (based largely on Postma 1970:110, 133, 184, 188, et passim, and Postma 1975).[8]

8. Postma's recent work (1970, 1975) is the first quantitative analysis of the Dutch slave trade to shed much light on the problem of slave provenience, but it was not intended to present a picture of the slave trade from the perspective of Suriname. For a

The most important challenge raised by these data is the suggested down-ward revision of the proportion of slaves coming to Suriname from the Gold Coast, especially during the early years of the colony. We now know that during the seventeenth century, the infamous Dutch castles along the Gold Coast, such as Elmina, were centers of trade mainly in commodities *other than slaves* (in particular, gold). As Postma's painstaking review of the records reveals, prior to 1700 "it seems unlikely that more than three or four WIC [West India Company] slavers acquired their cargo on the Gold Coast" (1970:184). (Note that this would represent only about 2 percent of the approximately 180 Dutch shipments for this period [Postma 1970:97].) And though the Gold Coast was being transformed into a major slave exporter during the first decades of the eighteenth century, it seems to have become really important, numerically, in the Dutch trade only toward the 1720s (Postma 1970:134, 184), when it finally began to rival the Slave Coast as the major supplier to the West India Company. A second point of interest is that during the seventeenth century the Dutch substantially bypassed many slav-ing regions exploited by other Europeans, such as Senegambia, Sierra Leone, the Grain and Ivory Coasts, and the Bight of Biafra (Postma 1970:29-30). Third, it is worth noting that during the course of the eighteenth century, the focus of the Dutch trade on the Guinea Coast moved gradually but persist-ently westward until, by the end of the century, more than half of their slaves were coming from the broad region which Postma calls the Windward Coast. Finally, these data reveal that Bantu-speaking slaves, from Loango/Angola, made up a steady one-fourth to one-third of all imports *at every period of Suriname's history,* making them in all probability the single most important group of imports from a quantitative viewpoint.

As to the precise tribal or ethnic identity of the slaves filtering through the ports of these various slaving regions, a good deal still remains obscure. But even the preliminary attempts to deal with this enormously complex problem—from Herskovits 1941:33-53 and Aguirre Beltrán 1946 to Patterson 1967 and Curtin 1969—permit the drawing up of tentative tribal lists for each of the major slaving regions. Though the details of these lists are not germane for present purposes, I shall mention two findings of particular relevance for understanding the trade to Suriname. First, the Windward Coast—though "one of the longest stretches of coastline where the Dutch slaved" (Postma 1970:189)—was not exploited uniformly. A sample of fifty-six Dutch ships suggests that perhaps 50 percent of the Windward Coast slaves were shipped from Cape Lahu, and nearly 20 percent from the region around the town of River Cess (Postma 1970:187). Because of this "eastern bias," there must

general review of the literature on the Dutch trade, see Emmer 1972. I would suggest that a careful study, using written records of the slave trade to Suriname and comparable to, for example, the work now being done by Debien and his associates for Saint-Dominigue (see, for references, Fouchard 1972) still remains to be undertaken.

have been many more cultural (and linguistic) affinities between Postma's "Windward Coast" and "Gold Coast" than one would otherwise expect (see also Postma 1975 and Curtin 1975).[9] Second, while the Ewe-speaking peoples of the Slave Coast can be said to exhibit considerable cultural homogeneity, a significant number of the slaves shipped by the Dutch through their ports came from wars with their eastern neighbors, particularly the Yoruba (often called, in the literature, Nagos).

Further important light can be thrown on slave provenience by viewing the problem from the Suriname side of the ocean, though present knowledge does not yet permit quantification here. One important finding based on this approach is that there were *some* slaves imported from areas which were, from a gross demographic viewpoint, touched little by the Dutch trade. For example, in one brief period during the late seventeenth century, there were three shiploads of slaves brought to Suriname from "the Calabar" (in the Bight of Biafra, normally little trafficked by Dutch slavers—van der Linde 1966:91); and "Calabari" slaves were well-enough known to the planters to permit generalizations about their alleged "national character" (van der Linde 1966:91; Benjamins and Snelleman 1914-17:638). Moreover, during the English period, "Cromantees" were certainly present in some numbers— Aphra Behn makes much of them in her novel about Suriname (1688), and Jermes, an English-period maroon leader discussed later in Part One, is known to have been a "Coromantijn" (Hartsinck 1770:755).[10] There were, then, always exceptions to the general picture presented in Table 3.

Nevertheless, taken as a whole, the lists of African "nations" compiled in colonial Suriname add nuance without contradicting the basic data on slave provenience compiled from the African perspective. Planters and slave dealers in Suriname (as elsewhere) showed a keen interest in the "characteristics" of slaves from different regions, and there are more than a half-dozen historical works which discuss the slaves using these colonial categories. Such lists are

---

9. Philip D. Curtin, in a personal communication (1973), reported on ongoing research relevant to this point: "I have done some further recalculations based on Postma's and some other new data, and have tried to reconstruct the probable route of the supply to Cape Lahu. The slaves shipped from that point appear to have come not so much from the immediate coastal area as from the further interior. This means that they would almost certainly have passed through Baule country on the way, in which case they would, of course, be Akan, like the people of the southern Gold Coast. On the other hand, I have not encountered any evidence yet to suggest that the shipped slaves, as opposed to those who shipped them, were Baule. They may well have been people following down this trade route from wars further north, particularly those involved in the formation of the kingdom of Kong." On this subject, see now also Curtin 1975:121.

10. In seventeenth- and early eighteenth-century Suriname, "Calabari" seems to have meant slaves shipped through Kalabari, that is New (rather than Old) Calabar; they would, then, more likely have included a predominance of, say, Ibo or Ijo than Efik or Ibibio (see Barbot 1732:380-83; Curtin 1969:188). "Coromantijn," a designation derived from the Dutch fort at Koromantin, referred in Suriname to Fanti, Ashanti, and members of a large number of other interior Gold Coast tribes.

problematical, however, not only because they provide no quantification but also because the major ones (Hartsinck 1770:919-22 [see Price and Price 1972:13]; Stedman 1796, I:207, II:254-55, 268-69, *et passim*; Teenstra 1835, I:179-84; and Hostmann 1850, II:247-50) all postdate 1770, leaving us with little systematic information from the Suriname side of the Atlantic about which "types" of slaves were important (and in what ways) during the whole first century of the colony's history, when local Afro-American institutions, languages, and other cultural systems were being forged.[11] For the present, then, we will probably have to be content with the general picture in Table 3, modified by the kinds of exceptions noted above, until further archival research permits a more comprehensive treatment.

SLAVE SOCIETY: THE EARLY SYNTHESIS

Colonial Suriname was a plantation society par excellence. Relatively large-scale estates developed early, and some 80 percent of the population continued to live on plantations until the end of the eighteenth century. It is true that during the first two decades after the Dutch began rebuilding the ruined English colony, estates tended to be small, and the labor force included white indentured servants who worked alongside American Indian and African slaves. For example, in 1684, the plantation of Johannes Basseliers, one of the largest in Suriname, included four white servants; five Indians (plus their children) who served as domestics, hunters, and fisherman; and fifty-one black slaves (plus their children) who labored in the fields and at the sugar mill (van der Linde 1966:75). But the size of plantations, almost all of which in this early period were devoted to sugar production, increased rapidly, and by 1700 the agricultural sector could be described as "very flourishing," and the success of the colony such as might inspire "the envy of all the others in the Americas" (Nassy 1788, I:56). At their height during the eighteenth century, "average" sugar estates are said to have had a slave force of 228, and "small-sized" estates 137 (van Lier 1971:161-62)—somewhat larger than those in Jamaica at its height (Sheridan 1973:223, 231), and more than seventeen times as large as average contemporary plantations in Virginia or Maryland (Fogel and Engerman 1974:22).

Though on the whole plantation Suriname was an enormously profitable colony (Nassy argued that per capita it produced more total revenue and

---

11. Several modern anthropologists and historians have examined these Suriname lists and have had fairly good success in identifying the names with African slave ports, place names, and tribal or language designations. (This work, begun by Lichtveld [1928-30] and Lindblom [1924], has been carried forward by van Lier [1971] and Wooding [1972], who were able to draw on comparable work for the rest of the Americas by Herskovits, Aguirre Beltrán, and others.)

consumed more imported manufactures than any Caribbean colony—1788, II:40), its economy experienced considerable fluctuations over time. While most of the English plantations had been established well up the Suriname River on high ground, the Dutch, in rebuilding the colony after 1667, began developing the richer soils of the area closer to the coast, using their special knowledge of polder agriculture. And, as in other colonies with large wilderness areas (e.g., Jamaica or the United States), new plantation areas were periodically opened up during the eighteenth century, as older lands became exhausted—a process that is vividly illustrated in an excellent series of historical maps recently published in Amsterdam (Bubberman *et al.* 1973).

Throughout the early period of Dutch control, the economic future of the colony remained in doubt, since internal political difficulties, threatened and actual invasions by foreign powers, and serious depredations by Indians sapped much of the colonists' strength. Until the early eighteenth century, with the slave force building toward its maximum size, agriculture was practically limited to sugar cane, with only a few estates being devoted to timber and the production of foodstuffs. The introduction of coffee in 1720, and experimentation with other crops (e.g., cacao, tobacco, indigo, roucou and, later, cotton) led to diversification, and by 1750 coffee had actually outstripped sugar as the colony's most valuable export (see Fig. 3). Yet in terms of the organization of plantations, the introduction of coffee seems to have done little to alter the scale of estates; while late eighteenth-century sugar estates averaged 228 slaves, the comparable figure for coffee plantations was 247 (van Lier 1971:161).

In the 1760s and 1770s, a serious economic and social crisis developed as planters began relying for the first time on European credit. Heavy speculation, a trend toward overappraisal of estates, and rapid changes in ownership occurred. These events unfolded in the context of significantly diminished land fertility, a rapidly aging slave population (compared to earlier periods), sharply increased slave unrest and maroon depredations, and problems of massive slave uprisings in neighboring Berbice, for the suppression of which the colonists had to contribute both troops and supplies. Absentee ownership of plantations, relatively rare in earlier periods, became more common; by 1788, fully 77 percent of the plantations under cultivation had owners who lived in Holland (Nassy 1788, II:10).

Very little has been written about the nature of the social and cultural life of slaves on Suriname's plantations. However, my own ongoing research suggests that here, as elsewhere in the Americas (Price 1973:27-28; Mintz and Price n.d.), imported Africans very early created distinctively Afro-*American* ways of dealing with life. Indeed, there are indications that in Suriname, the process of creolization was both more rapid and more thorough than in most other New World colonies. But "creolization" must be distinguished from "assimilation" or "acculturation." Suriname's African slave force, while creat-

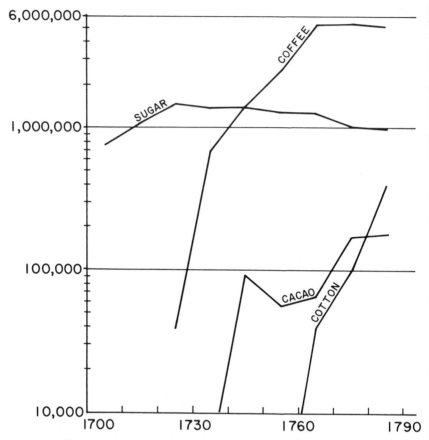

Fig. 3. Value of four major agricultural products 1700-89
(in constant guilders).

NOTE: The graph uses mean figures for each decade plotted at the decade's midpoint. Production figures are from Nassy 1788, II:88-95, extrapolated for 1788-89. These figures cannot be considered definitive, as there are considerable unexplained discrepancies between those given by Nassy and those of Fermin (1778:369). Moreover, Fermin indicates that his figures, and by implication Nassy's, refer only to products shipped to Amsterdam, and he cites figures for one year, 1771, showing that the value of Rotterdam's Suriname imports fully matched those of Amsterdam (1778:372). Values in the graph were figured in constant guilders, using Fermin's prices, which seem to represent an average for the period 1750-74: a barrel of sugar (1000 pounds) @ 60 guilders; one pound of coffee @ 8 1/2 sous; one pound of cacao @ 6 1/2 sous; one pound of cotton @ 8 sous (Fermin 1778:371).

ing new institutions with what may have been unusual speed, did so with remarkably little reference to the models afforded by their masters. And this early, distinctive cultural synthesis fashioned by slaves on Suriname's plantations became the base from which all modern variants of Afro-Suriname culture eventually developed.

For reasons that remain somewhat problematical Suriname slaves seem, from the first, to have organized themselves less in terms of ethnic affinities than in terms of their New World situations (compared, say, to those in Jamaica, Saint-Domingue, or Demerara). It is true that there is a report from 1665 which says that "they are a mixture of several Nations, which are always Clashing with one another" (Warren 1667:19), and another which documents a 1738 "Coromantin" revolt on a sugar plantation (Nassy 1788, I:91). But careful study of contemporary accounts—which were highly sensitive to alleged behavioral differences among slaves of different African proveniences—does not indicate that slaves from particular groups often formed organized collectivities within plantation complements. Rather, in Suriname loyalty to those slaves with whom one shared a common physical and institutional setting seems quite early to have taken precedence over Africa-based ties.

One reason for this may be that the slave complements on early Suriname plantations seem to have been quite heterogeneous ethnically; in contemporaneous Barbados, which was supplied by the same Dutch ships (see above), Ligon noted that "there is a third reason, which stops all designs of that kind [conspiracies], and that is, They are fetch'd from several parts of *Africa,* who speak several languages, and by that means, one of them understands not another" (1673:46). And in Suriname, on the arrival of a shipment from Africa, planters—using a divide-and-rule strategy—are said to have

> put 'em, some in one, and some in other Lots [groups of slaves destined for the same plantation] . . . . they sold 'em off, as Slaves to several Merchants and Gentlemen; not putting any two in one Lot, because they would separate 'em far from each other; nor daring to trust 'em together, lest Rage and Courage should put 'em upon contriving some great Action, to the Ruin of the Colony [Behn 1688:166].

A second reason originated in the policy of the Suriname planters during the first hundred years of the colony's history not to break up slave families by selling members to different masters, and to take special care to avoid separating mothers from children, or husbands from wives. Indeed, the Suriname plantation slaves were considered, in effect, to belong to the soil, and were to be sold, not as individuals or family groups, but only when the estate itself changed hands; transfers of whole complements from one plantation to another, always strongly resisted by the slaves, required special approval by the governor (Benjamins and Snelleman 1914-17:638; van Lier 1971:154-55). Along with the early development of extended, localized kinship groups that was fostered by these practices, strong ritual attachments began to bind slaves to particular localities (see Mintz and Price n.d.). Indeed, not only did the slave force of each plantation eventually develop a distinctive character and identity (many even possessing their own style of drumming [Wooding 1972:259-60]), but its members used a special term of address with one another, *sibi*, which had originated as an address term for slaves who had shared passage on the same ship (Voorhoeve and Lichtveld 1975:55).

Perhaps the clearest indicator of the speed with which Suriname slaves developed a culture of their own is language. Before the departure of the English slaves (almost all of whom were transferred out of Suriname within the first twenty years of the colony), a new creole language had become the mother tongue of the slaves.[12] During the several years when the newly imported Dutch-owned slaves overlapped with the soon-to-be-departing English ones, this language must have been passed on to them; for ever since that time this English-based creole (called Sranan, Negro-English, Taki-Taki, or Surinaams) has been the "national language" of Suriname (Voorhoeve and Lichtveld 1975:275-76). This language—a completely new Afro-American creation—was, then, "firmly established" within the colony's first two decades (Voorhoeve 1971:307).

Equally striking, perhaps, because it is so much at the core of Afro-Surinamese culture and society, is the apparent earliness with which a complex, integrated, and distinctive religious system developed. Although the ignorance and lack of interest of contemporary commentators makes early documentary accounts of local slave religion rare, there is strong indirect evidence for an early synthesis (see Mintz and Price n.d.). When the ancestors of the Saramaka maroons escaped from the plantations along the Para Creek and the Suriname River to establish an independent society in the forested interior (during the seventeenth and very early eighteenth centuries), they must have carried with them a religious system that had already been rather fully shaped on the plantations; for there are remarkable similarities today between the religious systems of the Saramaka and that of the Creoles of the

---

12. I should say a word about my use of the term "creole," which is employed in such diverse ways by different scholars, and so differently in various regions in the Americas. In this book, lower-case "creole" refers only to a special class of languages (see Hymes 1971). Upper-case "Creole" refers to Suriname-born individuals of African ancestry; this is the common Suriname term for Afro-Surinamer. "Creolization" refers to the process by which new sociocultural forms were forged in the interactions among Africans of diverse origins, Europeans, and American Indians in the colonial New World. An African immigrant who is more "creolized" is not, then, in my usage necessarily more "Europeanized" but, rather, further acculturated toward a new, developing Afro-American sociocultural synthesis.

Para region, similarities which range from countless specific belief-rite complexes (such as that surrounding the killing of a tapir), to broad-based principles like those relating corporate groups and their ancestral gods, and these similarities cannot be explained adequately on the basis of subsequent contact (Price and Price n.d.; Wooding 1972). Moreover, today—now that there is freedom of movement for Saramakas going to the coast—a specific group of Saramakas will commonly visit, worship with, and exchange specialized ritual information with those Creoles who are precisely the descendants of slaves who lived on the same plantation from which the ancestors of that particular group of Saramakas had fled, over two and a half centuries ago.

We can assert with some confidence, then, that within the earliest decades of the African presence in Suriname, the core of a new language and a new religion had been developed; and the subsequent century of massive new importations from Africa apparently had the effect merely of leading to secondary elaborations. Similar early syntheses undoubtedly occurred in other realms of life as well. In material culture, for example, Amerindians strongly influenced the slaves' horticultural adaptations (for growing and processing the bulk of their own food), their hunting and fishing techniques, their knowledge of crafts (such as basketry), their use of therapeutic plants, and so forth. Since Amerindians largely disappeared from the plantation scene after the first decades of the colony, I believe that we can infer that those of their techniques which are present in Afro-Surinamese culture must date from this early period.

It does not seem difficult to account for the striking "non-Europeanness" of this early synthesis. Suriname's ratio of Africans to Europeans was always extreme—more than 25:1 for much of the eighteenth century, with figures ranging up to 65:1 in the plantation districts (van Lier 1971:53). This may usefully be compared to Jamaica's ratio of 10:1 in 1780, "the highest in the British West Indies," and to those of "4:1 for Barbados, parity for Bermuda, Virginia and Georgia, and a white preponderance of 15:1 for the American Middle Colonies" (Craton 1975:254).

Why the early African population of Suriname became less Europeanized than that of many other plantation colonies, then, seems to be rather clear. But why it so rapidly "creolized," in terms of forging new, Afro-American institutions—rather than grouping itself along older African tribal or linguistic lines—is more resistant to any neat or simple explanation. It seems at least possible, however, that more detailed sociohistorical research will reveal that in plantation America, strong manifestations of African ethnicity as the central organizing principle for slave complements were actually more the exception than the rule, occurring only under special conditions (see Mintz and Price n.d.), and that inter-*African* "syncretism," with more or less European and Amerindian influence, was almost everywhere the central process in the forging of new, Afro-American cultural forms.[13] In any case, I would argue that current cultural differences among Suriname's various Afro-American populations (which, in the extreme case, speak mutually unintelligible languages) have tended to mask their underlying similarities, and that these are grounded in the common and profound experience of their ancestors having shared directly in the process of forging together a wholly new society and culture in the early plantation colony.

Before turning to the Suriname maroons themselves, I want quickly to note again some of the features of the plantation society that especially encouraged their presence and strongly influenced their ultimate success. This summary list may serve as a bridge to the remaining two sections of Part One.

Suriname plantations, after the initial, faltering years of the colony, were consistently large. Moreover, they contained from the first unusually high ratios of Africans to Creoles, and of recently arrived Africans to seasoned slaves. The colony as a whole was marked by a no less remarkable preponderance of blacks to whites and slaves to free. Manumission was rare by any comparative standard, and freedmen were few; as late as 1787, freedmen comprised only 1 percent of the nonwhite population (van Lier 1971:97), so that the distinction between free and slave corresponded almost exactly to that between white and black. In general, plantations were run as business enterprises, and the paternalism so characteristic of certain other plantation colonies did not mark the relationship between Suriname's masters and slaves. A seemingly inpenetrable rain forest grew up to the very doorsteps of the cultivated settlements, adding still another barrier to effective control of the work force. International difficulties, which caused confusion and consternation on the plantations, occurred periodically throughout the colonial era. And slave treatment, always harsh by comparative standards, grew visibly worse during the several periods of real economic crisis.

Such characteristics of colonial Suriname were, I believe, among those which made this colony the unintended matrix of the longest-lived and most successful of all maroon societies in the Americas.

MARRONAGE AND THE COLONIAL REACTION

In Suriname, as elsewhere in the Americas (see Price 1973), flight, or marronage, began at the time of the very first importations of African slaves.

---

13. A notable feature of the Afro-Suriname cultural synthesis—whether in religion, song, or dance—is that the gradual creation of a new system, involving a fundamental New World commitment from its participants, in no way negated or denied the African elements which contributed to it. And these systems seem to have been structured in

Indeed, when Willoughby's men arrived in 1651 to found the first permanent settlement, it is possible that—with the exception of a handful of surviving Jewish settlers (van der Straaten 1973:68)—the only non-Indian inhabitants of the colony were maroons who had escaped from the short-lived settlements of Captain Marshall in the 1630s and 1640s, or from those of the French during the same period (Scott 1668; Benjamins and Snelleman 1914-17:667). The supporting evidence on this point is admittedly unclear (see Douglas 1930:5), but were it in fact to have been the case it would mesh nicely with Saramaka oral accounts of their own earliest history (see Morssink n.d.; Price and Price n.d.).

In any case, we do know that the slaves of Willoughby's colony were prone to marronage. Warren, a contemporary observer of slavery, wrote:

> These wretched miseries not seldome drive them to desperate attempts for the Recovery of their Liberty, endeavoring to escape, and, if like to be re-taken sometimes lay violent hands upon themselves [1667:19].

During this same period of English control, one group of maroons, under the leadership of a Coromantyn slave named Jermes, had established a fort in the Para region, from which they raided nearby plantations (Hartsinck 1770:755). And there are other references to slave mutinies and marronage during the English period (Rens 1953:35). By 1678, a decade after the Dutch took over, the maroon threat to the colony had continued to grow, and Samuel Nassy was commissioned to hunt down and capture "the runaway rebel slaves" (Oudschans Dentz 1927:14-15). In that same year, Indian raids against the plantations brought the colony to the brink of ruin; sugar production came to a standstill and there was insufficient food for the slaves, who became for the moment an economic liability. During this period of great uncertainty, many slaves seized the opportunity to escape to the forests along the Suriname River (Buve 1966:17, 23).

In 1679, Governor Heinsius estimated that there were 700 to 800 runaways in the forest (Buve 1966:24). Since this figure would place some 25 percent of the colony's total black population in the forests, it is probably exaggerated, though I doubt that it represents more than twice the true number. Two years later, black rebels were posing a serious threat to the young colony. Ganimet, a slave who had had an ear cut off by his master, had joined a number of rebellious Indians in the forest and made forays to plantations where he incited slaves to revolt and join him. In 1681, government troops attacked and destroyed Ganimet's fort in the Para region, killing fifty

---

such a way that, for an individual, special identification with, say, Ashanti or Yoruba features, could enrich without taking precedence over commitment to the plantation-based slave community.

maroons. The others escaped, fleeing toward the Saramacca River (van der Linde 1966:93-95; Buve 1966:24). In 1684, having already concluded treaties with rebellious Indians, the government signed a peace treaty with a group of maroons under Jermes, then living on the Coppename River (Hartsinck 1770:649; Wolbers 1861:137). Throughout the 1680s there were incidents of slave rebelliousness, and the number of runaways increased substantially (van der Linde 1966:95). Most commonly, slaves escaped singly or in twos and threes, sometimes after committing acts of violence, but there were occasional larger revolts during this period as well. For example:

> there was in the year 1690 a revolt on a plantation situated in the Cassowine kreek . . . belonging to a Jew named Imanüel Machado where, having killed their master, they ran off, taking all that he owned with them [Nassy 1788, I:76, my translation].

However, organized revolts of this kind seem to have been rare until the 1730s, 1740s, and 1750s (see below).

By the beginning of the eighteenth century, the maroon population was estimated to have reached 5000 to 6000 (Hartsinck 1770:757)—again, clearly an inflated figure, but indicative of the fear in which the colonists held the rebels. As early as 1685, the colonial government had established bounties for the capture of runaway slaves. In the beginning, it was set at 5 guilders; two years later it was increased to 300 pounds of sugar if the runaway had been expressly hunted down, and 100 pounds otherwise; in 1698, it was increased to 25 to 50 guilders, depending on the specific circumstances of capture; and in 1717 bounties of 1500 guilders each were earmarked for the discovery of two notorious maroon villages, and 600 guilders for any other village, plus a 10-guilder bonus per inhabitant (which was later expanded to the granting of freedom in addition to the usual bounty to any slave or runaway who disclosed the whereabouts of a maroon village) (Hartsinck 1770:756-57).

From the earliest years of the colony, special punishments were reserved for maroons. In the 1660s, Warren observed of runaways that

> if the hope of Pardon bring them again alive into their Masters power, they'l manifest their fortitude, or rather obstinancy in suffering the most exquisite tortures can be inflicted upon them, for a terrour and example to others without shrinking [1667:19].

And a half-century later, Herlein reported that

> If a slave runs away into the forest in order to evade work for a few weeks, upon his being captured his Achilles tendon is removed for the first offence, while for a second offence, if he wishes to increase the

punishment, his right leg is amputated in order to stop him from running away; I myself was a witness to slaves being punished thus [1718:112, translated in van Lier 1971:133].

Perhaps the most common punishment for maroons recaptured quickly, in the vicinity of their own plantation, was one that is still remembered by Saramakas, the so-called *Spaanse bok* (Spanish whip). As one eighteenth-century observer described it:

> . . . the hands are tied together, the knees drawn up between them, and a stick inserted through the opening between the knees and the hands and fixed firmly in the ground, around which they then lie like a hoop and are struck on the buttocks with a guava or Tamarind rod; one side having been struck until the skin is completely broken they are turned over to have the other side similarly injured; some use hoop-sticks for this, although this is an extremely dangerous practice, as it generally results in the slave's death, even though the chastisement is less than with the abovementioned rods [Nepveu, translated in van Lier 1971:130].

A missionary, on a trip up the Suriname River in 1779, reports that he twice stopped for the night at plantations where recaptured runaways who had received this torture several days before remained tied at the posts with "maggots running around in their pus-filled wounds" (Staehelin 1913-19, III(2):178-80).

Although a law promulgated in 1721 specified a mandatory death penalty for the act of marronage (Hartsinck 1770:757), it appears that planters continued to act largely at their own discretion when it came to punishing runaways (van Lier 1971:132-36). Indeed, the Suriname planters' reputation for unusual brutality, sometimes attributed merely to the eloquence of Stedman's widely read work (1796), seems to me to have solid grounding in fact. Van Lier cites several earlier sources, written by foreigners and local writers, which concur in this opinion (1971:131) and I have seen a number of others. Even Voltaire, in 1759, chose Suriname as the platform from which to launch a satirical discussion of New World slavery—doubly chilling today because this conscious attempt to ridicule-by-exaggeration comes so close to sounding like objective contemporary reports.

> As they drew near the town they came upon a Negro lying on the ground wearing only half his clothes, that is to say, a pair of blue cotton drawers; this poor man had no left leg and no right hand. "Good heavens!" said Candide to him in Dutch, "what are you doing there, my friend, in that horrible state?"
>
> "I am waiting for my master, the famous merchant Monsieur Vanderdendur."

"Was it Monsieur Vanderdendur," said Candide, "who treated you in that way?"

"Yes, sir," said the Negro, "it is the custom. We are given a pair of cotton drawers twice a year as clothing. When we work in the sugar mills and the grindstone catches a finger, they cùt off the hand; when we try to run away, they cut off a leg. Both these things happened to me. This is the price paid for the sugar you eat in Europe" [*Candide*, ch. 19].

Two actual cases can illustrate the treatment which recaptured maroons could expect in eighteenth-century Suriname. Recounting a contemporary incident, Herlein reported that a recaptured town slave, "whose punishment shall serve as an example to others," was sentenced

> to be quartered alive, and the pieces thrown in the River. He was laid on the ground, his head on a long beam. The first blow he was given, on the abdomen, burst his bladder open, yet he uttered not the least sound; the second blow with the axe he tried to deflect with his hand, but it gashed the hand and upper belly, again without his uttering a sound. The slave men and women laughed at this, saying to one another, "That is a man!" Finally, the third blow, on the chest, killed him. His head was severed and the body cut in four pieces and dumped in the river [Herlein 1718:117; my translation].

Several years later, the following sentence was meted out by the criminal court to eleven maroons captured on a punitive expedition of 1730:

> The Negro Joosje shall be hanged from the gibbet by an Iron Hook through his ribs, until dead; his head shall then be severed and displayed on a stake by the riverbank, remaining to be picked over by birds of prey. As for the Negroes Wierai and Manbote, they shall be bound to a stake and roasted alive over a slow fire, while being tortured with glowing Tongs. The Negro girls, Lucretia, Ambia, Aga, Gomba, Marie and Victoria will be tied to a Cross, to be broken alive, and then their heads severed, to be exposed by the riverbank on stakes. The Negro girls Diana and Christina shall be beheaded with an axe, and their heads exposed on poles by the riverbank [Hartsinck 1770:763-65; my translation].

As is evident from these cases, the colony's judiciary was often as brutal as the individual planters. And such sentences were not merely isolated extremes. Van Lier has examined the records of the local judiciary for the mid-eighteenth century, and found that during one twenty-two-year period at least sixteen recaptured slaves had a leg amputated, and four their Achilles tendon severed; that between 1731 and 1750, slaves were hanged by a meathook inserted through the ribs on at least twelve occasions (see Stedman 1796, I:facing 111, for an illustration of this punishment); and that "burning at the stake, quartering and the breaking of limbs were repeatedly imposed as punishment" (van Lier 1971:136). It may help put these enormities into perspective (though not in any way to diminish them) to report that Saramaka maroons, recounting the horrors of slavery according to their own oral traditions, dwell less on such mutilations and executions than on what they remember as the crushing day-to-day reality of contending with whippings by drivers, symbolic humiliations forced upon them by masters, and the like (see Price n.d.). All in all, the excesses of colonial Suriname—in terms of both the brutality and the luxury amid which the planters lived—must be constantly kept in mind in building toward some understanding of the slaves' response.

Flight from the plantations, revolts by the slaves, and armed raids by maroon bands were a ubiquitous feature of plantation life during the eighteenth century. Colonial lists of the major maroon raids—always partial, at best—show a devastating monotony: in 1701 or 1702, the maroons murdered a planter; in 1713, they killed a plantation carpenter; a few years later, they seriously wounded another planter, violated his wife and carried off their possessions; about 1721, another plantation was sacked, with both slaves and possessions liberated; during the early 1730s, a large number of plantations were systematically pillaged, with a number of slaves as well as the whites being killed and many slaves liberated. The frequency and seriousness of these attacks increased as time went on (Hartsinck 1770:757-58; Nassy 1788,I:77). As for revolts—which were often closely tied to maroon activity (see Price n.d.)—they, too, increased dramatically through time, with that of 1690 (see above) being followed by similar, single-plantation uprisings in 1738 and 1749, and then by the much larger rebellions of 1757 and 1758, which led to sharply increased raids against the plantations (Nassy 1788, I:77-78).

Special opportunities for flight—such as the unrest of 1678, referred to above—continued to be seized by the slaves. For example, when French Admiral Jacques Cassard, accompanied by eight warships and 3000 soldiers, attacked the colony in 1712, most of the male colonists went to defend the fort at Paramaribo, but many women and children—from both the city and the plantations—were sent to hide in the surrounding forest, in the care of their slaves. Meanwhile, a number of urban slaves seem to have been secreted by their masters at the forested edge of the city, in order that they not be taken by Cassard as part of the ransom he demanded. There were sizable desertions from both groups of slaves, with the new runaways joining those already in the forest (Herlein 1718:93; Hartsinck 1770:700-4; Wolbers 1861:90; Morssink n.d.). Nevertheless, in spite of such mass desertions and those occasioned by maroon raids, the majority of runaways during the eighteenth century, as before, escaped by slipping away alone or in small groups (Price n.d.).

The organized pursuit of maroons, and expeditions to destroy maroon settlements, date at least from the 1670s, when a citizens' militia was established for this purpose (see above). During the late seventeenth and early eighteenth centuries, numerous small-scale military expeditions were mounted, sometimes at the personal expense of particular planters, but these rarely met with success, for the maroons had established and protected their settlements with great ingenuity, and had become expert at all aspects of guerrilla warfare (see Price 1973).

One captain of the Jewish militia led more than thirty such expeditions during his life, and another citizen was reported to be on his seventeenth in 1749 (Nassy 1788, I:90, 96). By 1718, larger military expeditions began to be organized and included Indians trained in the use of firearms as well as slaves (*ibid.*). But it was in the 1730s and 1740s, when "the colony had become the theater of a perpetual war" (Nassy 1788, I:87), that such expeditions reached their maximum size and frequency. Among the several sent out in 1730, for example, was one that included fifty citizens and 200 slaves, which in addition to killing sixteen maroons, captured four men, twelve women, and ten children (who were among those to whom the sentences quoted on p. 26 were applied—Hartsinck 1770:759-65). And others on the same scale were mounted throughout this period, for example, that of 1743, which was comprised of twenty-seven civilians, twelve soldiers, fifteen Indians, 165 slaves, and sixty canoes (Nassy 1788, I:93). Though the most successful of the military expeditions listed by Hartsinck and Nassy during the 1730s and 1740s returned with as many as "47 prisoners and 6 hands of those whom they had killed" (Nassy 1788, I:92), most such expeditions were fruitless. Indeed, by the 1740s the financial costs to the colonists had become overwhelming, as typical expeditions were costing "more than 100,000 guilders each," and often had to traverse "forty mountains and sixty creeks" before reaching a maroon hideaway (Hartsinck 1770:766-68). By this time, it had also become clear to the colonists that the expeditions themselves were contributing to increased marronage, as they made known to the slaves both the escape routes from the plantations and the locations of maroon villages (*ibid.*).

The increasingly costly guerrilla warfare between maroons and colonists, which by the mid-eighteenth century had lasted nearly one-hundred years, finally culminated in a decision by the whites, during the late 1740s, to sue their former slaves for permanent peace. The complicated events surrounding the making of the treaties with the two largest maroon groups (the Djuka and the Saramaka) in 1760 and 1762, and with the Matawai in 1767, have been recounted by a number of authors, as has the history of the major new revolts and large-scale war of the subsequent decades, which witnessed the use of an army of mercenaries imported from Europe, and culminated in the formation of the Aluku as well as the Paramaka and Kwinti tribes. I therefore choose here merely to refer the reader to the literature discussed in Part Two, but with the caution that most available accounts are written from a strongly Euro-centric or colonial perspective.[14] It should be added that while the nominal pacification of the major tribes, and the subsequent settling of the new Aluku tribe under the wing of the Djukas, seem to have diminished somewhat the frequency of marronage, flight from the plantations and acts of rebellion by the slave force continued to occur until the very eve of Emancipation. Indeed, perhaps the most dramatic act of slave violence in the colony's history—the burning of much of the capital—occurred in 1832 and, as late as 1860, the entire slave complement of a plantation escaped to the forests en masse (see references in Part Two, below).

Within the limits of this book, it is not possible to broach the complex issues surrounding the internal organization of the early maroon groups in Suriname. However, another work devoted to this subject is in active preparation, and it will analyze in some detail how the original bands were organized largely on the basis of social ties stemming from life on the plantations, rather than in terms of African tribal or linguistic affiliation; how the devastating raids which nearly brought the colony to its knees were motivated by economic necessity and the need for recruits rather than simply a lust for revenge; how religion served as the central focus for political authority throughout the war years; and, more generally, how these maroons were able to become highly successful guerrillas and, at the same time, to elaborate remarkably complex and integrated social and cultural forms upon the base which they and their fellow African slaves had established on the plantations (see also Price 1973).

Here we may turn instead to outlining the history of tribal differentiation and its implications for an understanding of the ethnography of the several maroon tribes. For I am becoming convinced that the widely different dates at which the maroon tribes were formed had a truly major impact on the shape which their respective institutions and cultural systems were eventually to take.

THE FORMATION OF
MAROON SOCIETIES: CHRONOLOGY AND IMPLICATIONS

Although it is only during the past several years that serious research has been initiated into the precise origins of the several maroon tribes, and though many details remain unclear, the general outlines are becoming

---

14. I am currently at work on an extensive analysis of this period based in large part on oral history accounts gathered in the field.

known. I present here what is simply a summary of the relevant chronology, leaving the documentation as well as the geographical details for another publication (Price n.d.).

Of the six current tribes, the Saramaka (and the Matawai, who split from them in the mid-eighteenth century) are the oldest. Hartsinck claimed that

> The Saramaka maroons originated with slaves who escaped from the English [that is, prior to 1667] and who established themselves along the Suriname, Saramacca, and Coppename Rivers, especially in the heavily forested areas, where they established a kind of republic [1770:755, my translation].

But it is unclear whether the group led by Jermes (see above) actually became the core of the Saramaka tribe (as Hartsinck suggests [1770:755-56]) or gradually disappeared as a group through marriage with local Indians (as Wong [1938:299] and Abbenhuis [1943:67-68] assert). And Ganimet's contemporaneous group is not, to my knowledge, discussed further in the historical literature at all, though it may also have been an early element of the Saramaka population. We do know that Riemer, who carried out first-hand missionary work among the Saramakas in 1779-80, and recorded a good deal of oral history, wrote:

> The oldest of these [maroon] nations is the Saramaka, which has existed for over 100 years [Staehelin 1913-19, III(2):249].

And Herlein, writing of a recent expedition against a Saramaka stronghold, noted:

> These runaways had lived here [in the forest] so long that they had already-married children who in their whole life had never seen a white man [1718:116, my translation].

However, my main evidence on the Saramaka and the Matawai comes from the fragmentary but enormously valuable genealogical information gathered by missionaries who lived and worked with them on the Upper Suriname River and the Saramacca River in the 1760s, 1770s, and 1780s, together with more recent oral data that can be correlated with it. These data make clear that (1) the last significant influx into this tribal population came from slaves who escaped during the 1712 invasion of Cassard, and (2) these new recruits fit themselves into a nascent society that was already—in cultural terms— relatively well formed (see Price n.d.).

But while the defections at the time of Cassard's invasion gave the Saramakas their last large demographic input, they seem to have constituted the earliest core of the yet-to-be-formed Djuka tribe (Wong 1938:302). In the many revolts, raids, and defections which followed 1712, the great bulk of new runaways, rather than joining the Saramakas, fled toward the southeast, in the direction of the younger and smaller Djuka group, with increasing numbers of recruits coming during the 1730s and 1740s, and an even greater influx during the Tempati revolts of 1757. Indeed, the Djukas continued to receive large new demographic inputs right up until 1760 (Hartsinck 1770:779; Nassy 1788, I:77-78, 98; Wolbers 1861:153-54), and the tribe became effectively closed to new recruits only after the treaty of that same year (Nassy 1788, I:125).

Three smaller tribes grew from the core of slaves who escaped in the years immediately following the treaties with the Djuka, Saramaka, and Matawai in the 1760s. The original historical ties among the three new groups remain, as of this writing, problematical, though there is increasing evidence that their early histories were intertwined. It now appears that a tiny group of maroons, a few of whom had escaped as early as 1715, managed to survive on the fringe of the cultivated area in the eastern region of the colony into the 1760s (and these later became the core of the Aluku tribe—Abbenhuis 1964:23-24). Once the treaties with the Djuka, Saramaka, and Matawai (which bound these tribes to return all future runaways) had closed off the slaves' escape routes to the south (see Nassy 1788, I:125-29), the majority of new maroons settled in the same area as this nearby group, and participated actively with them in inciting the revolts and defections of the late 1760s, the 1770s, and the 1780s. During this period, these groups lived in a wilderness region within the famous "protective cordon"—a remarkable 60-meter-wide defensive perimeter manned at short intervals by soldiers, which the colonists set up across the whole of the heavily forested southern border of the plantation region in the 1770s to prevent escapes and maroon raids. By the 1790s, having gone through rather different historical experiences, these maroons had coalesced into three main groups: the ancestors of the Aluku (Boni), who were the leaders of military resistance during this period, the Paramaka, and the Kwinti. The first of these groups, moving eastward, finally settled in the Upper Marowijne basin; the second migrated much more slowly toward the Lower Marowijne; and the third moved quickly westward toward the Coppename, whence they later joined the Matawai on the Saramacca River and, still later, again settled, in part, on the Coppename (see Green 1974:58-62; Hurault 1960; Lenoir 1973:18-29; Nassy 1788, I:129-30; van der Elst 1975:10-12; and other references cited in Part Two, below).

Let us consider briefly some of the implications of this tentative chronology, in light of the demographic and sociohistorical data presented above. First, it should be clear that the initial composition of each major group was a direct product of the historical period during which it was formed. Focusing, for example, on the oldest of the tribes, it should be evident that only a very tiny minority of the slaves who escaped to become Saramakas (and, probably, Matawais) were not born in Africa. Those slaves who ran off prior to 1680 must have all been African-born, since the slaves from the English period who had not become maroons (including their "Creole" children) had already been removed from the colony, and the oldest Suriname-born children of the slaves of the post-English period would have been only twelve years old by this time. Moreover, by 1690, there would have been only about eighty-five Creoles over the age of fifteen in the colony—representing less than 2 percent of the total slave population. By 1715—the date we can use as the approximate end of significant new population input into these groups—there still would have been only about 400 to 500 Suriname-born slaves over the age of fifteen, or about 2 percent of the total slave population (see Tables 1 and 2, above). It seems clear, then, that those runaway slaves who formed the Saramaka tribe were almost all African-born "salt-water Negroes." And a glance at Table 2 will reveal that nearly two-thirds of them were, at the time of taking flight, less than ten years away from their African homelands (if one makes the conservative assumption that runaways were distributed randomly among plantation slaves, in terms of their time in the New World).

Incidentally, it may be worth stressing that those few Creoles who numbered among the pre-1715 runaways should not be confused with some sort of prototypical antebellum United States (or nineteenth-century Suriname) Creoles, for all of them had parents who were born in Africa. It is true that the early Creoles in Suriname, who represented such a small proportion of the population, were generally given privileged positions in plantation society because of their more western language skills and styles of social interaction. Indeed, the original generation gap between these early Creoles and their African-born parents is perpetuated linguistically in Saramaka today; youths, who are expected to invent or develop styles or fashions of their own that in some sense elaborate on or run counter to those of their elders are still called *kióo* (Creoles). Nevertheless, I would stress that the original Creole runaways to Saramaka were but a single generation removed from Africa; and though they may have had a *relatively* broad knowledge of the world of the whites, they remained in an excellent position to understand and communicate fully within that of their African-born brothers as well.

It must be reiterated also that those slaves who became Saramakas, though almost all African-born, were nevertheless very far from being a homogeneous group. We have already seen that they represented a variety of African ethnic backgrounds, with all the linguistic and cultural diversity that this implies. But they also must have represented a variety of personal adjustments to their New World situations, including varying degrees of creolization, differing attitudes toward whites and their society, and so forth. In Suriname as elsewhere in the Americas (Price 1973:24), it seems likely that Africans who were literally just off the ships in their first days or weeks in the New World attempted to escape especially frequently—though they always would have represented a minority of the total runaway population. Nor should one underestimate the numerically small but potentially influential contribution of skilled or privileged slaves, many of them urban, who had already spent many years in the colony, though the proportions of such maroons may have been relatively small in the early years. But the great majority of pre-1715 runaways were plantation slaves who had already made some adjustment to their Suriname situations (the precise nature of which would have varied significantly depending on whether they lived on estates devoted primarily to sugar, coffee, or timber, on their particular task assignments, on the character of their supervisory staff, and so forth). And it is notable that such slaves seem to have run off particularly when they or their kinsmen or friends had been victims of brutality considered excessive even by the ordinary standards of the plantation. And, in considering the formative influences on the nascent ideology of these early maroon groups, it is worth noting that these runaways—who constituted a majority—may have represented a particularly embittered segment of the total slave population.

In this context, I would stress also that the overall alternatives open to slaves of any one category—whether sugar-cane cutters or house servants—were much greater than has usually been recognized, and that the individual adjustments which were achieved must often have been complex. As Mintz has written, "the house slave who poisoned her master's family by putting ground glass in the food had first to become the family cook" (1971:321). Therefore, any attempt to classify the early maroons in terms of a unilinear gradient from "accommodation" to "resistance to slavery" would represent considerable oversimplification. Coming from a variety of African ethnic groups, having had divergent experiences in Suriname, and therefore possessing differing views of the world and ways of interacting with people, the mass of early maroons was far from being monolithic, culturally or socially. What most of them did share, and what became the cornerstone of their new societies and cultures, were certain central historical experiences and values—most notably, a recently formed Afro-American plantation culture and strong ideological (or at least rhetorical) commitment to things "African" (see Price 1973:26).

What are some of the ways in which the initial composition of the other maroon groups differed from that of the Saramakas? First, the proportion of Creoles over the age of fifteen in the general slave population ranged from 10 to 15 percent during the period of Djuka formation to 30 to 35 percent during the time when the bulk of Aluku, Paramaka, and Kwinti ancestors were making their escapes. (This means that the proportion of Creoles was between five and seventeen times as great as it was during the period of Saramaka and Matawai formation.) Second, the tribal and linguistic provenience of the African-born maroons, who continued to form the bulk of the new runaways, had changed significantly since the earlier period (see Table 3, above). For example, the Slave Coast, which provided the bulk of imported Africans well into the early decades of the eighteenth century, supplied almost none of the new slaves after 1735; or again, the Gold Coast and the Windward Coast, which during the period of Saramaka and Matawai formation supplied less than 8 percent of the slaves to Suriname, accounted for fully 75 percent of the imports during the formative years of the Djuka, Aluku, Paramaka, and Kwinti.[15] And many other changes that took place in the slave society of Suriname between, say, the late seventeenth century and the late eighteenth century undoubtedly influenced the ways in which the different maroon societies took shape.

But our rough chronology of tribal formation has further implications as well. Scholars of slave resistance and marronage have sometimes argued that as slave societies became more "mature," a serious ideological cleavage developed between the increasingly creolized slave group and the more African-oriented maroons, with the more Europeanized slaves regarding the maroons as culturally "distant" and "strange."[16] While such a view may be defensible from the perspective of the antebellum American South, the situation in Suriname was far more complex. Consider as an illustration the following. At any time after about 1720 (until the slave trade ended in the nineteenth century), plantation society was in much more direct contact with Africa than was that of the Saramakas (or Matawais). In 1770 (to choose an arbitrary date), a large proportion of the plantation slaves were still recent arrivals from Africa, owing to the very high replacement rate of slaves—equivalent to some 5 percent per year for the slave population as a whole and probably closer to 10 percent for the field laborers throughout the second half of the eighteenth century (see Tables 1 and 2). But while about one-third of the field slaves would at that time have been temporally removed from their African homelands by less than five years, about 99 percent of the Saramaka population would have been Suriname-born. With these figures in mind, it would not be surprising to find on the plantations of the late eighteenth century much purer "Africanisms" in certain realms of life than existed in Saramaka at that time. (For example, the contrast between the strikingly "African-looking" calabash art on nineteenth-century plantations and that of contemporary Saramaka might well be explained in this way—see Neumann 1961 and Price 1970.) And whatever ideological or other cleavages

---

15. Ongoing research to improve Table 3 may permit in the future far more precise estimates of slave provenience for particular subperiods, e.g., the 1770s and 1780s, when the Paramaka tribe took shape.

16. Professor Eugene Genovese, referring particularly to Jamica and the Guianas, developed this view forcefully in his Frederick Douglass Memorial Lecture at Morgan State College, February 13, 1975.

had developed between slaves and maroons would be far more complex than a contrast between "African" maroons and "creolized" plantation slaves.

The full implications of a historical perspective for explaining the differences and similarities among Suriname's Afro-American populations remain largely unexplored. But if we focus, for example, on the late eighteenth century, many of the potentially interesting contrasts are thrown into sharp relief. To consider, for a moment, only the three major groupings: the Saramaka population at this time would have been almost wholly Suriname-born, the plantation population heavily (some two-thirds) African, and the composition of the Djuka tribe somewhere in between. And I would suggest that the greater similarities of many aspects of Djuka culture with that of coastal Suriname (than obtains between Saramaka and the coast) can be traced to the relative lateness of their "separation." To choose two random examples, the prevalence of "day-names" and the importance of *bakru* (dwarf-like supernaturals who can be commissioned to do evil) among coastal Creoles and Djukas, and the "foreignness" of these concepts to Saramakas, can probably be related to the great westward expansion of the Dutch slave trade during the course of the eighteenth century, as both concepts were probably brought over by Gold Coast and Ivory Coast peoples, who were only sparsely represented in the initial Saramaka population (see Price 1975:n. 5).[17] But the clearest illustration of the explanatory power of our chronology of tribal differentiation comes from examining language. The several pages which follow, and which close out this introductory part, use language history—developed here in only a preliminary fashion—to suggest the more general usefulness of a historical perspective for an understanding of cultural differences in Suriname.

There are three main creole languages spoken in Suriname today: (1) Sranan, once the language of the plantation slaves, now the "national language" of Suriname; (2) Saramaccan, spoken by the Saramaka and Matawai; and (3) Ndjuka, spoken by the Djuka, Aluku, and Paramaka.[18] A first approximation of their differences, in terms of vocabulary, can be grasped by examining, for each, the origins of the two-hundred lexical items in the standard Swadesh "200-item list." Table 4 summarizes the analysis of Jan Voorhoeve, expressed as percents (1973:138).

But, it should be added that this word list, consisting of so-called basic, core vocabulary, cannot be taken as representative of the total lexicons of these languages for historical purposes. In the initial contact situation on the

---

17. The cultural interrelationships among the maroon tribes and plantation Suriname (and even among the subdivisions of each of these populations, which are by no means culturally uniform) are in fact more complex than these examples indicate. I am merely trying to suggest a historical *strategy* for approaching the explanation of these similarities and differences.

18. The language of the Kwinti has not yet been adequately described (see van der Elst 1975:14-15).

Table 4. Origin of 200 Lexical Items, in Percents

Origin =	English	Portuguese	Dutch	African
Sranan	77	5	16	3
Ndjuka	81	3	14	2
Saramaccan	54	37	4	4

plantations, basic vocabulary could be expected to be especially strongly influenced by the masters' speech, since discourse dealing with these items would have constituted the bulk of communication between slaves and whites. Indeed, I have suggested elsewhere that the percent distribution of origins for a *complete* Saramaccan dictionary would be more like: English = 20, Portuguese = 20, Dutch (and Amerindian) = 10, and African = 50 (Price 1975).[19] Of the three languages, Saramaccan is least like the others. It is fully a tone language, and by any measure is mutually unintelligible with Sranan. Yet Sranan and Ndjuka speakers can converse with one another with little difficulty.

The problem of explaining these differences has puzzled investigators for well over a century, but recent work by Voorhoeve (1973), building on that of earlier scholars, has done much to shed light on the issue. In his brief but rich presentation, Voorhoeve argues that the original speakers of both Sranan and Saramaccan arrived in Suriname with a basic knowledge of Portuguese Pidgin; that Sranan "relexified" rather fully toward English on the plantations, while Saramaccan relexified only partially, as its early maroon speakers fled relatively quickly to the forests; and that Ndjuka, though similar in form to Sranan today, developed not through a process of relexification, but directly out of eighteenth-century African English Pidgin. For present purposes, I think it is fair to summarize Voorhoeve's underlying historical assumptions under five headings:

1. When a group of African slaves arrived in Suriname, its members already possessed a common basic knowledge of a European pidgin;

2. The ancestors of the Saramaccan speakers escaped from the plantations at a much earlier period than did those of the Ndjuka speakers;

3. Portuguese Pidgin was gradually supplanted by English Pidgin as the lingua franca of the West Coast of Africa, during the course of the early eighteenth century;

---

19. In an unpublished paper, Virginia Dominguez has pointed out that the European nouns in Saramaccan tend strongly to be generic terms, with many African items referring to more specific levels of contrast; thus tree = *páu* (from Portuguese) but *kinds* of trees are largely non-European in origin. I would go further and suggest that the very frequent synonymy on the species level is due in part to the existence of alternative items drawn from different African languages.

4. The language of Suriname slaves was essentially uniform; that is, there were not (as many previous writers have claimed) two speech communities among the early slave population, one (speaking early Sranan) on the English/ Dutch plantations, and another (speaking a highly Portuguized variant) on the estates of the Portuguese Jews.

5. It can be assumed that the ancestors of the Ndjuka speakers and those of the Saramaccan speakers had identical experience on the plantations not only as regards language exposure, but also in terms of the time they spent on plantations, the proportions of recruits to each tribe who were African or Creoles, and so forth.

Voorhoeve's first assumption, which fits with recent research from other New World colonies, seems a useful hypothesis (so long as the stress in "basic knowledge" remains on the first term). The second, which he suggested as a tentative hypothesis, has been amply documented in previous portions of Part One. The third, already powerful, can be further strengthened by considering the westward shift in the Dutch slave trade during the relevant period, increasingly drawing on English-controlled areas. But I believe that the fourth and fifth assumptions are unpersuasive, and that a reconsideration of them can suggest somewhat different conclusions about language history in Suriname.

I would suggest, first, that the ancestors of the Saramaccan speakers were exposed to significantly more Portuguese language influence on the plantations than were those of the Ndjuka speakers. Voorhoeve's argument against the existence of a separate Portuguized slave language on the Jewish plantations rests largely on his identifying the so-called *Djutongo* (a term used by contemporary writers) as Saramaccan, largely on the basis of two late eighteenth-century quotations. But my own reading of these same quotations suggests a rather different conclusion, i.e., that *Djutongo* referred to a Portuguese-influenced creole spoken both by Saramaka maroons *and* by the slaves on Jewish plantations (Voorhoeve 1973:140-41).[20] As late as 1767, a German missionary in Suriname, who worked on the Upper Suriname River, noted:

> The language of the town [Paramaribo] Negroes is quite a bit different from the language of the [Suriname River] plantation Negroes. They

---

20. The relevant quotations, taken from Voorhoeve 1973:140-41, are: (1) "Djutongo is the name by which the Negroes here [Sranan speakers] call the mixed Portuguese-Negro language. Saramakas have [speak] Djutongo"; (2) "In town [Paramaribo] this word [*bringi*] is not used much; it is Djutongo: but many plantations have [use] it." And Voorhoeve's use, as further support for his thesis of linguistic uniformity, of a 1693 Dutch traveler's report that "The English made here a colony, and that language is mostly spoken by the slaves," seems a very weak straw on which to lean, in terms of the apparent lack of the traveler's linguistic sophistication—his not mentioning *any* special slave speech patterns, etc. (*Ibid.*)

[the latter] have many broken Portuguese words. They can describe different things in three or four different ways [Staehelin 1913-19, III(1): 75-76].

No less an authority than Schumann, who wrote the pioneering eighteenth-century dictionaries of Sranan and Saramaccan, explicitly attributed the Portuguese influence in Saramaccan to the Jewish plantation experience [Staehelin 1913-19, III(1): 347]; and he noted elsewhere that Sranan was "spoken in Paramaribo and *the majority* of plantations" (my italics), and added that "on some plantations the Negroes have their own distinctive language" (1778:64-65). Finally, I would note that by the mid-nineteenth century, though the Portuguized slave speech on Jewish plantations was said by one lexicographer to be "fast disappearing from the colony" (Wullschlaegel 1856:vi), another could still point to words that were only "used by the Negroes of the Portuguese Jews" (Focke 1855, s.v. *foegà*, cited in Schuchardt 1914:xxix).

I would contend, then, first, that there were significant differences in speech patterns that distinguished the slaves on Jewish plantations from those on other plantations. Second, it seems clear that this difference disappeared through time, with the period before 1715—when the Portuguese planters were still within a half-century of their Brazilian experience—witnessing a stronger degree of Portuguese influence than there was later. Third, the proportion of eventual Saramaccan speakers who escaped from Jewish plantations was higher than that of Ndjuka speakers (since a greater proportion of the Djuka-Aluku-Paramaka ancestors fled from the eastern region, and these Tempati and Commewijne plantations had a much smaller proportion of Jewish owners—see Nassy 1788, II:71-72). And finally, on the basis of the data developed earlier in this part, I would reiterate that the original ancestors of the Saramaccan speakers were, demographically, significantly more African (in terms of overall proportions and time in the New World) than those of the Ndjuka speakers, who would have included a significant number of Creoles.

This last observation helps explain, I think, both the greater African language influence in Saramaccan than in either Ndjuka or Sranan, and the greater similarities between the latter two languages. With the other modifications of Voorhoeve's interpretations, they suggest the following scenario: The ancestors of both Saramaccan and Sranan speakers arrived in Suriname with some knowledge of West African Portuguese Pidgin. A significant number of the future Saramakas found themselves on Portuguese-owned plantations, where there was relatively little interference from English or, later, Sranan. And many other future Saramaccan speakers, on non-Jewish plantations, escaped to the forests before their language had fully relexified toward English. Thus, I would contend that the Portuguese influence in Saramaccan is *both* Old and New World, and·that we cannot with present information assign a relative weight to each of these inputs. Meanwhile, Ndjuka would seem to be the product of later imports who arrived in Suriname with some knowledge of an English (not a Portuguese) Pidgin, who came into a linguistically "supportive" Sranan environment, and who tended to be relatively well-acculturated by the time of their escapes. In other words, in the case of Ndjuka, as in that of Saramaccan, I would not underestimate the importance of the New World influence. My differences with Voorhoeve, then, are only about the extent to which differential New World experiences must be taken into account; indeed, his general historical approach to language differences in Suriname has opened the whole field to new study.[21]

These three languages, Ndjuka, Sranan, and Saramaccan—like the other cultural systems of Suriname's Afro-American populations—emerge from this still-preliminary analysis as complex products of historical processes that link inextricably the Old World and the New. And we see that maintaining a time perspective—the chronology of the differentiation of the maroon groups, the pace of development of plantation society, changes along the slave coasts of Africa—may go far toward helping us unravel the observed cultural differences in Suriname today.

REFERENCES CITED

[Item numbers refer to Bibliography in Part Three]

Abbenhuis 1943. Item *2*.

Abbenhuis 1964. Item *5*.

Aguirre Beltrán, Gonzalo 1946. La población negra de México, 1519-1810. Mexico: Ediciones Fuente Cultural.

Barbot, John 1732. A description of the coasts of North and South Guinea. *In* Awnsham Churchill (ed.), A collection of voyages and travels. London. Vol. 5.

Behn, Aphra 1688. Oroonoko; or the Royal Slave. *In* Montague Summers (ed.), the works of Aphra Behn, London: William Heinemann, 1915, V, pp. 125-208.

Benjamins and Snelleman 1914-17. Item *235*.

---

21. Though a stress on New World (as opposed to African) influence on the Suriname creoles, in particular Saramaccan, has been out of fashion at least since Herskovits's important paper (1930/31), it would be misleading to view my position merely as a kind of backward step. Essentially, my findings reject an exclusivistic argument of *either* persuasion, both the view that the Portuguese in Saramaccan must be African (which Herskovits so eloquently argued, and Voorhoeve, on the basis of new evidence, has supported) and that which saw it as simply a product of the Jewish plantations (e.g., Wullschlaegel 1856). The data, as presented here, do not support an either/or formulation and demonstrate, I believe, that adherents of both theories were, in part at least, historically correct.

Bridenbaugh, Carl and Roberta Bridenbaugh 1972. No peace beyond the line: the English in the Caribbean 1624-1690. New York: Oxford University Press.

Bubberman *et al.* 1973. Item 282a.

Buschkens, W.F.L. 1973. Het familiesysteem der volkscreolen van Paramaribo. Proefschrift, Leiden.

Buve 1966. Item *299*.

Byam, William 1667. An exact narrative of ye state of Guyana of ye English colony in Surynam. *In* V.T. Harlow (ed.), Colonising expeditions to the West Indies and Guiana, 1623-1667. London: Hakluyt Society, 2nd Series, No. LVI, 1924, pp. 199-222.

Craton, Michael 1975. Jamaican slavery. *In* S.L. Engerman and E.D. Genovese (eds.), Race and slavery in the Western Hemisphere: quantitative studies. Princeton: Princeton University Press, pp. 249-84.

Curtin, Philip D. 1969. The Atlantic slave trade: a census. Madison: University of Wisconsin.

Curtin, Philip D. 1975. Measuring the Atlantic slave trade. *In* S.L. Engerman and E.D. Genovese (eds.), Race and Slavery in the Western Hemisphere: quantitative studies. Princeton: Princeton University Press, pp. 107-28.

van Dantzig 1968. Item *350*.

Douglas 1930. Item *383*.

Dunn, Richard S. 1972. Sugar and slaves. New York: Norton (1973 edition).

Emmer, Pieter C. 1972. The history of the Dutch slave trade: a bibliographical survey. Journal of Economic History 32:728-47.

Fermin 1778. Item *406*.

Focke 1855. Item *414*.

Fogel, Robert W., and Stanley L. Engerman 1974. Time on the cross. Boston: Little Brown.

Fouchard, Jean 1972. Les marrons de la liberté. Paris: Editions de l'Ecole.

Franco, José Luciano 1968. Cuatro siglos de lucha por la libertad: los palenques. *In* J.L. Franco, La presencia negra en el nuevo mundo. Havana: Casa de las Americas, pp. 91-135.

Friederici, Georg 1960. Amerikanistisches Wörterbuch und Hilfswörterbuch für den Amerikanisten. 2 Auflage. Hamburg: Cram, de Gruyter and Co.

Green 1974. Item *472*.

Guillot, Carlos Federico 1961. Negros rebeldes y negros cimarrones. Montevideo: Fariña Editores.

Hartsinck 1770. Item *510*.

Herlein 1718. Item *521*.

Herskovits 1930/31. Item *528*.

Herskovits 1941. Item *535*.

Hostmann 1850. Item *561*.

Hurault 1960. Item *574*.

Hymes, Dell (ed.) 1971. Pidginization and creolization of languages. Cambridge: Cambridge University Press.

King 1973. Item *675*.

Lenoir 1973. Item *777*.

Lichtveld 1928-30. Item *782*.

van Lier 1971. Item *793*.

Ligon, Richard 1673. A true & exact history of the Island of Barbados. London.

Lindblom 1924. Item *827*.

van der Linde 1966. Item *833*.

Mintz, Sidney W. 1971. Toward an Afro-American history. Cahiers d'Histoire Mondiale 13:317-32.

Mintz and Price n.d. Item *893*.

Morssink n.d. Item *905*.

Nassy 1788. Item *914*.

Neumann 1961. Item *919*.

Oudschans Dentz 1927. Item *933*.

Oudschans Dentz 1938. Item *938*.

Parris, Scott 1972. The role and influence of third parties on relations between European colonial establishments and the maroons: a survey of selected areas. Ms.

Parry, J.H. and P.M. Sherlock 1965. A short history of the West Indies (2nd ed.). London: Macmillan.

Patterson, Orlando 1967. The sociology of slavery. London: MacGibbon and Kee.

Postma, Johannes 1970. The Dutch participation in the African slave trade: slaving on the Guinea Coast, 1675-1795. Unpublished Ph.D. dissertation, Michigan State University.

Postma, Johannes 1975. The origin of African slaves: the Dutch activities on the Guinea coast, 1675-1795. *In* S.L. Engerman and E.D. Genovese (eds.), Race and slavery in the Western Hemisphere: quantitative studies. Princeton: Princeton University Press, pp. 33-49.

Price 1970. Item *1022*.

Price 1973. Item *1025*.

Price 1975. Item *1028*.

Price, Richard n.d. Toward an Afro-American history: Saramaka society in the eighteenth century. Ms in preparation.

Price and Price 1972. Item *1030*.

Price, Richard and Sally Price n.d. Values, history, and society: the Saramaka maroons of Surinam. Ms. in preparation.

Rens 1953. Item *1052*.

Sahlins, Marshall D. 1968. Tribesmen. Englewood Cliffs: Prentice-Hall.

Schuchardt 1914. Item *1118*.

Schumann 1778. Item *1122*.

Scott, Major John 1668. The description of Guyana. *In* V.T. Harlow (ed.), Colonising expeditions to the West Indies and Guiana, 1623-1667. London: Hakluyt Society, 2nd Series, No. LVI, 1924, pp. 132-48.

Sheridan, Richard B. 1973. Sugar and slavery. Baltimore: Johns Hopkins University Press.

van Sijpesteijn 1854. Item *1130*.

Simons, A.J. 1934. Het verval van Suriname. West Indische Gids 15:299-308.

Simons 1960a. Item *1137*.

Simons 1960b. Item *1138*.

Staehelin 1913-19. Item *1154*.

Stedman 1796. Item *1161*.

van der Straaten, H.S. 1973. Suriname, een volksplanting; van Willoughby tot Crijnssen. Verre Nasten Naderbij 7(3):65-84.

Teenstra 1835. Item *1180*.

van der Elst 1975. Item *1217*.

Voltaire 1759. Candide ou l'optimisme.

Voorhoeve 1971. Item *1244*.

Voorhoeve 1973. Item *1245*.

Voorhoeve and Lichtveld 1975. Item *1249*.

Warren 1667. Item *1280*.

Wolbers 1861. Item *1314*.

Wong 1938. Item *1317*.

Wooding 1972. Item *1318*.

Wullschlaegel, H.R. 1856. Deutsch-Negerenglisches Wörterbuch. Löbau.

PART TWO

A GUIDE TO THE SOURCES

PRELIMINARIES

This bibliographical survey represents one scholar's choice of the major sources for the study of Bush Negro history and ethnography. The bulk of the survey is organized chronologically and, for the nineteenth and twentieth centuries, tribe by tribe, so that the reader can follow the cumulative growth of knowledge about a particular tribe through time. I have, however, complemented this chronological presentation with four topical sections devoted to specialized aspects of Bush Negro life that have received sufficient attention from commentators to warrant setting them off from the rest.

A number of the minor items listed in Part Three are not covered here, as I have attempted to trade absolute completeness for clarity and usefulness. Many of these fall under the rubric of popular literature: (1) "sensational" pieces written at least in part for their shock value, ranging from Papillonlike views of the Marowijne Bush Negroes to accounts of miraculous magical cures by "jungle witchdoctors" (e.g., *356-358, 556, 1141, 1206, 1212, 1300-1302*); (2) journalistic accounts and travelogues, which tend to be affected by their dependence for information on city guides, cooks, and interpreters who, while willing to speak with authority about Bush Negro life, often rely on the stereotypic misconceptions about these peoples widespread among Creoles (e.g., *178a, 283, 508, 751, 752, 855, 856, 913*); the recent, more explicitly commercial literature directed at luring tourists to an exotic vacationland (e.g., *365, 471, 1142a*, and most issues of *Surinam Adventure* and the *Surinam Sun*); and (4) the sizable body of fiction inspired by Bush Negroes and the initial runaways, much of it written by missionaries, frequently directed at children, and often based directly on historical accounts (e.g., *227, 272, 411, 701, 752a, 761, 766, 767, 916, 1057, 1169, 1261*). I might mention also that this popular literature includes many photos of ethnographic interest, though they are often unidentified, even as to which tribe they represent (see, e.g., *206, 245, 308, 559, 571, 945, 1002, 1009, 1010*).

Bush Negroes, like other "exotic" peoples, have been subject to more than their share of distorted reportage. Indeed, their special history and physical isolation has until very recently guaranteed their being viewed as something distinctly "other," by other Afro-Americans as well as by European and American whites. Though I have long intended to analyze at length the images of Bush Negroes in the literature, here I can merely mention in passing a few of the more persistent perspectives.

The Bush Negro as Noble Savage is probably the most tenacious of the stereotypes. In fact, thanks to Behn's depiction of Oronooko—the African prince/rebel slave—Suriname boasts one of the earliest representations of the Noble Savage in all world literature (*227*). A century later, Stedman's glowingly romantic vision of his maroon adversaries (*1161*), held a mirror up to the morals and mores of European society, revealing a very similar sensibility. The 1920s witnessed a renaissance of this romantic view, with larger-than-life heroes stalking the pages of several widely read authors (e.g., *632-643, 1206-1214*). Hints of exotic sex and jungle mysteries, rivers swarming with piranhas, and the ever-present beat of the tomtom permeate many works of this period, and ethnographic fact was often distorted. Vandercook, for example, reports that "So vain are they of their magnificent physiques that all young men who do not attain a stature of at least six feet are driven out to die" (*1210*:227-28). Nor has the Noble Savage been absent even from more serious ethnographic writing; for example, the works of Hurault (*572-584*) contain certain passages that conduce to this image. The recent, much publicized discovery of the Suriname maroons (renamed "bush Afro-Americans") by a team of black Americans has again revivified this image, this time as "the Original Brother" (see *331a, 550, 682a, 846, 1216, 1319*).

Other persistent stereotypes may be mentioned even more briefly. When not portrayed as Noble Savages, Bush Negroes have often been depicted as childlike innocents, carefree despite their allegedly limited intellectual and cultural capacities. Language often serves as the vehicle for conveying this particular message (as does a heroic physical type in portrayals of the maroon as Noble Savage), and Bush Negroes—who are in fact unusually elegant rhetoricians—are portrayed speaking a broken-English baby talk (e.g., *637, 913, 1277*). And this has even found its way into the language section of the *Guiness Book of World Records* (1971 edition, p. 166), where one learns under the heading "Least Complex" that "the language with the smallest vocabulary is Taki taki spoken by bush blacks in French Guiana, South America. It boasts only 340 words." Many missionary authors adopt another perspective, viewing "their" Bush Negroes as souls gone astray, living in terror under the sway of the powers of darkness (see, among many others, *344, 382, 745, 760*, but note that this view of Bush Negroes terrorized by their gods is not confined to missionaires, e.g., *796*). Finally, an image of Bush Negroes as at worst rapacious outlaws and at best sneaky liars dominates much of the more strictly colonial literature, from the original war years through the works of certain twentieth-century government officials (see, e.g. *616-631*).

That all authors have a viewpoint is a truism, and the preceding paragraphs are in no way intended to impugn journalistic, popular, or missionary writings in general. Indeed, in the essay that follows, I point frequently to useful works of these types. However, I have been sobered, in preparing this essay, by the dreary regularity with which the most sensational, bizarre, and inaccurate observations of the past continue to be recycled—in disregard of the often excellent but modestly toned admonitions of contemporaneous authors as well as more modern ethnographic research. That these inaccuracies may be pressed into the service of more sympathetic ideological positions in no way enhances their legitimacy, for Bush Negroes, "objectified" anew, remain as ever largely mute victims. Nevertheless, recent years have witnessed an encouraging increase in solid scientific research, and for the first time Bush Negro works of poetry, fiction, and ethnography are making their appearance (e.g., *8b, 615, 948, 1309*). Until there are more Bush Negroes who can tell their own story, however, it would seem a foremost responsibility of those scholars who have been their guests to grant them their full say, just as it is the responsibility of their readers to insist always on an inside view, whoever reports it.

FORMATIVE YEARS:
THE SEVENTEENTH AND EIGHTEENTH CENTURIES[22]

Contemporary descriptions of the colony of Suriname, published periodically during this era largely for the consumption of readers in the metropole, often contain a good deal of historical synthesis. Warren (*1280*) provides observations on marronage and punishments for recaptured maroons during the English period, and Aphra Behn's well-known fictionalized account of these themes (*227*) covers the same early years of the colony. Herlein, writing a half century later (*521*), gives a vivid sense of the perceived threat posed by organized maroon bands, and offers details on expeditionary forces sent against them; his work presents rich details on slave life during the early eighteenth century as well. The detailed history of the Jewish colony on the Suriname River, compiled in the late eighteenth century by David Nassy (*914*), is sprinkled with references to marronage, rebellions, raids by Bush Negroes, and the numerous colonial expeditions against them. Hartsinck's

22. For this as well as later periods of Suriname history, the maps included in *282a* are indispensable aids.

monumental 1770 history (*510*) contains the most complete synthetic account of the maroon bands—always, however, from the colonial perspective. It includes the most extensive published descriptions of expeditions against the Bush Negroes, with names and locations of villages, their estimated populations, the names of their leaders, and so forth; it discusses the seventeenth-century band led by Jermes (see Part One, above, for other references on Jermes, Ganimet, and the seventeenth-century maroon groups); it is the standard published source on the negotiations leading to the abortive 1749 treaty with the Saramaka, and those of the 1760s with the Djuka, the Saramaka, and the Matawai; and it includes as well the texts of the treaties themselves (on this, see also *490* and *675*).

Much of the other published historical writing that covers the first one hundred years of Suriname's history is derivative and of little value, though this might not be evident at first glance. For example, van Berkel's 1695 description (*238*) is plagiarized almost word for word from Warren (*1280*), and it seems likely that he was never in Suriname at all; Accarias de Sérionne (*6*) appropriates large sections of Hartsinck (*510*), simply translating them into French; and the historical portion of Stedman's narrative that deals with Bush Negroes (*1161*) is little more than an abbreviated version of Hartsinck's discussion.

Several later synthetic works of history present useful overviews, though except in those rare cases when the author refers to an archival source, there seems little reason for the interested student not to consult directly the eighteenth-century works already mentioned. Wolbers' general history of Surinam (*1314*) is the major nineteenth-century history of the colony, but it depends very heavily on Hartsinck and Nassy for the sections relating to maroons. The brief amateur history (*383*) of Douglas, a retired planter, draws—albeit somewhat uncritically—on a much broader range of published sources in attempting an overview of early maroon history (for a similar, earlier attempt, see *1130*). More recently, van der Elst has offered an ambitious synthetic presentation (*1215*), still relying, however, on the standard published sources. The only serious attempts to synthesize historical sources on the Guiana maroons in general, drawing on archival as well as published materials, are van Panhuys's encyclopedia article (*972*) and a lengthy paper by Wong (*1317*), who integrates into his account oral-history data gathered during his service as district commissioner on the Marowijne.

The bulk of the literature devoted to eighteenth-century maroons centers on the wars of the 1770s and 1780s and the formation of the Aluku (Boni) tribe. Stedman (*1161*) offers the most dramatic eyewitness account of the wars (which has been widely plagiarized). In addition to detailed discussions of military strategy, this work provides numerous bits of ethnographic information on the rebels (albeit often romanticized) including drawings of items of material culture. For the planters' perspective on the wars and the extent to which they nearly ruined the colony, see, in addition to Stedman, *27, 30, 31, 278, 510, 662, 845a,* and *1082.* For discussions of these war years which focus more strictly on the rebels themselves and on their developing communities, see *5* (which includes maps of early village sites), *453,* and *574;* for important oral accounts of the period, gathered from Alukus in the nineteenth century, see *335;* on the historical controversy surrounding the rebel leader Baron, see *32, 934,* and *361.* André Pakósie, a young Djuka, has recently written an intereseting revisionist account of early Aluku history, based on oral transitions (*948*), as has "Ajax" (*8a*). On the rebellion of the Black Rangers, who first fought against the maroons but later joined them, see the recent study by de Groot (*487* and *493*) as well as *33b, 207, 396, 574, 952,* and *966.* De Groot provides an excellent overview of the "Boni war" in *492c.*

Early maroon communities in the Guianas were not confined to Suriname, though it was only there that they flourished. Secondary sources on early maroon bands in French Guiana include *359, 360,* and *519.* For first-hand descriptions by outsiders, see *595, 596,* and *403.* A unique maroon perspective is provided by *894.* Late eighteenth-century plans by the French government to move the Suriname Bush Negroes into French territory are discussed in *359, 574,* and *858;* the documents reveal a chilling continuity from the eighteenth century to the present day in the ways in which the colonial powers have attempted to make major policy decisions about Bush Negroes— unilaterally and without any informed consideration of the consequences for the populations themselves. For Guyana (British Guiana), Synnott's overview of slave rebellions (*1173*) complements the standard accounts of the great Berbice uprising of the mid-eighteenth century, in which an attempt was made by the rebel leaders to join the maroons in Suriname (see *189, 349a, 349c, 509a, 510, 667, 918, 1006a, 1069,* and *1282a*).

As for ethnography—information on the internal organization and daily life of the early Suriname maroons—we are fortunate to have a major body of data on the Saramaka beginning almost immediately after the treaty of 1762, thanks to the aggressive attempts of the Moravians to missionize that tribe during the second half of the eighteenth century. The key work remains Staehelin's collection of German missionary diaries and letters (*1154;* see also *29, 33, 33b*), which I am currently editing and annotating for publication in English. Supplementary works of genuine ethnographic importance, all by eyewitnesses, include Quandt's report (*1039*), which is particularly good on maroon-Indian relations, Riemer's book (*1060*), which is rich in Saramaka ethnography and history, and Schumann's excellent dictionary of Saramaccan (*1122*).

Oral history relating to the eighteenth century has been collected by several missionaries, government officials, and others, usually in small bits and pieces. In addition to the works of Staehelin (*1154*) and Riemer (*1060*), and the varied Aluku materials mentioned above, Morssink's manuscript (905) is a rich ethnohistorical source, as are works by King (673, 675), van Coll (321), and Junker (616, 617).

I end this sketch of early sources with a caveat: serious work on early Suriname history can no longer depend simply on the traditional mix of eighteenth-century histories and nineteenth- and twentieth-century rehashes of them. To reconstruct a picture of the development of the Guiana maroon societies, long-term research must be undertaken, on the one hand, to squeeze out every last bit of relevant information from archival sources (as in 492c) and, on the other, to gather oral data from the descendants of the original maroons, among whom very strong historical traditions persist.[23] Preliminary ethnohistorical research of this latter kind has been carried out by Lenoir among the Paramaka (777), Green (472) and the de Beets among the Matawai (225a), and by de Groot, particularly on the Djuka (492). My own current research is focused on analyzing, comparatively, colonial accounts and Saramaka oral traditions gathered in the eighteenth, nineteenth, and twentieth centuries by other outsiders, as well as those which I collected and am continuing to gather from Saramakas in the field.

THE NINETEENTH CENTURY

From an ethnographic viewpoint, the richness of the eighteenth-century German missionary reports on Saramaka derives largely from the fact of the authors' having resided in Bush Negro villages, permitting descriptions, though often naive, of daily social interactions, as well as rudimentary case histories. The lack of materials of a comparable kind for the greater part of the nineteenth century is perhaps the largest gap in our knowledge of the development of these societies.

From the first half of the nineteenth century, we have only a few brief, generalized ethnographic accounts, which usually offer a few sentences each on such subjects as houses, clothing, diet, government, trade, and so forth. Von Sack (1079) and van Heeckeren (515) provide typical examples for the early years of the century. Van Eyck, a government postholder for the Saramaka, wrote a more comprehensive, generalized mini-ethnography about

---

23. The major unpublished resources on this period would seem to be: (1) the diverse government records now on deposit at the Rijksarchief in the Hague, and (2) the diaries, reports, letters, and records of the German Moravian missionaries who lived among the Saramaka during the second half of the eighteenth century, most of which were deposited at Herrnhut. The former materials are currently being catalogued and examined in detail by Silvia W. de Groot and her students at the University of Amsterdam. The state of the materials at Herrnhut is unknown to me, though much was allegedly damaged during the Second World War. Those materials from Herrnhut pertaining to Saramaka and Matawai that are included in Staehelin's collection (1154) will become available in the English edition I am preparing currently.

1830 *(401)*. Hostmann, a physician and amateur naturalist, wrote a similar though longer account of Djuka, based on a visit there in 1840 *(561*, ch. 7). Benoit's book of engravings on Suriname *(236)* includes Bush Negro (apparently Djuka) clothes and other material culture of the 1830s, as well as a brief first-hand description of relations between them and the government. And Hurault gives extensive citations from several unpublished official reports of visits to the Aluku/Boni that pertain to this period *(574, 582)*. During the first half of the nineteenth century, occasional trips into the interior by missionaries produced data on locations and names of villages as well as fragments of diverse ethnographica; one of the best examples is *1231*, which describes a trip to the southernmost Saramaka villages. I suspect that whatever still "undiscovered" material there may be on daily life during this period would be found either in the archives of the Moravians or in missionary journals of the time.

As discussed in Part One, marronage and violent slave resistance continued far into the nineteenth century, until the very eve of Emancipation. Recent runaways who lived on the fringes of coastal territory without joining the organized tribes constituted a continuing problem in the relationship between the government and the tribes throughout the period. For discussions of the 1832 conspiracy, in which recent runaways played a major role, and which culminated in the burning of a large portion of Paramaribo and the heroic death by torture of its youthful leaders, see *663, 1062, 1179,* and *1181*. On problems of slave control and marronage among the volatile border population of Nickerie during this period, see *514*, and on the contemporaneous Coronie rebellion, see *1053* and *1250*. The major dispute of 1835 between the government and the Saramakas about the harboring of new runaways, which led to the removal from office of the Saramaka *gaamá* and the drawing up of revised treaties with the Saramaka, Djuka, and Matawai, is treated in *63, 186, 492d, 620, 906, 941,* and *1317*, and see also *834*. The largest group of nineteenth-century runaways established their own village close by the cultivated regions, and included a substantial number of new maroons from as late as 1860; a first-hand ethnographic sketch of this community before its post-Emancipation assimilation into coastal society was written by the missionary van Coll *(321*; see also *223, 225, 328, 383, 555,* and *1230)*.

The Eastern Tribes. Small bits of first-hand ethnographic information on the tribes along the Marowijne River begin to appear after the mid-nineteenth century, largely as a by-product of the economic development of the region for goldmining, logging, and so forth. Problems of access by outsiders to the interior as well as intertribal relations on the Marowijne—particularly between the Aluku and the Djuka—took on a new importance during this period (see *1128, 481, 574,* and *582)*. Preliminary explorations of the Marowijne in 1860 and the major Franco-Dutch expedition of 1861, which opened the region to outsiders, were prompted by these concerns, and were written up by Ronmy, Vidal, Kappler, and Cateau van Rosevelt *(1072, 1226, 1227, 648, 311)*, producing information on village names and locations, headmen, and diverse ethnographic fragments. Similar data are included in the accounts of contemporaneous trips by Charrière (*315, 316, 317*), Kappler (*649*), and Bouyer (*273, 274*). Kappler, a German colonist who did much to open up the eastern part of Suriname to settlement, had relations with Bush Negroes, particularly those from the Cottica and Marowijne regions, from the 1840s through the 1870s, and his books include a good deal of ethnographic data as well as information on interethnic relations (*646, 647, 650, 651, 652*). Coster, a sawmill owner, was in close contact with Bush Negroes in this same region during the 1850s and wrote a brief general ethnography, organized topically (*328*); this report provided the bulk of the Bush Negro "ethnography" presented in Bonaparte's study of 1884 (*254*). This latter work, a lavish catalogue of the Colonial Exposition of 1883 in Amsterdam (for which several Djukas and Saramakas were transported to Europe along with items of material culture) includes some rare early photographs.

The French explorer Jules Crevaux visited the Marowijne tribes in the late 1870s, and produced the most astute reports of ethnographic detail and oral tradition yet recorded for that region (*335-340*). Coudreau's observations on the same area a decade later, while much less impressive, provide additional data (*329-331*). The diary of Father Brunetti's mission trip of 1886 to the Aluku and the Djuka (*281, 282*) contains many ethnographic observations of interest, and includes a number of important sketches (as well as some purely fanciful ones). Professor Joest's expedition of 1890 resulted in both a museum collection brought back to Germany and some generalized ethnography that combined secondary sources with his own strongly biased observations (see *600-604*; *603* also includes several excellent photos). Reports of other expeditions to the Marowijne during this period include *841, 842, 1146,* and *1147.*

During the final years of the nineteenth century, L.C. van Panhuys resided at Albina on the Marowijne and made investigations into several aspects of Bush Negro culture in that region. His publications, usually in the form of brief, particularistic papers in scholarly journals, appeared over a period of more than fifty years. His contributions to the *Encyclopaedie van Nederlandsch West-Indïe* (*972, 973*) represented the best scholarly summary to that date of what was known of the history, society, and culture of the Guiana maroons. His numerous contributions in the field of art and folklore, the great bulk of which concern the Marowijne tribes, are discussed below.

I know of very few reports from this period by people actually living in Bush Negro settlements in the Marowijne or Cottica region. The brief general "ethnography" of the missionary-teacher J.G. Spalburg (*1144*), who lived in the village of the Djuka chief during the final years of the century, demonstrates how valuable such first-hand observations can be (see also *1143*). Although my list of items includes seven other missionary manuscripts on this region for the second half of the nineteenth century (*39, 44, 50, 282b, 282c, 282d, 1160*), it would be surprising if archival research in the Netherlands, Germany, France, and Suriname did not uncover other valuable documents of this kind. For Moravian missionaries were all required to keep journals and did so rather faithfully until well into the twentieth century. One of the most interesting contemporary perspectives on the events along the Marowijne during the second half of the century can be found in the works of the Matawai prophet Johannes King, whose father was a Djuka, and who writes in considerable detail about his attempts to missionize that tribe (see below for further discussion of his work).

Finally, the Dutch historian Silvia W. de Groot has produced two careful studies of the relationsihip between the Djukas and the government in the mid-nineteenth century (*481, 483*), with important data on economics as well as politics.

The Central Tribes. In comparison to the Marowijne region, the Suriname River, where the Saramaka live, was visited only rarely during the second half of the nineteenth century. A few pages on Kappler's several-day trip to the Saramaka villages closest to the coast are included in *647*. Professor Martin's geological expedition of 1885 got only as far as the villages now under the artificial lake, but he presents some useful general ethnography, including several drawings, in his reports (*859-861*; see also *41*). Baron A. Klinckowström's zoological expedition of 1890 to the Sara Kreek and nearby Saramaka villages (which also included a visit to the Cottica Djuka) resulted in a varied ethnological collection still in Sweden (see *681* and *827*). The only expeditions of the period to reach the confluence of the Gaánlío and the Pikílío were those of Cateau van Rosevelt, aimed at mapping this still uncharted territory during the 1860s and 1870s. His reports provide invaluable data on village locations as well as a good deal of incidental ethnography (*310* and *312*). By the 1870s, foreign investors in Suriname such as the Australian I. Rosenberg, who accompanied Cateau on his 1862 trip, were involved in gold and timber operations in the lower stretches of Saramaka territory.

There is little during the nineteenth century on Saramaka to compare with the rich materials of the eighteenth-century missionaries. Ledderhose (*734*) gives an account of the reopening of the Moravian Mission, which had been closed for nearly thirty years, during the 1840s (see also *837a* and *873a*), and Schneider covers in summary fashion missionary work for the rest of the century (*1110*); the works of Johannes King, who was married to a Lower River Saramaka woman, include some incidental material on Saramaka (see below). Except for the fragmentary but ethnographically interesting diary of Albitrouw (*8d*), I am unaware of accounts during the remainder of the century written by people *living* in Saramaka villages. The only exception is the literature surrounding the Messianic figure Anake, whose social-religious experiment completely transformed one village for the half century following 1891 (see *8c, 51, 219, 625, 1235, 1250*).

Materials on the Matawai and the Kwinti are relatively rich for the latter part of the nineteenth century. J. King's writings (*669-679*) focus on the Matawai, and contain a great deal of information about intratribal politics, history, attitudes about religion, and diverse ethnography. (For commentary on King and his work and for bibliographical guidance see *428, 677, 773, 831, 1121, 1234, 1236, 1241, 1242, 1248, 1249,* and *1321a*). King's picture of Matawai politics can be rounded out with the help of *62*, which cites archival, newspaper, and other sources, and with the oral accounts synthesized in *472*. Burkhardt's 1898 mission history (*286*) includes a chapter on the Matawai, as does Schneider's 1893 work (*1110*); Wehle describes a late nineteenth-century mission visit (*1283*); and there may well be manuscript materials by missionaries dating from this period for the Matawai, in the Moravian archives (see also *36*). On the Kwinti during this period, see, in addition to King's work, contemporary accounts in *286* and *1163*, and recently collected oral data in *472*.

TWENTIETH-CENTURY ETHNOGRAPHY

The Eastern Tribes. The early years of the twentieth century saw continued visits by explorers and travelers to the eastern region. Van Cappelle made a brief visit to the Cottica Djuka, commenting on diverse aspects of their culture and publishing several excellent photographs (*302, 306*). Guffroy explored the Lawa and Tapanahoni rivers about 1902 and wrote a report (which I have not been able to examine) on their inhabitants (*496*). The two major Dutch expeditions up the Lawa (1903-4) and the Tapanahoni (1904) produced a good deal of incidental ethnographic information on the Djuka, Aluku, and Paramaka. The main reports are those of Franssen Herderschee (*422, 423*), Versteeg (*1225*), and de Goeje (*451*)—which include maps and important photos relating, for example, to religion as well as to material life. A brief first-hand description of the burial of a *vodu* god dating from this period is included in *457*. De Goeje was especially interested in relations between these Bush Negroes and Indians, and discusses the trade language used between the Djuka and the Trio and Wayana (*449* and *451*); for more recent discussion of this special relationship, see *26, 582,* and *1066*. Brief missionary reports on the region appeared throughout the period, and include *81, 295, 426, 427, 698, 735,* and *1310-1312*.

Prior to the professional ethnographic work of the 1960s, the most important interpreters of Djuka life were W.F. van Lier and F. Morssink. Thanks to de Groot's detailed study of van Lier's relations with the Djuka (*486*), we know a great deal about the kinds of contact on which his ethnographic observations are based. Though his earliest works (*794, 795,* and *796*) include a good deal of material directly from his field diary, his subsequent writings tend to be more synthetic. His single most important work is probably his monograph on Djuka religion (*806*), which includes considerable comparative information on the other tribes and numerous bibliographical references. Its format, however, is catalogue-like, treating diverse terms, beliefs, and practices discretely, with little attention to their social context. As the representative of the Suriname government to the Djuka during the 1920s, van Lier includes in his works information on official attitudes toward Bush Negroes as well as on the political organization of the Djuka. (On this, see also *486* and *1149.*) For a careful analysis of the government's attempt at community development among the Djuka (1917-26), in which van Lier played the central role, see *486.* My bibliographical list of van Lier's works (*794-826*), compiled with the generous help of, among others, Silvia W. de Groot, supersedes the partial listing in *486,* pp. 251-52.

The Redemptorist Father F. Morssink also collected a great deal of significant data on the Djuka during this period, and was a frequent critic of van Lier's work. In spite of Morssink's fiercely proselytizing attitude, his general ethnographic observations, collections of oral historical accounts, and discussions of religion and political succession represent—to my mind—the most important nonprofessional corpus in twentieth-century Bush Negro studies (see, in particular, *905*, unfortunately never published). Morssink was involved with the Djuka for more than three decades, beginning about 1910, but worked with each of the other tribes as well; his major work (*905*) treats each tribe separately.

Modern anthropological field research among the Djuka—the first with any Bush Negro tribe—began in 1961, with the work of André Köbben, H.U.E. Thoden van Velzen, and W. van Wetering, whose excellent studies comprise the standard ethnographic sources on that tribe. Köbben, who lived for a year in a village on the Cottica River, concentrated on social organization and has written, in English, a series of clear and concise papers on the kinship system (*685*), social roles (*688*), sociocultural change (*687*), religion (*689a*), the field work experience (*684*), politics (*689b*), and law (*689*). (Other references on Bush Negro law include *924a, 1083, 1274a,* and *1305.*) At the same time, Thoden van Velzen and van Wetering, then Köbben's students, worked in the village of the Djuka tribal chief on the Tapanahoni River, and they have produced rich full-length monographs on political organization (*1190*) and witchcraft (*1294*), papers on aspects of religious, domestic, and political organization (*1189, 1295, 1293, 1191, 1192a, 1192b, 1193*), and a film (*1187a*). They are now engaged in research relating to the new messianic movement of Aklari (see *1192, 1193a*), and are writing a book on Djuka religious leaders (*1193b*). During their initial field work period, H.E. Lamur studied migrant Djuka laborers in Paramaribo for a period of several months (*723*).

For the Aluku, we do not have ethnographic coverage of the same quality, in my opinion, as we have for the Djuka. Although Morssink devotes a section of his *Boschnegeriana* to the Aluku, his work with them was less intense than with the Djuka, Saramaka, or Matawai. Léon Damas, the French Guianese poet of *négritude*, records his personal vision of the Aluku in *349b*. But the major work with this tribe was accomplished by the French geographer Jean Hurault, who made eight expeditions to the interior of French Guiana between 1948 and 1965. Though he never carried out long-term field work in a community, his considerable exposure to the Aluku has resulted in extensive publications—a comprehensive general ethnography (*576*), a monograph on material culture and economy, particularly horticulture (*579*), which is the only detailed work on this subject thus far for any Bush Negro tribe (but see also *205, 436, 437, 714, 715*), a book on aesthetics (*581*), papers on demography (*573*), canoes (*575*), and hunting and fishing (*577*), and a film of funeral rites (*585a*). Anthropologists working with other Bush Negro tribes have questioned certain of Hurault's conclusions about the Aluku and about Bush Negroes in general (see *683, 686, 1023, 1186*), noting, for example, some tendency toward romanticization; an assumption of considerable sameness in the culture and societies of the various tribes, so that misleading generalizations about "Bush Negroes" are frequent in his works; and an undue stress on normative (as opposed to behaviorial) data, which imparts a certain quality of rigidity and uniformity to the society, which one would not expect to find, given the considerable amount of conflict and manipulation present in the other tribes. Nevertheless, Hurault's works, all in French, contain a great deal of important information on many aspects of Aluku life. Shorter-term field work among the Aluku has been carried out by de Lamberterie (*720*); Sausse, who was primarily interested in medical problems (*1089, 1090*); and the North American anthropologist Thomas Price, who discusses the "cultural self-image" of the Aluku, comparing it to that of other Afro-Americans with whom he has worked (*1035* and *1036*).

The Paramakas have been described in any detail by only three authors during this century. Morssink, who began working among them in 1910, devotes a section of his book (*905*) to their history and includes field journal data from his visits. H. Leerdam, a Creole schoolteacher who lived among them (as well as among the Saramakas and Djukas) for a number of years between 1926 and the 1950s, wrote a series of articles which constitute a serious if untutored attempt to deal with diverse ethnographica (*739*). His work is particularly interesting in its attempt to deal comparatively with the Paramaka data, and shows how much could be done by more sophisticated work that considers Bush Negro societies and cultures as a set. The North

American anthropologist John Lenoir conducted field research among the Paramaka in 1970-73, and his dissertation (*777*) focuses on religion, particularly the influence of the Moravian and Roman Catholic missions on traditional beliefs and rituals; this work also contains valuable historical data on the formative years of this tribe. Lenoir is currently doing work on the messianic movement of the Djuka prophet Aklari, who visited Paramaka during the summer of 1974, and he is continuing to write on the political ramifications of church affiliation among the Paramaka, viewed through time (*777a* and *777b*).

The Central Tribes. Two major Dutch expeditions in 1908 and 1910-11 explored the Suriname River and the Gaánlío under the leadership of Eilerts de Haan, who died of malaria during the second trip. His report, published in 1910 (*395*) contains many significant ethnographic observations (e.g., on cicatrization, marriage, and language), important maps of village locations, and several photos. Kayser's report on the second expedition (*661*) covers the same itinerary, but with little detail. In the mid-1920s, further exploration of this territory was reported by Stahel and Ijzerman. Stahel's work (*1158*) includes some rich ethnographic passages, with descriptions of religion, village life, and fauna, drawings of house and canoe construction, and a reproduction of Cateau van Rosevelt's important mid-nineteenth-century map. Ijzerman's massive geological report (*593*) contains incidental ethnography, detailed maps, lists of village names, and other useful geographical information.

For more than two decades, beginning in the teens of the present century, two highly opinionated amateur ethnographers—Father Morssink (see above) and the part-time government official L. Junker—wrote on the Saramaka. Junker, whose authoritarian and paternalistic attitude toward the Saramakas caused serious confrontations with them on several occasions, published on a variety of ethnographic subjects, often presenting data and viewpoints in open conflict with those of Morssink. Two of Junker's papers (*616, 617*) include important collections of oral history; three (*618, 619,* and *623*) are devoted to Saramaka religion; two discuss problems of succession to the office of *gaamá* (*620, 631*); two include telling accounts of Junker's own confrontations with Saramakas (*622, 630;* see also *1134*), the first also including a discussion of a visit to Djuka; there is a first-hand account of Anake's millenarian experiment (*625*); and there are papers on gold and balata concessions, hunting, and fish drugging (*627, 626, 629*). Staal provides a "reminiscence" on the Saramaka *gaamá* during this period, in *1150*. A good deal of missionary ethnography by Moravians residing in Saramaka villages appeared during the first half of the century. The most important are probably *739, 763,* and *765,* but see also *85, 99, 106-110, 262-267, 294, 736, 737, 741-744, 746, 753-762, 764, 766-773,* and *1098*.

During the 1920s, changes in the intellectual climate of the United States fostered a new interest among urbane educated North Americans in the "exotic" black cultures of the New World. Artists and dancers, as well as readers of the popular intellectual magazines "discovered" black culture, though strongly romanticized and seen through western lenses. It was in this atmosphere that several American expeditions to Saramaka territory were undertaken during the 1920s, the most important of which were those of Morton Kahn and Melville and Frances Herskovits. Kahn, an American physician, made three brief trips to the interior, chiefly to collect woodcarvings and other items of material culture (now housed in the American Museum of Natural History, New York City). He did not hesitate to publish prolifically on his experience, in spite of having only a most superficial understanding of what he saw. Because of their tendency toward sensationalism, his publications—from *Djuka* (which is based largely on experiences with the Saramaka) to articles such as "Africa's lost tribes in South America; an on-the-spot account of blood chilling African rites of 200 years ago preserved intact in the jungles of South America by a tribe of runaway slaves" (*632-643*)— unfortunately remain among the most heavily used sources by American journalists and other popular writers about Bush Negroes. Dutch scholars, however, were quick to criticize the superficiality of his work (see, e.g., *231* and *897*).

Melville Herskovits, pioneer in Afro-American anthropology, spent part of two summers among the Saramaka (accompanied during one summer by his wife) in his first foreign field work. From his later works, it is clear that Herskovits's Saramaka experience deeply affected his later intellectual orientation. In one of her last publications, Frances Herskovits noted of her husband that "His field experience in Surinam in 1928 and 1929 had a profound influence on his thinking .... In the Guiana bush, among the Saramacca peoples (sic), he saw, as he often told his students, nearly all of western sub-Saharan Africa represented" (*543*: vii). And it is probably significant that at the time of her recent death, Frances Herskovits was working on a revision of *Rebel Destiny* (*544*), their major work on Saramaka. Though their field work was brief and by modern standards superficial, and was informed both by some romanticism and by what appears to be a sturdy (if not always conscious) desire to uncover African retentions among the Saramaka, their book succeeds where Kahn's fails in conveying a convincing portrait of village life, insofar as a traveler could observe it. The Herskovitses made the first field recordings of Bush Negro music, which were transcribed and published along with numerous proverbs (*545*). This latter work, which primarily concerns the culture of the Paramaribo Creoles, is perhaps the most important statement to date of the need to analyze Bush Negro cultural materials in the broader context of Afro-Suriname and of Afro-America more generally. In addition to these two books, Herskovits's Saramaka research resulted in papers on Bush Negro social organization (*527*), art (*525, 537, 542*), language (*528*), divination (*540*), and the "African" game of Adjiboto (*524, 530*); in

Herskovits's more general writings on Africanisms in the New World, Bush Negroes often played a pivotal role (see, e.g., *532, 533, 536,* and many of his more general theoretical works, not listed in my bibliography). Herskovits's initial field work with the Saramaka was never followed up by him or by any of his students.

In the two decades following the Second World War, to my knowledge only two relatively brief pieces of descriptive ethnography appeared on the Saramaka—an account of funeral practices and beliefs by a Roman Catholic missionary in the northern area of the tribe *(373)* and a thirty six-page general ethnography written by O.J.R. Jozefzoon, an educated, Christian Saramaka from the same region *(615).*

In 1966 and 1967-68 and briefly in 1974 and 1975, Richard and Sally Price engaged in general ethnographic work on the Pikílío. To date, this has resulted in a monograph on Saramaka social structure *(1029),* and papers on emigration and social change *(1021),* the belief system *(1024),* aspects of verbal and graphic arts *(1033, 1031, 1032, 1022, 1023, 1027a, 1030),* and historical linguistics *(1028).* Saramakas and other Bush Negroes are placed in the broader comparative context of Afro-American maroons in *1025.* Currently in progress are: a general ethnography on the Saramaka, the historical reconstruction of the society in the eighteenth century, discussed above, and an integrative work on Saramaka arts. During the period of the Prices' field work, Jan de Vries, who served as a schoolteacher at the Moravian mission at Djoemoe, carried out investigations on education and medical programs, resulting in several papers and a dissertation for a degree in education *(1262-1267;* see also *324).*

The massive transmigration, involving more than 6000 Saramakas in the 1960s as a result of the hydroelectric project, has not yet received systematic study and remains a subject of considerable political sensitivity. It is worth noting that far more publicity and public concern was devoted to the international rescue operation for the animal population displaced by the artificial lake than to the displaced human inhabitants. Articles with titles like "Pity the poor jungle animals" *(1139)* were commonplace, but there was almost complete silence about the Saramaka. Perhaps the sole exception was the reports by Drs. Jan Michels—the government official whose difficult task it was to inform the Saramakas of the decision and to see them through the period *(881, 883, 884,* and, most recently, *890).* (It was also Michels who initiated the international rescue operation for the jungle animals.) For studies of Bush Negro land rights with particular relevance to the transmigration, see *1041, 1042,* and *1043.* For journalistic treatments of the transmigration, see *119-122, 125, 128, 129, 132, 211, 326, 1290c.* The Roman Catholic bishop provides his views on the transmigration in *717.* The most widely read of the animal rescue sagas (including photos of inundated Saramaka villages), later condensed in *Reader's Digest,* is *1277* (see also *133, 134, 137, 138, 139,*

1139, 1140). A review of the literature, mostly biological, concerning the effects of the lake appears in *1291*. Studies on the potential medical effects of the creation of the lake include *195, 1183*, and *1184*. A brief scholarly report on the social effects of the transmigration was prepared by Guda in 1967 (*495*). Paerl provides a more "politicized" analysis in *947*. Adiante Franszoon, a Saramaka by birth, has recently completed a report on current social conditions in the new villages (*423a*). And currently, Silvia W. de Groot is analyzing the transmigration as part of her broader research on the history of government/Bush Negro relations.

The Matawai and Kwinti are described in expedition reports dating from the earliest years of the twentieth century. Van Stockum's account (*1165* and *1166*) includes varied incidental data on the Matawai. Bakhuis's report of the Coppename expedition of 1901 (*203*) includes key ethnographic data on the Kwinti, covering, for example, demography, education, and aesthetics, and including sketches and photos. Moravian Bishop R. Voullaire wrote about the Matawai in the following years (see in particular *1258* and *1259*), as did his confrere, Burkhardt (*289, 290*), and other missionaries (e.g., *65, 87, 102, 218, 750, 917, 1114*). The early 1920s report of the Gonggrijp and Stahel expedition to Matawai (*464*) includes a map with village locations and several excellent photos.

Exploratory ethnographic field work among the Matawai was carried out by A.A. Trouwborst in 1963 (see *1202*), but this work has not been published. Edward Green conducted research among the Matawai in the early 1970s, and in his dissertation presents an overview of their society and culture, focusing particularly on "acculturation" (*472*). Chris and Miriam de Beet have recently concluded dissertation research on the Matawai, with his field work focused primarily on religion and demographic change, and hers on household and domestic organization; the results are currently being written up as a joint project (*225a*).

The Kwinti remain the least known of the Bush Negro tribes (see, e.g., *154*), though during the summer of 1973 Dirk van der Elst conducted field-work among them (*1217, 1218* and *1219*), and Green includes in his dissertation (*472*) discussion of their historical relation to the Matawai, based on oral accounts collected from Matawais. Van der Elst is planning further field work with this group.

Scholarly interpretations of Bush Negro society and culture based solely on secondary sources include several studies worthy of mention. Sir Harry Johnston's treatment of Bush Negroes in *The Negro in the New World* (*606*) prefigured a number of works in the Afro-Americanist tradition. Delafosse, writing from his Africanist perspective, attempted to tease out Africanisms on the basis of data collected by Crevaux (*362, 363*), as did Fagg (*402*) using materials from Herskovits and Kahn. Lindblom, working with the late nineteenth-century collection of Bush Negro material culture made by Klinckowström (see above), produced a careful, well-documented analysis of Amerindian and African influences which includes numerous drawings (*827*); nonmaterial "traits" such as personal names, dueling with seconds, and so forth are given similar treatment in the same work. Among the more recent interpreters of Bush Negro culture from afar are: Angelina Pollak-Eltz, whose neo-Herskovitsian analyses are based on a very selective use of the sources (see *1013, 1016, 1017*); the late Roger Bastide, whose interesting theoretical orientation is combined with ethnographic data drawn almost exclusively from the somewhat problematical works of Hurault (*215, 216, 216a, 217*); Debbasch, whose interpretive overview of maroons in the Caribbean touches particularly on the Aluku, with strong historical emphasis (*359*); Lowenthal, a geographer, who includes a synthetic section on Bush Negroes as one of his groups of "ethnic outcasts" in the Caribbean (*844*); Neumann, who draws on a very wide range of published secondary sources and archival and museum materials in East Germany to present a Marxist interpretation of Bush Negro society, economy, and culture (*920, 921, 922*); and van der Elst, who attempted a synthesis of information available up to the late 1960s in his dissertation (*1215*).[24]

Changes in the political consciousness of Bush Negroes vis-à-vis the national society during the twentieth century can be gleaned from many of the works by W.F. van Lier, Junker, and S.W. de Groot, cited above. For various negotiations about land- and transport-rights, and other matters of economic importance, as well as the texts of revised treaties made during this period, see *63, 68, 1151, 1317*. For Saramaka *gaamá* Djankuso's letter to the League of Nations, see *252*. On the current rapidly changing consciousness of Bush Negroes, and their participation in national politics, an overview has yet to be written; but see *611, 1290c*, and *368*. On this subject, Suriname newspapers, which I have not examined systematically for this bibliography, are an indispensable source; I have, however, listed several brief reports that have come my way (e.g., *150, 153, 158, 160, 162, 165, 176a, 182a*, and *564a*). Likewise, I have not had the opportunity to examine Dutch newspapers systematically, to follow political and social developments among the many Bush Negroes now living in the Netherlands. In late 1970, the tribal chiefs of the Djuka, Saramaka, Matawai, and Paramaka were sent by the national government on a visit to West Africa. Silvia W. de Groot, who was their official escort, has published several accounts of the journey (*488, 489, 491*,

---

24. There are two belief-rite complexes which have captured the imagination of several authors writing in the folkloristic tradition—one involving magical protection against the bite of poisonous snakes, the other regarding the relationship between leprosy and the breaking of certain taboos (see, for example, *232, 233, 399, 602, 653, 722, 784, 935, 978, 995, 1136*). Since neither of these complexes is confined to Bush Negroes, the articles about them lean heavily on data from other Afro-Surinamers.

and, in particular, *492*). On the current plan of the Suriname government to integrate the Bush Negro populations into national life by means of consolidating them in large planned towns to be built in the interior, see *178, 182b, 1124,* and *1290c* (and for a related plan to build a series of hydroelectric dams throughout the interior, *398a*). Hesselink, a social geographer, outlines the implications of the company-town syndrome in a recent analysis of Moengo (*546*).

LINGUISTIC STUDIES

Many of the early commentators on Bush Negroes made incidental remarks about language (see, e.g., *328, 337, 860, 1154*). The first systematic work was accomplished by the eighteenth-century German missionaries in Saramaka, who produced an excellent dictionary (*1122*) and Saramaccan translations of a number of Christian texts (many of which are reprinted in *1118*; see also *1248*, pp. 106-9, for a complete description of these works, which are not otherwise listed in the present bibliography). Twentieth-century word lists include *185* (on Ndjuka), *449*, and *451* (mainly on the trade language used between the Djuka and the Trio and Wayana), *1304* (on Saramaccan), and *585* (on Aluku). The first modern dictionary on a Bush Negro language is *376*, on Saramaccan, which compares current forms with those in Schumann's eighteenth-century dictionary. More recently, serious lexicographic work has been undertaken in Saramaccan and Ndjuka by the Summer Institute of Linguistics, of which *587* (including Ndjuka, Saramaccan, and Sranan forms) is the first product. A comprehensive, comparative dictionary of the Suriname creoles is currently in preparation under the direction of Jan Voorhoeve.

For the past several years, the Summer Institute of Linguistics has been sponsoring research directed toward increasing literacy in Saramaccan and Ndjuka. In addition to pilot textbooks in Ndjuka (*591, 590*), they have produced a large number of texts for local consumption—translations of biblical fragments, historical works and, more recently, a number of native-authored texts (*13-24a, 142, 145, 151, 152, 157, 161, 169, 170, 173a, 175, 181a, 181b, 182d, 183, 184, 191, 198, 199, 589, 1091-1096,* and see also *949a*). The publication of numerous additional texts is planned for the near future. A large collection of materials, recorded and transcribed in Saramaccan, including songs, traditional tales and proverbs, council meetings, and diverse religious ceremonies, was collected by Price and Price and is available in *1033*. Recently, Arthur Licht, a young Saramaka man using the pen name "Akanamba," brought out what is probably the first printed poetry in Saramaccan (*8b*).

A considerable number of articles and a good deal of controversy has arisen around the problematical "Djuka script" of Afaka, which dates from the early twentieth century. I merely list here the relevant references, several of which argue the case for African continuities (*260, 347, 348, 387, 388, 460, 461, 462, 463, 637, 903, 1046, 1172*); the Africanist perspective receives its fullest treatment in *1196*.

Except for a brief paper by Donicie (*375*) and the pioneering work of Voorhoeve (*1237, 1239,* and *1240*), modern descriptive linguistics on Bush Negro languages began with the Summer Institute of Linguistics in the late 1960s. Grimes has described a standard orthography for the Bush Negro languages (*475*); Huttar and Huttar have written on Ndjuka phonology (*588*), and Park on Ndjuka discourse (*998a*); Glock, Grimes, and Rountree have written a series of papers on Saramaccan tone, phonology, verb structure, and narrative style (*447, 448, 448a, 476, 1074, 1075, 1075a*), and Smith has written a brief discussion of Saramaccan vowel harmony (*1141a*). Two papers by R. and S. Price treat aspects of Saramaka language use, one on names and naming (*1031*), the other on secret play languages (*1032*). Sociolinguistics has been largely neglected, though Eersel offers some astute observations on Bush Negro/Creole interaction (*394*).

For many years now, serious scholarship has been devoted to the historical development of the Suriname creoles. Schuchardt, a pioneer in creole studies, made a first attempt to describe the historical position of Saramaccan in the broader context of New World creoles (*1118*). Van Panhuys includes historical data and speculation in his encyclopedia section on Bush Negro languages (in *972*). Lou Lichtveld, whose fiction has brought him international renown under the pen name Albert Helman, has argued for decades for the importance of a Pan-Caribbean approach to creole studies and for a serious effort to uncover their underlying African components (see, e.g., *782* and *785*). A 1930 paper by Melville Herskovits (*528*), which lay in obscurity for years, was the most detailed treatment to that date of the historical relationship between the Bush Negro languages, particularly Saramaccan and Sranan. His argument that the relatively high proportion of Portuguese lexical items in Saramaccan stemmed largely from the use of a maritime Portuguese Pidgin on the coast of West Africa prefigured a very large body of "creolist" literature written during the 1960s and 1970s concerning the New World more generally. Jan Voorhoeve mapped out a program for the comparative study of Suriname creoles in 1959 (*1238*) and, in addition to those of his works already cited, has developed his ideas about historical relationsihips in two important papers (*1244* and *1245*). The work of Douglas Taylor, which has been so important in fostering a comparative approach to creoles, deals historically with Bush Negro languages, particularly Saramaccan, in greatest detail in *1176* and *1178*. Hancock has used Saramaccan and Sranan materials in developing an argument about the historical relationships of these and the other so-called "English-derived Atlantic creoles" (*502, 504*), but his evidentiary base is considerably weaker than that of Voorhoeve. Alleyne makes extensive use of Saramaccan materials in his historical-comparative study of Afro-American languages (*11*). Huttar explores syntactic similarities between Ndjuka and the Kwa languages (*587a*). Smith compares Saramaccan and Lingala (Bantu) vowel harmony (*1141b*). Father Daeleman, writing from an Africanist perspective, attempts to demonstrate the lexical influences of KiKoongo on Saramaccan (*345, 346*); R. Price has written a commentary on this paper, raising further questions about historical relationships with Africa (*1028*). (On historical linguistics, see also Part One, above.)

MEDICAL RESEARCH

Because I have not surveyed the medical literature on Bush Negroes with the same care as I tried to show for other topics, the following remarks are no more than a preliminary guide. A useful survey of medical research for Suriname as a whole can be found in *716*.

Since the eighteenth-century reports by missionaries in Saramaka, malaria has dominated observations on Bush Negro pathology. Twentieth-century studies of malaria include *250, 259, 412, 628, 713, 971, 994, 1133, 1183*, and, in particular, *712*. Since 1957, the Anti-Malaria Campaign of the World Health Organization, affiliated with the Suriname Department of Public Health, has worked intensively in the interior of Suriname. Their mimeographed annual reports contain substantial quantitative data on malaria incidence and the prevention program among Bush Negroes, as well as data about the difficulties encountered by them in attempting to carry out relevant public health measures. (On the related difficulties encountered by a missionary physician in the decade following the Second World War, see *477-480*.)

Several other topics have been singled out for attention. Studies on blood and blood groups include *297, 638, 781*, and *1282*. Works on parasitology include *195, 196, 197, 249, 251, 279*, and *1184*. Peri-natal disease is treated in *598*, and tuberculosis in *639* as well as *1089, 1090*, and *1097*. Items containing general observations on pathology among Bush Negroes (covering many of the topics mentioned above) include *1158, 1089, 1090*, and *1097*, all of which include comparative data on Amerindians. A useful source on the relative incidence of various medical conditions are the annual reports of the Moravian medical teams in the interior (see *117*). These make clear the importance of local ecological differences for health problems among Bush Negroes; epidemiological problems are quite different, for example, for Saramakas living on the Upper Suriname River, for those on the Lower River, for Tapanahoni Djuka, and so forth. Such reports make clear that it is as misleading to generalize about Bush Negroes in matters of health as on other aspects of their social and cultural life.

Studies of human biology—physical anthropology, nutrition, and so forth—have appeared irregularly since the late nineteenth century. They include *254, 379, 656, 657, 1228,* and in particular *377* on the growth and development of children in the Upper Marowijne, and *850, 851,* and *852.* It is worth noting not only that the epidemiological environments are subtly different from region to region in the areas inhabited by Bush Negroes, but that differences in diet and nutrition also contribute to the considerable degree of variation in medical problems.

HISTORY OF MISSIONS

A large number of the works appearing in the bibliography relate to the missionizing effort. Nevertheless, this is the area in which my list could most easily be expanded by more systematic work in specialized journals as well as in archives.

The primary sources on the eighteenth-century mission among the Saramakas were mentioned earlier in this chapter. Secondary accounts focusing on this period—all written by Moravians—include *333, 334, 517, 557, 907, 1064,* and *1287.* Later works dealing synthetically with the history of Moravian missions among the Bush Negroes, again all written by members of that church, include *100, 213, 221, 275, 285, 592, 718, 757, 764, 1048a, 1110, 1163, 1253, 1256,* and *1284.* A look at *175a, 382,* and *1221,* recent overviews of the Moravian effort written from the inside, disclose how consistent the church's point of view about these missions has been during more than two centuries of labor in the interior. The best work of serious scholarship on the Moravian effort in Suriname, which contains material of relevance to the Bush Negro missions, is by van der Linde (*831*), and see now also *1043a.*

For general information on the more limited Roman Catholic missionary activity among Bush Negroes, see *4, 73, 271, 146,* and *441a,* as well as the several works of Father Morssink which are discussed under Twentieth-Century Ethnography (see above). Morssink's appendix to *905* gives a detailed chronology of Roman Catholic mission work among the Bush Negroes.

STUDIES ON THE ARTS

Probably no single ethnographic subject has received more attention in the literature on Bush Negroes than the arts—in particular woodcarving. The following brief survey is intended as an introductory guide to this very uneven literature. Because of the visual saliency of woodcarving, cicatrization, and the other graphic arts in these societies, almost every visitor to a Bush Negro village beginning in the mid-nineteenth century, has included comments, drawings and, more recently, photos in his report. Yet until the middle of the nineteenth century, there is no mention of decorative woodcarving or cicatrization among the maroons; neither the letters collected by Staehelin based on long residence with the Saramaka (*1154*) nor the detailed first-hand observations and descriptions of maroon material culture by Stedman (*1161*) nor Benoit's pictorial account of the colony (*236*) gives any indication that the practice of these arts had yet been initiated. Indeed, Hurault (*581*) and R. and S. Price (*1022, 1023, 1030*), who have independently carried out the only serious historical investigations of these arts, conclude that these arts began to develop for the first time only 150 years ago (on the basis of this negative evidence combined with rich documentation of historical development and change in travelers' reports and museum collections since the 1850s).

Cateau van Rosevelt mentions decorated stools in his mid-nineteenth-century report on the Saramaka (*310* and *312*). Crevaux, during his 1877 expedition to the Djuka and Aluku, made an important collection, now housed in the Musée de l'Homme, and commented on cicatrization (*340*). Bonaparte's extensive catalogue of the 1883 exposition at Amsterdam (*254*) includes excellent photos of cicatrization and items of material culture. Reports resulting from the expeditions carried out during the next quarter century enrich substantially our knowledge of late nineteenth-century graphic arts, not only woodcarving and cicatrization, but also decorative sewing. All of the following items (except the first) include either sketches or photos of these arts, as well as some commentary: *321, 281, 282, 859, 302, 395, 203*; for information on the tribes represented, see above. Several contemporaneous expeditions resulted in collections of material culture: *658* (on a collection brought to Leiden), *1146, 681* (on the important collection brought to Stockholm and discussed at length in *827*, the first serious attempt to disaggregate African and Amerindian influences on Bush Negro material culture), *603* (on a collection brought to Berlin), and *422, 423,* and *451* (three reports on collections brought to Leiden, the first two of which were of major importance and were discussed with numerous sketches by van Panhuys in items *963* and *964*; see also *54*).[25]

Until the last two decades, only three investigators focused their attention on the ethnography of Bush Negro woodcarving *in the field*: van Panhuys,

---

25. Among collections of Bush Negro material culture not mentioned in this essay are those in Frankfurt, Rochester, N.Y. (Museum of Arts and Sciences), Bloomington (Indiana University Museum), Philadelphia (the University Museum), Los Angeles (Museum of Cultural History, U.C.L.A.) and, of course, Paramaribo (Surinaams Museum).

Kahn, and Herskovits. The extensive descriptions and analyses of van Panhuys are based primarily on his residence during the 1890s at Albina, though he also analyzed several later collections made by others. His more important works on art are *963* and *964* (see previous paragraph), *967* (which includes some excellent sketches of cicatrization), and *982, 983,* and *991* (the last of which includes details on cicatrization, and all three of which present numerous sketches of woodcarvings and analyses of their "meaning"). Other of his studies (usually short notes) bearing on the same subjects include *953, 955, 958, 959, 962, 965, 968, 979, 984, 985,* and *986.* A large collection of diverse woodcarvings from the same period as those in van Panhuys's descriptions is currently housed in the Tropen Museum in Amsterdam. The Kahn and Herskovits expeditions of the late 1920s (see above) resulted in several publications on art, especially woodcarving, and two major field collections largely from Saramaka. Kahn's discussions of woodcarving (see in particular *636* and *637*) are marked by the same superficiality and misinformation that typify the rest of his ethnography. Kahn's collection, now housed in the American Museum of Natural History in New York, includes a log containing some information on the provenience of pieces; photographs of many of the objects in this collection are found in item *351*. The Herskovitses' studies of art (*525, 537, 539, 542, 544*) show a firmer grasp of ethnographic realities, though their willingness to expound in an authoritative fashion on what are complex and subtle issues, on the basis of two very brief visits, makes these works as valuable for the questions they implicitly raise as for their substantive conclusions. The fine personal collection made by the Herskovitses has recently been deposited in the Field Museum in Chicago; photos of some of these pieces appear in *351*. A collection by the Herskovitses of nearly 200 pieces (of which less than half survived the war) is in the Museum für Völkerkunde, Hamburg.

Two scholars have written analyses of woodcarving, drawing very heavily on the Kahn and Herskovits materials. Dark, whose book (*351, 354*) includes excellent photographs, presents a formal analysis of the objects at his disposal. However, his uncritical reliance on the works of Kahn and Herskovits reduces the value of the rest of his text (see also *352, 353*). Crowley's interesting formal analysis of some combs from the Herskovits collection suffers from similar limitations (*342*).

Brief comments on the graphic arts, including often excellent photographs, are included in many of the journalistic, touristic, and missionary accounts of twentieth-century visits, and a number of brief articles devoted to the subject are included in the bibliography (where they are easily identifiable by title); examples of this genre are *393, 408, 923, 1268-1271*. Likewise, several brief studies of the arts by authors with no first-hand knowledge of Suriname appear in the bibliography (e.g., *332, 466,* and *513*).

Two substantive issues dominate serious scholarship on Bush Negro woodcarving—the nature of its symbolism and the origin and development of the art. Extensive discussions of symbolism range from the catalogues of motifs and their alleged meanings compiled by van Panhuys (e.g., *963, 964, 982, 983,* and *991*) through the discussions of Herskovits and Kahn (see above) to a small book by Muntslag (*912*) which asserts that the motifs form a writing system and that their juxtaposition on a particular piece composes a literal message. But by far the most sophisticated and scholarly study of symbolism is Hurault's lavish book (*581*). Like the earlier authors cited, Hurault argues that motifs are named and meaningful, that they are composed of more or less abstract representations of people, animals, or objects, and that their meanings are primarily sexual. Indeed, for him, sexual symbolism is the *raison d'être* of Aluku carving, and the messages transmitted by the carver are more highly valued, the more indirect and abstract the form in which they are expressed. R. Price, in a paper which reviews in some detail both Hurault's claims and the "symbolist" literature to date, calls into question many of these assertions, on the basis of field data from Saramaka (*1023;* for further discussion of "meaning" in Saramaka arts, see *1030, 1031*). As of this writing, it must be said that the question of the "meaning of meaning" in the woodcarvings of the various tribes remains unresolved.

In contrast to the continued controversy surrounding the issue of symbolism, our knowledge about the origins of Bush Negro woodcarving has been substantially expanded and clarified during the last several years. For decades, scholars had assumed that woodcarving was an "original" African art form, and formal similarities (the shapes of combs, stools, and so forth) on one side of the Atlantic and the other were taken as proof of direct historical continuity (see, e.g., *525, 636,* and *1232*). However, recent historical research, based on oral sources, field ethnography, and the examination of documents and museum collections, points to a nineteenth-century origin for this art, an efflorescence only around the turn of the present century, and continued development and change since then. R. Price (working on Saramaka materials) and Hurault (focusing on the Aluku) have arrived at strikingly similar progressions of distinctive "styles" in woodcarving during the past century, and both stress the central role of aesthetics in daily life and the importance of creativity, innovation, and change, of fads and fashions (*1022, 1023, 581*).

Such research suggests a reorientation of our focus, from trying to explain similarities of form considered in isolation to comparing broad aesthetic ideas, the implicit principles which generate these forms. One would no longer assume that the very real formal similarities between the art of Bush Negroes and that of some West African peoples is evidence of static "retentions" or "survivals," but approach them rather as products of independent development and innovation within historically related and overlapping sets of broad aesthetic ideas. Recent research into other realms of Bush Negro aesthetics—cicatrization (*1030*) and onomastics (*1031*)—suggests parallel conclusions. Such work does not ignore the existence of direct formal continuities with Africa, such as the wooden door locks discussed in *827, 937,* and *980* (see *893* for discussion of different types of continuities in general, and the circumstances in which they developed). But it does direct our attention toward new questions in the historical study of African continuities in the New World (see *892*: 55-58), and suggests the necessity of close collaboration with sophisticated art historians of Africa (see *1194-1196*).

A related suggestion, implicit especially in the work of Hurault and R. and S. Price, is the necessity to consider aesthetic principles and forms across, as well as within, specific media. While we must have field studies which take seriously men's and women's calabash decorations, embroidery and clothing styles, the designs on cassava cakes, men's and women's hairdos, body ornamentation, jewelry, and of course woodcarving, we must also have studies which view these expressive media within a more general aesthetic framework into which would also fit music, dance, the verbal arts, postures, and so forth (see *1027a*). Currently, the Prices are working on an integrative book on Saramaka esthetics, to be published by the UCLA Museum of Cultural History. If the recent past teaches any lessons, we can expect that the ongoing integration of Bush Negroes into the national society will bring rapid and far-reaching changes, and in some cases extinction, in these arts. Indeed, the recent price list of a large collection of "antique Bush Negro items" (*143*), advertised on the open market by a California dealer, suggests that further field research on the history of Bush Negro arts cannot afford to be long postponed.

Compared to woodcarving, the verbal arts have received relatively little serious attention in the literature. And perhaps because of the linguistic knowledge necessary for an analysis of, say, tales or proverbs in their social contexts, much of what has been written is laced with errors. To cite just one example, Hurault, who has published a series of tales, writes that "Anansi toli" (spider-trickster stories—an important tale-type throughout Afro-Suriname) are "never of a licentious nature" (*576*:268), though in fact prodigious and explicit sexuality is a prominent characteristic of their protagonist.

Analyses of any of the verbal arts have been few. The Herskovitses (*545*) deal with Saramaka proverbs and song texts in the comparative context of both Afro-Suriname and Afro-America more generally; the Summer Institute of Linguistics is continuing research on narrative style in Saramaccan (see *476, 448a,* and *1075a*); and R. and S. Price have discussed Saramaka play languages and naming and are continuing field research on the verbal arts (*1032, 1031, 1033*). I would suggest that on both stylistic and historical grounds, analyses of the verbal arts must eventually encompass, comparatively, *all* the Afro-Suriname cultures. Indeed, the literature on Creole (as opposed to Bush Negro) verbal arts is already relatively rich (for an overview, see *1249*). Examples of Bush Negro proverbs, tales, and song texts are found in *18-22, 24, 24a, 173a, 303, 304, 306, 307, 328, 387a, 387b, 545, 576, 1091, 1118, 1129, 1153,* and *1237,* as well as in many of the ethnographic works already cited. The only extensive collection of recordings and transcriptions on the verbal arts is for the Saramaka (*1033*). The study of the verbal arts, which are so important an aspect of Bush Negro social and cultural life, represents a wide-open field of inquiry for future researchers.

From the earliest first-hand comments on Bush Negro culture (e.g., *1154, 1161*) to the latest touristic accounts (e.g., *172*), dance, drumming, and song have been singled out for comment. But in spite of the visibility of these expressive forms even to the most casual visitor, scholars have rarely seen fit to study them seriously. A comprehensive encyclopedia article, reviewing the literature on Bush Negro music and musical instruments, concluded more than six decades ago that "for the study of . . . Suriname Bush Negro music, a beginning has yet to be made" (*235,* s.v. *Muziek-instrumenten en muziek*); for a contemporaneous, complementary review of the literature, see *969.* Since that time, little has been written to change this general observation.

Van Panhuys discussed song, dance, and musical instruments in several papers, often in the more general context of Afro-Suriname culture (*969, 985, 988, 989, 992, 993*). Gilbert has written briefly on music and drumming, but is not a primary source (*442-445;* see also *564*). And Schipper provided a summary of the literature on Bush Negro music in the mid-1940s (*1101*). Two major sets of field recordings were made among the Saramaka, one by M. and F. Herskovits (*543a*) and one by R. and S. Price (*1033*), and both are now on deposit in the Archives of Traditional Music, Indiana University. Because of the poor condition and quality of the Herskovitses' recordings (which were made on wax cylinders, since transferred to tape), it is difficult to check them against the extensitve transcriptions and musicological analysis done at the time by M. Kolinski and published in *545.* This study, though suffering from the same weakness of insufficient time in the field as the Herskovitses' other Suriname work, remains the only serious attempt to deal with Bush Negro music. The Prices' collection, though more varied in the kinds of music included, has yet to receive detailed analysis. This collection includes recordings and field interviews on drum language, another little-studied subject (see also *967*). A phonograph record with selections from the Prices' collection, and with brief ethnographic notes, will be available shortly.

Dance has received even less attention than music, though it has been mentioned in numerous travelers' accounts. Attention to the seemingly "bizarre" rather than to aesthetic aspects of dance tend to dominate (e.g., *123, 172, 1008*). There has as yet been little scholarly recognition of the remarkable variation in types of styles of dance (that is, in distinctive dance forms) from one region and tribe to another, nor in the truly impressive and complex stylization many of these achieve. (R. and S. Price, in a work in progress, analyze dance in Upper River Saramaka.)

To summarize. The literature on the arts, while extensive, is—with the possible exception of woodcarving—shallow. While our knowledge of, say, the social structure or history of the several tribes has been markedly enriched during the past decade, nothing comparable has occurred with music, dance, or the verbal arts. Perhaps the next decade of studies will witness a serious beginning in the description, analysis, and appreciation of these central and highly developed areas of Bush Negro cultures.

PART THREE

A BIBLIOGRAPHY OF THE GUIANA MAROONS, 1667-1975

INTRODUCTION

It is safe to say that this bibliography would never have been written had I any idea at the outset how much time and effort it would entail. Begun innocently, in an attempt to review the seemingly limited literature on Bush Negroes, it became a major project continuing for some five years. (The two largest bibliographies to date on Bush Negroes listed 108 and 164 items, and many of these turned out upon inspection to be about Creoles, not Bush Negroes; my own compilation, below, includes some 1300 additional items.) In 1972, thinking myself close to completion, I sent out a mimeographed version of the list, which then included about 750 items, to colleagues. Their responses and encouragement were instrumental in bringing the bibliography to its present form.

Over the years, a number of students and colleagues have made contributions, some simply suggesting a lead on a reference or two, others spending many hours helping locate books in libraries, and others taking a great deal of time answering my frequent written queries. I would especially like to thank several students—Jeanne Devine, Jonee Feldman, Gary McDonogh, Scott Parris, and particularly Drexel Woodson; two fellow bibliographers—Timothy O'Leary and John Szwed; and most of all my colleagues in Bush Negro studies—Chris and Miriam de Beet, Naomi Glock, Ted Green, Silvia de Groot, André Köbben, John Lenoir, Jan Michels, Catherine Rountree, Bonno and Ineke Thoden van Velzen, Dirk van der Elst, and Jan de Vries. Two bibliographers in Leiden, Juliette Henket-Hoornweg and Bertie A. Cohen Stuart, whom I still have never met, have given most generously of their time to check countless errant references and to suggest new leads—and to them I am deeply grateful. The staffs of the libraries at Yale and The Johns Hopkins universities as well as at the Surinaams Museum and the Cultureel Centrum

Suriname have helped in many ways. Barbara Curtin expertly typed and retyped what became a difficult and typographically complex manuscript. And Sally Price, who helped only incidentally during the project's first several years, provided considerable assistance and advice during its final preparation.

My intent in this bibliography is to enumerate all items of ethnological and historical relevance. Nevertheless, there are areas in which it proved impossible to be completely systematic. For example, newspaper articles, schoolbooks, films, and very general works (e.g., travelogues on South America) are included only as they came to my attention. I was unable to examine the full runs of certain missionary journals (e.g., *Missions-Blatt der Brüdergemeine*, and *Suriname-Zending*), which would undoubtedly have yielded further relevant references. Archival materials are represented only sparsely in my list; their compilation would require a project of their own (but see now *240a*). I have tried to include book reviews of works on Bush Negroes only when they make a contribution in their own right. But here, as elsewhere in difficult decisions about inclusion, my criteria have probably wavered over the years. I have been rather strict in ruling out Afro-Suriname materials that do not deal with Bush Negroes, though here, too, marginal decisions were sometimes subjective and arbitrary. The treatment of maroon bands in what is now Guyana and French Guiana is certainly incomplete, though this list is broader in these regards than any other to date; fuller bibliography for these areas must await systematic historical research.

It will come as no surprise to anyone who has attempted to compile a comprehensive bibliography that behind the incomplete entires in my list lie many frustrating hours. Item **93* is an apt illustration. If memory serves, the sequence was roughly as follows: In reading the unpublished dissertation of Dirk van der Elst (*1215*), I came upon an intriguing reference to an article in the *Toronto Star* entitled "Black lords of the bush: Dutch Guiana, the only place where a nation of whites is subservient to a nation of blacks." Unable to obtain this newspaper in the United States, I corresponded over a period of months with the efficient reference staff of the Toronto Public Library who conducted several searches through the indicated issue and others, but drew a complete blank. I then wrote to Professor van der Elst who replied that though he had not himself ever seen the item, he had been given the reference to it some years before by his teacher, the late Melville Herskovits. I gave up hope. Then, a year or two later, while reading through the "new publications" section of the *West-Indische Gids* for 1933/34, I recognized this errant reference, and tried the Toronto Public Library once again, to no avail. My tentative conclusion is that Herskovits saw the *West-Indische Gids* announcement (which was in error), noted it down for future use without having seen the article itself, and many years later passed the reference on to his student. Other incomplete or problematical references in the list could tell similar sagas, and many now complete items have nearly identical stories, only with happier endings.

Among the major bibliographies consulted to suggest new items to be reviewed for this project were:

Abonnenc, E., J. Hurault, R. Saban, *et al.*
1957 Bibliographie de la Guyane Française; Tome I. Paris: Larose.

―――
1859-1917 Catalogus der Surinaamsche Koloniale Bibliotheek. The Hague: Martinus Nijhoff; Paramaribo: H. B. Heyde.
Comitas, Lambros
1968 Caribbeana 1900-1965. Seattle and London: University of Washington Press.
Gordijn, W.
1972 Bibliografie van Suriname. Amsterdam: Nederlandse Stichting voor Culturele Samenwerking met Suriname en de Nederlandse Antillen.
Hiss, Philip Hanson
1943 A selective guide to the English literature on the Netherlands West Indies. New York: Netherlands Information Bureau.
Mevis, René
1974 Inventory of Caribbean Studies. Leiden: Caribbean Department of the Royal Institute of Linguistics and Anthropology.
Nagelkerke, G.A.
1971 Literatuur-overzicht van Suriname, 1940 tot 1970. Leiden: Koninklijk Instituut voor Taal-, Land- en Volkenkunde.
1972 Literatuur-overzicht van Suriname tot 1940. Leiden: Koninklijk Instituut voor Taal-, Land- en Volkenkunde.
O'Leary, Timothy J.
1963 Ethnographic bibliography of South America. New Haven: Human Relations Area Files.
Voorhoeve, Jan, and Antoon Donicie
1963 Bibliographie du négro-anglais du Surinam. Koninklijk Instituut voor Taal-, Land- en Volkendunde, Bibliographical Series 6. The Hague: Martinus Nijhoff.
Work, Monroe N.
1928 A Bibliography of the Negro in Africa and America. New York: H. W. Wilson.

The conventions used in this bibliography are relatively simple:
• Items are arranged alphabetically and numbered serially. (Numbers followed by "a," "b," or "c" are discrete entries, i.e., these number-letter combinations have no special meaning; moreover, in several cases, e.g., *48, 560,* numbers are missing from the list—again, this has no significance. Both the number-letter combinations and the number omissions result simply from additions and deletions made after the fundamental numbering system was established.)

• An asterisk preceding an item number indicates that the item was not seen by me; except for a very few items which were seen only by a colleague or correspondent, all nonasterisked items were reviewed by me personally.

• Titles of newspapers and journals are represented by abbreviations, listed in a separate section (Abbreviations for Periodicals). I attempt to provide as much publication data as possible about periodicals, especially those that would be unfamiliar to most anthropologists; in a few cases—e.g., HM, HS, V—I have been unable to locate these data, and list only minimal identification.

• I provide whenever possible a library or archival location for the items in this bibliography. Book locations are listed under each entry; locations for articles are listed under the abbreviation for the periodical in which they appear. Three locations are provided whenever possible: the first in the United States, the second in Europe, the third in Suriname. (When I knew of multiple United States locations, preference was given to the Library of Congress; on European locations, preference was given to the Netherlands.) Locations often proved extremely difficult to verify, especially for newspapers, and the absence of a location should not be read as definitive. The abbreviations used for library and archival locations are listed separately, below.

ABBREVIATIONS FOR LIBRARIES AND ARCHIVES

□	=	Location unknown.
ABA	=	Amerikaanse Bibliotheek, Amsterdam.
ABU	=	Archiv der Brüder-Unität, Herrnhut.
AGS	=	Library of the American Geographical Society, New York.
AHP	=	Archief der Herrnhutters (Evangelische Broedergemeente), Paramaribo.
AHT	=	Andover-Harvard Theological Library, Cambridge, Mass.
AHZ	=	Archief der Herrnhutters (Evangelische Broedergemeente), Zeist. [Currently housed in Rijksarchief, Utrecht.]
AM	=	American Museum of Natural History Library, New York.
AN	=	Archives Nationales, Paris.
ASC	=	Antropologisch-Sociologisch Centrum van de Universiteit van Amsterdam, Afdeling Culturele Antropologie, Amsterdam.
BCC	=	Bibliotheek Cultureel Centrum Suriname, Paramaribo.
BCL	=	Bedford College Library, London.
BHZ	=	Bibliotheek van de Zendingsgenootschap van der Evangelische Broedergemeente, Zeist.
Bi	=	Bischopshuis, Paramaribo.
BKH	=	Bibliotheek Katholieke Hogeschool, Tilburg.
BL	=	Bodleian Library, Oxford.
BLH	=	Bibliotheek Landbouw Hogeschool, Wageningen.
BM	=	British Museum Library, London.

BMB	=	Bibliotheek Ministerie van Buitenland Zaken, The Hague.
BPL	=	Boston Public Library, Boston.
BrU	=	Brown University Library, Providence.
BTH	=	Bibliotheek Theologische Hogeschool, Amsterdam.
BTHD	=	Bibliotheek Technische Hogeschool, Delft.
BV	=	Bibliotheek Vredespaleis, The Hague.
CaU	=	Catholic University of America Library, Washington, D.C.
CPL	=	Cleveland Public Library, Cleveland.
CrU	=	Cornell University Library, Ithaca.
CSL	=	California State Library, Sacramento.
CU	=	Columbia University Library, New York.
CvL	=	Collection of R. A. J. van Lier, Wageningen.
DLC	=	Library of Congress, Washington, D.C.
DV	=	Dienst Volksgezondheid, Paramaribo.
GI	=	Geografisch Instituut, Utrecht.
HSF	=	Hartford Seminary Foundation Library, Hartford.
HRAF	=	Human Relations Area Files, New Haven.
HU	=	Harvard University Library, Cambridge.
JHU	=	Johns Hopkins University Library, Baltimore.
KB	=	Koninklijke Bibliotheek, The Hague.
KI	=	Kriminologisch Instituut, Leiden.
KITA	=	Koninklijk Instituut voor de Tropen, Afdeling Antropologie, Amsterdam.
KITC	=	Koninklijk Instituut voor de Tropen, Centrale Boekerij, Amsterdam.
KTLV	=	Bibliotheek van het Koninklijk Instituut voor Taal-, Land- en Volkenkunde, Leiden.
LDS	=	Library of the Department of State, Washington, D.C.
LP	=	Landsarchief, Paramaribo.
LSE	=	London School of Economics Library, London.
LTS	=	Lutheran Theological Seminary Library, Philadelphia.
MI	=	Missiologisch Instituut, Leiden.
NSSR	=	New School for Social Research Library, New York.
NU	=	Northwestern University Library, Evanston.
NYAM	=	New York Academy of Medicine Library, New York.
NYP	=	New York Public Library, New York.
O	=	Not in National Union Catalogue or Union List of Serials
RPU	=	Rijksarchief der Provincie Utrecht, Utrecht.
SM	=	Surinaams Museum, Paramaribo.
SOAS	=	School of Oriental and African Studies Library, London.
SU	=	Stanford University Library, Stanford.
SUB	=	Library of the State University of New York at Buffalo.
TPL	=	Toronto Public Library, Toronto.
TU	=	Tulane University Library, New Orleans.
UBA	=	Universiteitsbibliotheek, Amsterdam.
UBG	=	Universiteitsbibliotheek, Groningen.
UBL	=	Universiteitsbibliotheek, Leiden.

UBU   = Universiteitsbibliotheek, Utrecht.
UC   = University of Chicago Library, Chicago.
UCB   = University of California at Berkeley Library, Berkeley.
UCLA = University of California at Los Angeles Library, Los Angeles.
UF   = University of Florida Library, Gainesville.
UI   = University of Illinois Library, Urbana.
UL   = University of London Library, London.
UML   = University of Minnesota Library, Minneapolis.
UP   = University of Pennsylvania Library, Philadelphia.
USB   = Universiteit van Suriname Bibliotheek, Paramaribo.
USDA = Library of the United States Department of Agriculture, Washington, D.C.
UV   = University of Virginia Library, Charlottesville.
UW   = University of Wisconsin Library, Madison.
VU   = Bibliotheek van de Vrije Universiteit, Amsterdam.
Y   = Yale University Library, New Haven.

ABBREVIATIONS FOR PERIODICALS

A   = Das Ausland. Wochenschrift für Länder- und Völkerkunde. Stuttgart and Munich. 1827-1893.
        [DLC/KTLV/□]

AA   = American Anthropologist. Journal of the American Anthropological Association. 1888-.
        [DLC/KTLV/□]

AAEU = Abhandlungen zur Anthropologie, Ethnologie und Urgeschichte. Frankfurt: Frankfurter Gessellshaft für Anthropologie, Ethnologie und Urgeschichte. 1908-25.
        [NYP/UBA/□]

ACIHR = Actes du Congrès International d'Histoire des Religions. 1900-.
        [Y/□/□]

ACu   = Amigoe di Curaçao: dagblad voor de Nederlandse Antillen. Willemstad.
        [O/KITC/□]

AESC = Annales: Economies, Sociétés, Civilisations. Paris. 1946-.
        [DLC/KB/□]

Af   = Afroamérica; revista del Instituto Internacional de Estudios Afroamericanos. Mexico: Fondo de Cultura Económica. 1945-46.
        [DLC/□/□]

AF   = American Forests. Washington, D.C.: The American Forestry Association. 1895-.
        [DLC/BLH/□]

Afr   = Africa. Journal of the International African Institute. London: Oxford University Press. 1928-.
        [DLC/KITC/□]

AG = Annales de Géographie. Paris: A. Colin. 1891-.
[DLC/UBA/□]

AHV = De Aarde en Haar Volken. Haarlem: A. C. Kruseman. 1865-.
[DLC/UBL/□]

AJH = American Journal of Hygiene. Baltimore: Johns Hopkins University. 1921-.
[DLC/UBA/□]

AJM = American Journal of Medicine. New York. 1946-.
[DLC/UBA/USB]

ALR = African Language Review. London: Frank Cass. 1967-.
[DLC/□/□]

ALS = African Language Studies. London: School of Oriental and African Studies. 1960-.
[DLC/□/□]

Am = Américas. Washington, D.C.: Pan American Union, Organization of American States. 1949-.
[DLC/UBL/□]

AMVD = Abhandlungen und Berichte des Staatlichen Museums für Völkerkunde, Dresden. Berlin: Akademie-Verlag. 1886-.
[DLC/KITC/□]

AMZ = Allgemeinen Missions-Zeitschrift. Monatshefte für geschichtliche und theoretische Missions-kunde. Berlin. 1874-1923.
[Y/KTLV/□]

An = L'Anthropologie. Paris. 1890-.
[Y/□/□]

Anth = Anthropologica. Ottawa: Research Centre for Amerindian Anthropology, University of Ottawa. 1955-.
[DLC/UBL/□]

Antr = Antropologica. Caracas: Instituto Caribe de Antropología y Sociología de la Fundación La Salle de Ciencias Naturales. 1956-.
[DLC/KITC/□]

AP = Algemeen Protestantenblad. Weekblad voor Nederlandsch-Indië. (Bandoeng?)
[O/KITC/□]

Ar = The Arts. Brooklyn, N.Y. 1920-31.
[DLC/□/□]

AR = The Annual Register, or a view of the history, politics, and literature, for the year—. London: J. Dodsley. 1758-.
[DLC/□/□]

AS = American Speech. Baltimore. 1925-.
[DLC/□/□]

ASo = L'Année Sociologique, 3e série. Paris. 1940/48-.
[DLC/UBA/□]

Av = Maandblad Avenue. Amsterdam: de Geïllustreerde Pers N.V. 1968-.
[O/□/BCC]

AWC = Algemeen Weekblad voor Christendom en Cultuur. Amsterdam.
        1924-39.
        [O/UBA/□]
BB   = Bouwkundige Bijdragen. Amsterdam: Maatschappij tot
        Bevordering der Bouwkunst. 1842-1881.
        [DLC/□/□]
BD   = Brabants Dagblad. 's Hertogenbosch. 1959-.
        [O/KB/□]
BFT   = Bois et Forêts des Tropiques. Paris: Société pour le
        developpement de l'utilisation des bois tropicaux. 1947-.
        [DLC/UBL/□]
BHW   = Berigten (Berichten) uit de Heiden-Wereld. Zeist:
        Zendelinggenootschap der Broedergemeente te Zeist. 1835-1928.
        [Y(1835-38, 1845-74)/KITC(1917-28); UBA(1835, 1839,
        1841-44, 1847-1903); AHZ/SM(1835-69)]
Bi   = Het Binnenhof. Katholieke dagblad voor's-Gravenhage en
        omstreken. The Hague. 1945-.
        [O/KB/□]
BI   = Boletín Indigenista. Mexico: Instituto Indigenista Interamericano.
        1941-.
        [DLC/KTLV/□]
BIZ   = Berliner Illustrirte Zeitung. Berlin. 1892-1945.
        [DLC/□/□]
BKM   = Bulletin van het Kolonial Museum te Haarlem. Amsterdam:
        Koninklijk Instituut voor de Tropen, Afdeling Tropische
        Producten. 1892-1913.
        [DLC/KTLV/□]
BMSA = Bulletins et Mémoires de la Société d'Anthropologie de Paris.
        2ᵉ série. 1866-1877.
        [DLC/□/□]
BNA   = Bijblad der Nederlandsch Antropologische Vereeniging. Leiden:
        Nederlandsch Antropologische Vereeniging. 1912-41.
        [O/UBL(1913-26); UBG(1913-18, 1926-28, 1937-38, 1941)/□]
Bo   = Boletín de Estudios Latinoamericanos y del Caribe. Amsterdam:
        CEDLA.
        [DLC/KTLV/□]
BSGE = Bulletin de la Société de Géographie de l'Est. Paris. 1879-1914.
        [DLC/UBA/□]
BSGP = Bulletin de la Société de Géographie de Paris. Paris. 1822-99.
        [DLC/□/□]
BSPE = Bulletin de la Société de Pathologie Exotique. Paris: Masson.
        1908-.
        [NYAM/UBL/USB]
BSRB = Bulletin de la Société Royale Belge de Géographie. Bruxelles.
        1877-.
        [DLC/UBA/□]

BT   = Bible Translator. London: United Bible Societies. 1950-.
         [DLC/KTLV/☐]
BTLV   = Bijdragen tot de Taal-, Land- en Volkenkunde van Nederlandsch
         Indië. The Hague: Koninklijk Instituut voor Taal-, Land- en
         Volkenkunde van Nederlandsch-Indië. 1852/53-.
         [DLC/KTLV/SM]
Bu   = Buiten; geillustreerd weekblad aan het buitenleven gewyd.
         Amsterdam: Scheltema & Holkema's Boekhandel. 1907-36.
         [HU/UBA/☐]
BW   = Black World. Chicago: Johnson Publishing Co..1942-.
         (Published as Negro Digest, 1942-April 1970.)
         [DLC/☐/BCC]
CH   = Craft Horizons. New York: American Crafts Council. 1941-.
         [NYP/UBL/☐]
CHi   = Current History. New York. 1941-.
         [DLC/BV/☐]
CI   = Cultureel Indië. Leiden: Afdeeling volkenkunde van het
         Koloniaal Instituut, Amsterdam. 1939-1948.
         [DLC/KTLV/☐]
CLA   = Country Life in America. New York: Country Life-American
         Home Corporation. 1902-42.
         [DLC/☐/☐]
CO   = Les Cahiers d'Outre-Mer. Revue de Géographie de Bordeaux
         et de l'Atlantique. Bordeaux. 1948-.
         [DLC/UBA/☐]
CR   = Caribbean Review. Hato Rey, Puerto Rico. 1969-.
         [DLC/KTLV/☐]
CRSG   = Comptes rendus des séances de la Société de Géographie et de la
         Commission Centrale. Paris. 1882-1899.
         [HU/KTLV/☐]
CS   = Caribbean Studies. Río Piedras: Institute of Caribbean Studies,
         University of Puerto Rico. 1961-.
         [DLC/KTLV/☐]
CSM   = Christian Science Monitor. New England edition. Boston. 1908-.
         [DLC/UBA/☐]
Cu   = Cultura; revista quadrimestral. Rio de Janeiro: Ministerio de
         educaçao e saúde. 1948-.
         [HU/☐/☐]
CW   = The Catholic World, a monthly magazine of general literature
         and science. New York: The Office of the Catholic World.
         1865-.
         [DLC/☐/☐]
D   = Daedalus. Journal of the American Academy of Arts and
         Sciences. Cambridge, Mass. 1846-.
         [DLC/UBA/☐]

Dj   = Djogo. Officiëel orgaan van de Vereniging "het Surinaams
          verbond." Amsterdam. 1958-?
          [O/KTLV/SM]
DMGT = Documenta de Medicina Geographica et Tropica. (Tropical
          and Geographical Medicine); quarterly journal of tropical
          medicine and hygiene. Amsterdam, London, New York. 1949-.
          (Published as Documenta Neerlandica et Indonesica de Morbis
          Tropicis from 1949-51.)
          [NYAM/KTLV/□]
E   = L'Europeo. Milan.
          [O/□/□]
EC   = De Emancipatie Courant. Paramaribo: Comité tot viering van
          1 Juli als Algemeene Dankdag ter versterking van het Rasgevool.
          1926-1938(?).
          [O/KITC/SM]
EGM   = Elsevier's Geillustreerd Maandschrift; versameling van
          Nederlandsche letterkundige Kunstwerken. Amsterdam.
          1891-1941.
          [DLC/KTLV/□]
EH   = Eigen Haard. Geïllustreerd volkstijdschrift. Haarlem/Amsterdam.
          1875-.
          [DLC/KTLV/□]
EJ   = Explorer's Journal. New York: Explorer's Club. 1921-.
          [DLC/KB/□]
El   = Eldorado; Maandblad ter behartiging van de belangen van
          Suriname en de Nederlandse Antillen. Bussum. 1949-1950.
          [O/UBA/SM]
EM   = Echo's uit de Missies. Roosendaal: de Zusters Franciscanessen
          van het Moederhuis Mariadal. 1927-(?).
          [O/□/□]
Er   = Erts. Maandblad van de Billiton Bedrijven. The Hague. 1949-.
          [O/KTLV/SM]
Et   = Ethnos. Stockholm: Statens Etnografiska Museum. 1936-.
          [DLC/KB/□]
Eth   = Ethnology: an International Journal of Cultural and Social
          Anthropology. Pittsburgh: University of Pittsburgh. 1962-.
          [DLC/UBL/□]
FCW   = Foreign Commerce Weekly. Washington: U.S. Bureau of Foreign
          and Domestic Commerce. 1940-.
          [DLC/□/□]
FMN   = Field Museum News; bulletin of the Chicago Natural History
          Museum. Chicago. 1930-.
          [DLC/□/□]
Fo   = Focus. New York: American Geographical Society. 1950-.
          [DLC/UBA/□]

FR   = The Fortnightly Review. London: Chapman and Hall.
      1865-1954.
      [Y/KB/□]

GA   = De Groene Amsterdammer, onafhankelijk weekblad. Amsterdam.
      1877-.
      [DLC/UBU/□]

Ge   = La Géographie, terre-air-mer; revue mensuelle. Paris: Société
      de Géographie, Société d'Éditions Géographiques, Maritimes et
      Coloniales. 1900-.
      [DLC/UBL/□]

Gem = Gemeenschap. (Driemaandelijks) Tijdschrift voor vragen van
      Evangelie en samenleving. Paramaribo: E. B. G. in Suriname.
      1952-(?). (Two numbers published in 1952; begun again, with
      Volume 1, in 1953 as "Driemaandelijks tijdschrift . . .".)
      [O/KITC/□]

GG   = Geneeskundige Gids. Tijdschrift voor Geneeskunst en
      Volksgezondheid. The Hague. 1923-.
      [NYAM/UBL/□]

Gi   = De Gids. Amsterdam. 1837-.
      [Hu/KTLV/BCC]

Gl   = Globus; illustrierte Zeitschrift für Länder- und Volkerkunde.
      Braunschweig: F. Viewegund. 1861-1910.
      [DLC/KTLV/□]

GM   = Geographical Magazine. London. 1935-.
      [DLC/UBL/□]

Go   = Gonini (Surinaams Weekblad). Amsterdam: Granma. 1972-.
      [O/KTLV/BCC]

GR   = Geographical Review. New York: American Geographical
      Society. 1916-.
      [DLC/KTLV/□]

Ha   = Hangalampoe. Maandblad dat zijn licht laat schijnen over
      Suriname. Paramaribo. 1973-.
      [O/KTLV/SM]

HA   = Het Handelsblad van Antwerpen. Onafhankelijk Vlaams
      Nieuwsen Sportblad. Antwerp.
      [O/KB/□]

HB   = Human Biology: a record of research. Baltimore: Warwick and
      York. 1929-.
      [DLC/UBG/□]

HBV = Hessische Blätter für Volkskunde. Leipzig: Hessische
      Vereinigung für Volkskunde. 1902-.
      [Y/KB/□]

He   = De Herrnhutter. Een blad voor het Christelijk Huisgezin.
      Orgaan der E. B. G. in Suriname. Paramaribo. (Bi-weekly.)
      [O/□/□]

HH   = Holland Herald; Newsmagazine of the Netherlands. Amsterdam.
     1966-.
     [DLC/UBA/□]

HI   = The Harvard Independent. Cambridge, Mass.
     [HU/□/□]

HM   = Herrnhutter Missionshilfe.
     [O/UBU/□]

HMa = Harper's (Monthly) Magazine. New York. 1850-.
     [DLC/UBA/□]

HP   = De Haagsche Post. The Hague. 1914-.
     [O/□/□]

HR   = Hardwood Record. Chicago: C. D. Strode. 1895-1939.
     [DLC/□/□]

HS   = Heilbronner Stimme.
     [O/□/□]

HUG = Harvard University Gazette. Cambridge, Mass. 1906-.
     [HU/□/□]

IAA = Ibero-Amerikanisches Archiv. Bonn: Ibero-Amerikanisches
     Forschungsinstitut; Berlin: Iberoamerikanisches Institut.
     1924-1944.
     [Y/UBU/□]

IAE = International Archives of Ethnography. Leiden: Internationale
     Gesellschaft für Ethnographie. 1888-1968.
     [DLC/KTLV/□]

IFM = International Folk Music Council Journal. Cambridge,
     England. 1949-.
     [DLC/□/□]

IJAL = International Journal of American Linguistics. New York:
     Columbia University. 1917-.
     [DLC/UBL/□]

IM   = De Indische Mercuur; orgaan voor handel, landbouw,
     nijverheid en mijnwezen in Nederlandsch Oost- en West-
     Indië. Amsterdam. 1878-1940.
     [NYP/KTLV/□]

In   = Indië. Haarlem: Weltevren; Kolff. 1917/18-1926/27.
     [CrU/KTLV/□]

InN = Het Indisch Nieuws. The Hague. 1945-1946.
     [HU/KB/□]

InNo = Indian Notes. New York: Museum of the American Indian,
     Heye Foundation. 1924-1930.
     [DLC/UBA/□]

IRM = The International Review of Missions. Edinburgh. 1912-.
     [DLC/KTLV/□]

Ja   = Janus; revue internationale de l'histoire des sciences, de la
     médecine, de la pharmacie et de la technique. Leiden: Société
     Historique Néerlandaise des Sciences Médicales. 1896-.
     [DLC/UBL/□]

JAL = Journal of African Languages. London. 1962-.
[DLC/UBG/□]

JI = Journal of Immunology. Baltimore: American Association of Immunologists. 1916-.
[DLC/UBL/□]

JMVL = Jahrbuch des Städtischen Museums für Völkerkunde zu Leipzig. Leipzig: Städtisches Museum für Völkerkunde. 1906-.
[Y/KB/□]

JNH = Journal of Negro History. Washington: Association for the Study of Negro Life and History. 1916-.
[DLC/UBA/□]

JRAI = Journal of the Royal Anthropological Institute of Great Britain and Ireland. London. 1871-1965.
[DLC/UBA/□]

JSAP = Journal de la Société des Américanistes, Paris, 2e série. Paris. 1904-.
[Y/UBA/□]

JSH = Journal of Social History. Berkeley: University of California Press. 1967-.
[DLC/UBL/□]

JTP = Journal of Tropical Pediatrics and African Child Health. London. 1955-.
[CU/UBG/USB]

JWVH = [Jahresbericht des] Württembergischer Verein für Handelsgeographie und Förderung deutscher Interessen im Auslande. Stuttgart. 1884-1932.
[DLC/UBL/□]

K = Kabul. Utrecht. 1969-.
[O/□/□]

KEB = Kerkbode van de Evangelische Broedergemeente in Suriname. Paramaribo: Drukerij "De West."
[O/□/□]

Kp = Kultuurpatronen. Bulletin van het Delfts Etnografisch Museum. Delft. 1959-1969.
[O/KTLV/□]

Ku = Kula. Uitgave van de Nederlandse vereniging van studenten in de culturele antropologie en de niet-westerse sociologie. Baarn: Hollandia N.V. 1959-69.
[O/KTLV/□]

KW = Koloniaal Weekblad. Orgaan der Vereeniging Oost en West. 1900-.
[O/KTLV/□]

L = Lingua; international review of general linguistics. Haarlem: J. H. Gottmer. 1947-.
[DLC/UBA/□]

La = Language. Baltimore: Linguistic Society of America. 1925-.
[DLC/UBA/□]

LA   = The Living Age. Boston: Littell and Gay. 1844-1941.
[DLC/□/□]

LD   = Literary Digest. New York: Funk and Wagnalls. 1890-1938.
[DLC/BV/□]

Li   = Lichtstralen op den Akker der Wereld. Uitgegeven met
aanbeveling van het Comité voor Nederl. Zendings-
Conferentïen. Zeist. 1895-1939.
[NYP/KTLV/□]

LI   = Life. International edition. Chicago: Time, Inc. 1946-72.
[DLC/ABA/BCC]

Lim   = Limburgsch Dagblad. Heerlen. 1919-.
[O/KB/□]

LMC = Les Missions Catholiques; revue éditée par les oeuvres
pontificales de la propagation de la foi et de saint-
Pierre-apôtre. Lyon. 1868-1964.
[CaU/BTH/□]

LS   = Language in Society. London and New York: Cambridge
University Press. 1972-.
[DLC/KTLV/□]

Ma   = Man. London: Royal Anthropological Institute of Great
Britain and Ireland. 1901-.
[DLC/KTLV/□]

MAG = Mitteilungen der Anthropologischen Gesellschaft in Wien.
Vienna: Carl Gerold's Sohn. 1871-.
[NYP/UBL/□]

Mar = Marineblad. Orgaan der Marine Vereeniging. Amsterdam:
Netherlands Historisch Scheepvaartmuseum in Amsterdam.
1886-1942; 1947-.
[O/KTLV/□]

MBB = Missions-Blatt der Brüdergemeine. Herrnhut: Mission der
Herrnhutter Brüdergemeine. 1837-.
[Y/UBA/□]

MC   = Las Misiones Catolicas. Barcelona.
[O/□/□]

Me   = The Mentor. New York. 1913-1931.
[Y/□/□]

MeN = Medische Nood in Tropenland. Officieel orgaan van de
Vereeniging "Simavi." Zeist. 1930-1940; 1951-.
[O/KTLV/□]

MMBS = Mitteilungen aus der Missionsarbeit der Brüdergemeine in
Suriname. Paramaribo.
[O/KITC/□]

MMo = Missionary Monthly. Reformed Review. Holland, Mich.
1927-.
[O/VU/□]

MN   = Mosquito News; official organ of the American Mosquito
Control Association. New Brunswick, N.J.: American Mosquito

Control Association. 1941-.
[NYAM/UBL/□]

Mo = Revista Montalban. Caracas: Universidad Católica "Andrés Bello." 1972-.
[Y/KITC/□]

MRW = Missionary Review of the World. Princeton, N.J.; London. 1878-1939.
[DLC/VU/□]

MS = Museum Service. Bulletin of the Rochester Museum of Arts and Sciences. Rochester, N.Y. 1928-1968.
[UCB/□/□]

MV = Masques et Visages. Revue Hebdomadaire Indépendente. Paris.
[O/□/□]

MW = Medisch Weekblad voor Noord- en Zuid-Nederland. Amsterdam. 1894-1925.
[NYAM/UBU/□]

N = Het Nieuws. Algemeen dagblad. Paramaribo. (?)-1961.
[O/KB/□]

Na = Nature; revue des sciences et de leurs applications aux arts et á l'industrie. Paris: G. Masson. 1873-.
[HU/BTHD/□]

NA = Nieuwsblad Noord-Amsterdammer (Nieuw Noordhollandsche Courant). Purmurend. 1935?-.
[O/KB/□]

Nat = De Natuur. Populair geillustreerd maandschrift gewijd aan de natuurkundige wetenschappen en hare toepassing. Utrecht: A. Oosthoek. 1881-1935.
[DLC/UBL/□]

NBC = Noord-Brabantsche Courant.
[O/□/□]

Ne = Neerlandia. Orgaan van het Algemeen Nederlands Verbond. Ghent; Dordrecht. 1897-.
[DLC/KTLV/□]

New = Newsweek. New York.
[DLC/BMB/□]

NeZ = Nederlandsche Zendingsbode. Centraalblad voor de Zending in de Koloniën. Ermelo/The Hague. Zendingsstudieraad. 1889-1918.
[O/UBG/□]

NH = Natural History; the magazine of the American Museum of Natural History. New York. 1900-.
[Y/KITC/□]

NMa = Het Nederlands Maandblad. Nationaal maandblad voor het Koninkrijk der Nederlanden. Batavia. 1941 (nrs. 1-6 only).
[O/KTLV/□]

NMGT = Nederlands Militair Geneeskundig Tijdschrift. The Hague. 1947-.
[NYAM/UBA/□]

NRC   = Nieuwe Rotterdamsche Courant. Rotterdam. 1844-.
        [UC/KB/□]

NTC   = Dagblad Nieuwe Tilburgsche Courant (Het Nieuwsblad van het
        Zuiden). Tilburg. 1911-.
        [O/KB/□]

NUAN = Northwestern University Alumni News. Evanston:
        Northwestern University Alumni Association. 1921-1965.
        [NU/□/□]

NV   = Nederlands Volksleven. Wassenaar: Nederlands Volkskundig
        Genootschap.
        [Y/KB/□]

NWIG = Nieuwe West-Indische Gids. The Hague: Martinus Nijhoff.
        1960-.
        [Y/KTLV/□]

NYT   = The New York Times. New York. 1851-.
        [DLC/BV/□]

NZ   = Nederlandsch Zendingsblad. Oegstgeest: Zendingsbureau.
        1921-53. (Continuation of Maandblad der Samenwerkende
        Zendings-corporaties. 1918-20.)
        [HSF/KITC/□]

O   = De Opbouw. Democratisch Tijdschrift voor Nederland en
        Indië. Utrecht. 1918-1938(?).
        [NYP/UBA/□]

OA   = Onze Aarde. Geïllustreerd Maandschrift. Amsterdam.
        1928-1940.
        [NYP/UBA/□]

OF   = Our Fourfooted Friends. Boston: The Animal Rescue League
        of Boston. 1902-.
        [DLC/□/□]

OH   = Op de Hoogte. Maandschrift voor de Huiskamer. Amsterdam;
        Haarlem. 1902-1939.
        [O/UBA/□]

OM   = Onze Missiën in Oost en West Indiën. Sittard: Indische Missie
        Vereeniging. 1911-63.
        [O/KITC; UBL (1917-30)/□]

Op   = Opbouw. Katholiek Maandblad onder redactie van de Fraters
        van Tilburg. Paramaribo. 1945-.
        [O/□/BCC]

OP   = The Osteopathic Physician: the independent voice of osteopathy.
        New York.
        [NYAM/□/□]

Or   = Oro. Maandelijks magazine over Suriname en het Caribisch gebied.
        The Hague: Stichting Oro.
        [O/KTLV/□]

OS   = Ons Suriname. Zeist: Zendingsgenootschap Evangelische
        Broeder Gemeente. 1929-49. (Continuation of BHW.)
        [Y/KITC/□]

OW   = Oost en West. The Hague. Koninklijke Vereeniging "Oost en
West." 1907-1971.
[AM/KTLV/BCC]

Pa   = Panorama, ons land. Leiden. 1913-.
[DLC/UBA/□]

PA   = Practical Anthropology. Tarrytown, N.Y. 1953-.
[Y/KTLV/□]

PD   = Petrus Donders. Tijdschrift van de eerw. Redemptoristen voor
hunnen missie in Suriname. Amsterdam. 1920-1934.
[O/KITC/□]

Pe   = De Periscoop. Algemeen Weekblad voor Suriname. Paramaribo:
Erven H. van Ommeren. 1924-29.
[O/KITC/□]

Ph   = Phylon; the Atlanta University Review of Race and Culture.
Atlanta: Atlanta University. 1940-.
[DLC/UBL/□]

PICA   = Proceedings of the International Congress of Americanists.
1875-.
[DLC/□/□]

PICAES = Proceedings of the International Congress of Anthropological
and Ethnological Sciences. 1934-.
[DLC/□/□]

Pl   = De Ploeg. Orgaan van de Brutusclub. Paramaribo. 1950-.
[O/□/SM]

PM   = Dr. A. Petermann's Mittheilungen aus Justus Perthes'
Geographischer Anstalt über Wichtige Neue Erforschungen auf
dem Gesammtgebiete der Geographie. Gotha: Justus Perthes.
1855-.
[DLC/KTLV/□]

Po   = Population; revue trimestrielle de l'Institut National
d'Études Démographiques. Paris: Presses Universitaires de
France. 1946-.
[NYP/UBG/USB]

PoA   = Political Anthropology; an international quarterly. Assen:
Van Gorcum. 1975-.
[DLC/KTLV/□]

PoD   = Politie Dierenbescherming. Vught: Bond van Politieambtenaren
in Nederland tot Bescherming van Dieren. 1919-.
[O/KTLV/□]

Pr   = Het Protestantenblad. Weekblad voor Suriname. Paramaribo:
Ned. Hervormde en Evang. Lutherse Gemeente. 1895-97,
1903-.
[O/KITC/□]

Pri   = De Prins. 1901-.
[O/UBA/□]

RA   = Revue d'Anthropologie, 3e série. Paris. 1886-1889.
[DLC/□/□]

RC   = Revue Coloniale, 2e série. Paris: P. Dupont. 1848-1858.
        [DLC/KTLV/□]
RCI   = Revue Coloniale Internationale. Amsterdam: J. H. Debussy.
        1885-1887.
        [DLC/KTLV/□]
RCS   = Revista de Ciencias Sociales. Rio Piedras: Colegio de Ciencias
        Sociales, Universidad de Puerto Rico. 1957-.
        [DLC/KTLV/□]
RD   = The Reader's Digest. Pleasantville, N.Y. 1922-.
        [DLC/UBA/□]
RE   = Revue d'Ethnographie. Paris. 1882-1889.
        [DLC/UBA/□]
RES   = Revue d'Ethnographie et de Sociologie. Paris: Institut
        Ethnographique International de Paris. 1910-1914.
        [DLC/KTLV/□]
RFEC = Revue Française de l'Etranger et des Colonies. Exploration et
        Gazette Géographique. Paris. 1885-1914.
        [DLC/UBA/□]
RFHO = Revue Française d'Histoire d'Outre-Mer. Paris: Société
        Française de l'Histoire d'Outre-Mer. 1913-.
        [HU/KTLV/□]
RG   = Revue de Géographie. Paris: C. Delagrave. 1877-1924.
        [NYP/□/□]
RGA   = Revista Geografica Americana. Buenos Aires: Sociedad
        Geografica Americana. 1933-.
        [HU/UBA/□]
RGI   = Revue Géographique Internationale; journal mensuel illustré
        des sciences géographiques. Paris. 1876-1903.
        [NYP/UBA/□]
RHC   = Revue d'Histoire des Colonies; revue française d'histoire
        d'outre-mer. Paris: Société Française de l'Histoire d'Outre-Mer.
        1913-.
        [HU/KTLV/□]
Ri   = De Rijkseenheid. Staatkundig economisch weekblad ter
        versterking van de banden tussen Nederland en de Indiën.
        Den Helder: C. den Boer Jr. 1929-40.
        [O/UBL/□]
RIE   = Revista del Instituto de Etnología. Tucumán: Universidad de
        Tucumán. 1929-35.
        [Y/UBL/□]
RMC   = Revue Maritime et Coloniale. Paris. 1834-(?).
        [Y/BTHD/□]
RMP   = Revista do Museu Paulista. Sao Paulo: Museu Paulista.
        1895-1938, 1947-.
        [DLC/□/□]
S   = Spektator, Tijdschrift voor Nederlandistiek. Amsterdam. 1971-.
        [NYP/KTLV/□]

SA = Surinam Adventure. Free monthly guide to shopping, fishing and hunting safaries. Paramaribo: Agmil. 1969-.
[O/□/□]

SB = Suriname Bulletin (voorheen Aluminium-Folie). Amsterdam: Het Suriname-Comité (v/h Aluminium-Comité). 1971-. [Appeared under the title Aluminium-folie, 1970.]
[O/KITC/□]

Sc = Schakels, Suriname. The Hague. Departement van Overzeese Rijksdelen. 1950-.
[CrU/KTLV/SM]

Sch = Schoolkrant. Paramaribo: Departement van Onderwijs.
[O/□/□]

SES = Social and Economic Studies. Mona: Institute of Social and Economic Research. 1953-.
[DLC/KTLV/□]

SF = Social Forces. Chapel Hill: University of North Carolina. 1922-.
[DLC/UBU/□]

SJ = Surinaams Juristenblad. Orgaan van de Surinaamse Juristen-vereniging. Paramaribo: Varekamp. 1963-.
[O/KTLV/USB]

SJA = Southwestern Journal of Anthropology. Albuquerque: University of New Mexico. 1945-.
[DLC/ASC/□]

SL = De Surinaamse Landbouw. Paramaribo: Departement van Landbouw Veeteelt en Visserij. 1953-.
[DLC/KTLV/SM]

SM = Suralco Magazine. Paramaribo: Suriname Aluminium Company. 1969-. [Continuation of Bauxco Nieuws.]
[O/KTLV/SM]

SMA = Sociaal Maandblad Arbeid. Alphen. 1946-.
[NYP/UBA/□]

SN = Surinaams Nieuws. The Hague. Commissariaat voor Surinaamse Zaken in Nederland. 1949-.
[DLC/KTLV/□]

SP = De Surinaamsche Politie. Orgaan van de Surinaamsche Politiebond. Paramaribo. 1920-(?).
[O/□/□]

SS = Surinam Sun. New York: Surinam Tourist Bureau. 1964?-.
[O/KITC/BCC]

SSMM = Stichting Surinaams Museum Mededelingen. Paramaribo.
[JHU/KTLV/SM]

St = Sticusa Journaal. Amsterdam: Nederlandse Stichting voor Culturele Samenwerking met Suriname in de Nederlandse Antillen. 1971-.
[DLC/KTLV/BCC]

ST = Spoor- en tramwegen; 14 daags tijdschrift voor het spoor- en tramwegwezen in Nederland en Indië. The Hague and

Utrecht: Moorman's Periodieke Pers. 1928-53.
[DLC/KITC/□]

StL = Stad en Land. Geillustreerd weekblad.
[O/□/□]

Su = De Surinamer. Paramaribo. 1894-?.
[O/KITC/SM]

Sur = Suriname (dagblad). Paramaribo. 1873(?)-1971.
[O/□/□]

SV = Sciences et Voyages. Paris. 1919-.
[DLC/□/□]

SXQ = Sigma Xi Quarterly (The American Scientist). Champaign,
Ill. and Burlington, Vt. 1913-.
[DLC/UBG/□]

SZ = Suriname-Zending. Zeist. (Continuation of OS.) 1950-.
[O/KTLV/SM]

TA = Trans-action. Social Science and the Community. St. Louis:
Washington University. 1963-.
[DLC/UBL/□]

TB = Tijdschrift der Nederlandsche Maatschappij ter Bevordering
van Nijverheid. Haarlem. 1833-.
[DLC/UBL/□]

TESG = Tijdschrift voor Economische en Sociale Geographie. Rotterdam:
Nederlandse Vereniging voor Economische en Sociale
Geographie. 1910-.
[NYP/KTLV/BCC]

Ti = Timehri; Journal of the Royal Anthropological and Commercial
Society of British Guiana, 4th series. Demerara: J. Thompson.
1934-.
[DLC/KTLV/□]

TKNAG = Tijdschrift van het Koninklijk Nederlandsch Aardrijkskundig
Genootschap. Leiden. 1876-.
[Y/KTLV/SM]

Tm = Time. New York. 1923-.
[DLC/□/□]

TM = Le Tour du Monde; nouveau journal des voyages. Paris:
Hachette. 1860-.
[DLC/KTLV/□]

TN = Tropisch Nederland. Tijdschrift ter verbreding van kennis
omtrent Nederlandisch Oost- en West- Indië. Amsterdam:
J. H. de Bussy. 1928-40.
[NYP/UBL/SM]

TNM = Tijdschrift uitgegeven vanwege de Nederlandse Maatschappij tot
Bevordering der Afschaffing van de Slavernij. The Hague:
Martinus Nijhoff. 1855-1862.
[O/KTLV/□]

Tr = Travel. New York: Travel Magazine, Inc. 1901-1961(?).
[DLC/□/□]

TS = The Toronto Star. Toronto: Toronto Star Ltd. 1892-.
[TPL/□/□]

V = Varia.
[O/□/□]

Va = Het Vaderland. The Hague. 1869-.
[O/□/□]

VBS = Verhandlungen der Berliner Gesellschaft für Anthropologie, Ethnologie und Ergeschichte. (Bound with ZE.) 1869-.
[DLC/UBG/□]

VG = Vox Guyanae. Paramaribo: Stichting ter Bevordering van Wetenschappelijke en Culturele Publicaties. 1954-1959.
[DLC/KTLV/SM]

VGE = Verhandlungen der Gesellschaft für Erdkunde zu Berlin. (Bound with ZAE.)
[DLC/KTLV/□]

VMVL = Veröffentlichungen des Städtischens Museums für Völkerkunde zu Leipzig. Leipzig: Städtisches Museum für Völkerkunde. 1907-.
[DLC/KB/□]

VN = Vrij Nederland; Onafhankelijk cultureel-sociaal en politieke weekblad. Amsterdam. 1940-.
[HU/UBU/□]

Vo = De Volksmissionaris: godsdienstig maandschrift. Roermond. 1879-1964.
[O/UBA/□]

Voe = Voeding. The Hague: Stichting tot wetenschappelijke voorlichting op voedingsgebied. 1939-.
[DLC/UBA/□]

We = Dagblad "De West." Paramaribo. 1909-1961; 1963-.
[UF/KB/□]

Wf = Weltfahrten. Beitrage zur Länder- und Völkerkunde. Berlin.
[O/□/□]

WH = Wolanda-Hindia. Zendings-tijdschrift voor jongeren. Amsterdam: Amsterdamsche Maatschappij voor Jonge Mannen. 1927-40.
[O/KTLV/□]

Wi = Wikor. Algemeen Kunsttijdschrift. The Hague. 1953-.
[DLC/KTLV/□]

WI = West-Indië; bijdragen tot de bevordering van de kennis der Nederlandsch West-Indische koloniën. Haarlem: A. C. Kruseman. (Appeared twice only—1855 and 1858.)
[O/UBU/SM]

WIG = De West-Indische Gids. The Hague: Martinus Nijhoff. 1919/20-1959.
[DLC/KTLV/SM]

Wk = Wereldkroniek: geillustreerd nieuwsblad. 1894/95-okt. 1970.
[O/UBA/□]

Wo   = Word; journal of the Linguistic Circle of New York. New York:
         Linguistic Circle of New York. 1945-.
         [Y/UBL/□]
WoT   = World Traveler. San Francisco, New York. 1908-31.
         [DLC/□/□]
WT   = De Ware Tijd. Paramaribo. 1958-.
         [O/□/□]
YAM   = Yale Alumni Magazine. New Haven. 1937-.
         [Y/□/□]
Ym   = Ymer; tidskrift utgifven af Svenska sällskapet för antropologi
         och geografi. Stockholm: Svenska sällskapet för antropologi
         och geografi. 1881-1965.
         [DLC/UBA/□]
Z   = Zaire: orgaan der vlaamsche kolonialen. Antwerpen: G. Foets.
         1924-26.
         [NYP/□/□]
ZAE   = Zeitschrift für Allgemeine Erdkunde. Berlin: Gesellschaft für
         Erdkunde zu Berlin. 1853-1944.
         [DLC/KTLV/□]
ZE   = Zeitschrift für Ethnologie. Berlin: Berliner Gesellschaft für
         Anthropologie, Ethnologie und Urgeschichte. 1869-.
         [DLC/UBU/□]
ZEBG = Zendingsblad van de E. B. G. in Suriname, N.W.I. Paramaribo:
         O. C. Marcus.
         [O/□/□]
ZVR   = Zeitschrift für vergleichende Rechtswissenschaft;
         einschliesslich der ethnologischen Rechts, und der
         Gesellschaftsforschung. Stuttgart and Berlin. 1878-.
         [Y/KTLV/□]

BIBLIOGRAPHY

ABBENHUIS, M.F.
1.   1943-46   Verhalen en schetsen uit de Surinaamse geschiedenis.
                 Paramaribo: Leo Victor. [O/KTLV/SM]
2.   1943   Volksplanting. Paramaribo: Eben Haezer. [O/KTLV/SM]
3.   1950   Bosnegers. *In* De Katholieke Encyclopaedie. 2^e druk.
                 Amsterdam: Joost van den Vondel N.V., vol. 5,
                 pp. 766-69. [DLC/UBU/□]
*4.   1956   De Katholieke Kerk in Suriname. VG 2:117-44.
5.   1964   Bonni. *In* Emancipatie 1863/1963 Biografieën.
                 Paramaribo: Surinaamse Historische Kring, pp. 23-39,
                 191-97. [O/KITC/SM]

ACCARIAS de SÉRIONNE, J.
6.   1778   La richesse de la Hollande. London: aux Depens de la
                 Compagnie. [NYP/□/□]

6a. 1780-83 Hollands rijkdom. Leiden: Luzac en van Damme.
                [Translation by E. Luzac of item 6.] [DLC/□/□]

ADHIN, J. H.

7.   1961   Suriname, een beknopte uitgave van de wereld.
                Sc 43:3-9.

AHLBRINCK, W.

8.   1956   Op zoek naar de Indianen. Amsterdam: Koninklijk
                Instituut voor de Tropen, Mededeling 117, Afdeling
                Culturele en Physische Antropologie 52.
                [DLC/KTLV/SM]

AJAX [pseud.]

8a. 1961   De vlucht van Bonni en Aloekoe. We 10 november-4
                december. [Typescript version is in SM.]

AKANAMBA

8b. n.d.   Mutjamah (regenboog). Paramaribo: H. v. d. Boom.
      [1970s] [JHU/□/□]

ALBITROUW, ISAAC

8c. n.d.   Tori Vo Dem begin vo Anakee en moro fara. 2 vols
      [c. 1900] [O/□/AHP]
8d. 1892-95 Vo da missionswroko na Goejaba ofoe Aurora. A bigin
                baka na 1891 en te moro na hoposei. MS. [O/O/AHZ]

ALEVA, G.J.J.

9.   1966   Reizen in Suriname. Er 18:71-77.

ALEXANDER, CAPT J. E.

10. 1833   Transatlantic sketches, comprising visits to the most
                interesting scenes in North and South America, and the
                West Indies. 2 vols. London: Richard Bentley.
                [DLC/BM/□]

ALLEYNE, MERVYN C.

11. n.d.   Comparative Afro-American (an historical comparative
                study of some Afro-American dialects of the New
                World). MS. 286 pp. [O/□/□]

AMERICUS

12. 1886   Les récents voyages du Dr. Ten Kate. RGI 11:214-16.

AMOIDA, DONISI

13. 1974   Mbeti u liba. Paramaribo: Instituut voor
                Taalwetenschap/Ministerie van Onderwijs. [DLC/□/BCC]
14. 1974   Mbeti u matu 1. Paramaribo: Instituut voor
                Taalwetenschap/Ministerie van Onderwijs. [DLC/□/BCC]
15. 1974   Mbeti u matu 2. Paramaribo: Instituut voor
                Taalwetenschap/Ministerie van Onderwijs. [DLC/□/BCC]
16. 1974   Wakama oto. Paramaribo: Instituut voor
                Taalwetenschap/Ministerie van Onderwijs. [DLC/□/BCC]
17. 1974   Wookoma oto. Paramaribo: Instituut voor
                Taalwetenschap/Ministerie van Onderwijs. [DLC/□/BCC]

AMOIDA, FANJEN

18.	1974	Bunu ku hogi 1. Paramaribo: Instituut voor Taalwetenschap/Ministerie van Onderwijs. [DLC/□/BCC]
19.	1974	Bunu ku hogi 2. Paramaribo: Instituut voor Taalwetenschap/Ministerie van Onderwijs. [DLC/□/BCC]
20.	1974	Dee dii womi. Paramaribo: Instituut voor Taalwetenschap/Ministerie van Onderwijs. [DLC/□/BCC]
21.	1974	Fufuu, huku, ku taanga. Paramaribo: Instituut voor Taalwetenschap/Ministerie van Onderwijs. [DLC/□/BCC]
22.	1974	Politiki. Paramaribo: Instituut voor Taalwetenschap/Ministerie van Onderwijs. [DLC/□/BCC]
23.	1974	Sö mi si ku sö mi jei. Paramaribo: Instituut voor Taalwetenschap/Ministerie van Onderwijs. [DLC/□/BCC]

AMOIDA, SAMO

| 23a. | 1974 | Wanlö fesiten oto. Paramaribo: Instituut voor Taalwetenschap/Ministerie van Onderwijs. [DLC/□/BCC] |
| 24. | 1974 | Wanlö Saamaka nöngö. Paramaribo: Instituut voor Taalwetenschap/Ministerie van Onderwijs. [DLC/□/BCC] |

AMOIDA, TIINI

| 24a. | 1975 | Köni miti wogi. Paramaribo: Instituut voor Taalwetenschap/Ministerie van Onderwijs. [DLC/□/BCC] |

AMSDORF, R. E.

| *25. | 1964 | Adieu Ganzee. We 20 juli. |

van AMSTEL, HANS

| 26. | 1946 | De laatsten der Wajarikoele's in Suriname. Bussum: P. Brand. [DLC/KTLV/SM] |

| 27. | 1761 | Summary of news from Surinam, dated February 23, 1761. AR 4:76. |

| *28. | 1773 | Authenticq relaas uit Surinamen, van de veroveringen van het dorp der gevaarlijkste wegloopers en muitelingen genaamdt Misalasi. Utrecht. [O/□/SM] |

| *29. | 1773 | Diarium der Geschwister unter den Frey-Negern in Suriname von Anfang May bis Ende August. MS. [O/ABU/□] |

| 30. | 1773 | Extract of a letter from Surinam, dated Sept. 5, 1772. AR 15:146-47. |

| *31. | 1773-81 | Papieren concernerende de expeditie van een corps troupes na Surinamen tegens de invasie der Bos-negers onder welke papieren ook is vervat het verschil tusschen 18 leden der Vergad van Holland en de stad Amsterdam |

over de inhouding van 's lands penningen door de
laatste stad met de Resolutien daartoe betrekkelyk.
1772 tot 1781. Z.pl., 1773-81. c.a. 25 stukken in 1
band. Met tabellen. MS. [O/KTLV/□]

*32. 1775 [On Baron.] Surinaamsche Courant, October 1776,
No. 65.

*32a. 1776 Missive van Gouverneur en Raden der Colonie van
Suriname, concerneerende het vormeren van het Cordon
van defensie, met een Plan en Berekening der Kosten
1776. [□/□/SM]

*33. 1799 Bericht des Frey Neger Gemeinleins ins Neu Bambey
von Ende Juni bis zu Ende des Jahres 1799. MS.
[O/ABU/□]

*33a. 1799 Berichten van den zendingen der Evangelische
Broedergemeente onder de heidenen. No. 4.
Amsteldam: Johannes Weppelman. [□/□/SM]

33b. 1813 Register der ordinaire Notulen, relatie hebbende tot het
binnen en buitenlandsche Defensie weezen deezer
Colonie, mitsgaders tot de Zaaken van de Bosch Negers
en 's Lands Vrije Corps, gehouden by Z. Exc. den H. E.
Gestr. Heer Pinson Bonham, . . . Gouverneur en
Commandant en Chef over de Colonie Suriname . . . en
de E. Achtb. Heeren Raaden van Politie en Crimineelse
Justitie der voorsz. Colonie. 1 Febr.-11 Maart 1813.
Paramaribo. [O/KTLV/SM]

34. 1834-35 Boschneger-aangelengenheden. "Aanteekenings-Boekje."
MS. [O/□/SM]

*35. 1835 1701-1801 Zendelings-arbeid onder de vrij-negers.
BHW, no. 3.

*36. 1861/62 Zending onder de Betoe-en Moesinga-negers. TNM 7:60.

37. 1864 Suriname. BHW 1864, Bijblad bij no. 10: 213-19;
1864, no. 11:237-38.

*38. 1867 Inventaris der kaarten berustende in het Rijks-Archief.
The Hague. Vol. 1, nos. 2124-2133. [O/□/□]

*39.	1869	Reise der Geschwister Raatz zu den Buschnegern der obern Commewyne. MS. [O/ABU/□]
40.	1885	Die Buschneger in Holländisch-Guiana. A 58:647-650.
41.	1885	[Report on Dr. K. Martin's trip up the Suriname River.] *In* Verslag der Zes en Veertigste Algemeene Vergadering van het Nederlandsch Aardijkskundig Genootschap gehouden te Amsterdam, 21 November 1885. TKNAG (2^e serie) 2:536-56. [pp. 550-53.]
42.	1886	Die Buschneger in Guiana. A 59:61-64, 88-90.
43.	1886	Reizen en onderzoekingen van Dr. H. ten Kate. TKNAG (2e serie) 3:706-10.
*44.	1887	Bericht über eine Reise zu den heidnischen Auka-oder Djokanegern an der obern Cottica. Coermotibo und Likanan vom 8.-17. März. MS. [O/ABU/□]
45.	1892	Bonis et Hollandais. RFEC 15:558.
46.	1892	Différences entre les Nègres Boni (Français) et les Nègres Bosch (Hollandais) à la Guyane. BSGE 14:322-23.
47.	1892	Van het Boschland te Suriname. BHW (9): 139-44.
49.	1893	Exode des Bonis. RFEC 17:477.
50.	1893	Suriname, Wanhatti. BHW (3):42-50.
*51.	1894	Auszug aus dem Tagesbuch Isaak Albitrouws von Aurora. MS. [O/ABU/□]
53.	1895	Suriname. BHW (1):4-16; (2):17-20.
*54.	1905	Catalogus van de Ethnographica verzameld door de wetenschappelijke expedities in de Binnenland van Suriname in de jaren 1903 en 1904. Leiden: Koninklijk Nederlandsch Aardrijkskundig Genootschap. [O/□/SM]

*55.	1912	De vrouw in Suriname. Amsterdam: Surinaamsche Sub-Comitee "de Vrouw 1813-1913." [O/KTLV/□]
56.	1912	Erste Nachrichten von Br. J. T. Hamilton. MBB 76:42.
*57.	1912	Hoe de toovenaar Atjarimikoele tot God der Djoeka's verheven werd. BHW (1):1-5.
58.	1913	Ein neuer Vorstoss ins Surinamer Buschland! MBB 77:3-5.
*59.	1913/14	Uit onze West, de boschnegers in Suriname. Pa 1:29-.
60.	1914	Aus den Buschland-Gemeinen an der oberen Suriname. MBB 78:249-52.
*61.	1915	Uit de rechtspleging der Auca-boschnegers. BHW oct.:179-84.
62.	1916	Hoofdenverkiezing bij bosnegers in Suriname. BTLV 72:590-98.
63.	1916	Politieke contracten met de Boschnegers in Suriname. BTLV 71:371-411.
64.	1916	Wie unter den heidnischen Buschnegern Surinames Recht gesprochen wird. MBB 80:221-26.

_____ [Mevr. W.H.M.]

*65.	1922	Naar Pakka-Pakka aan de Saramacca. AHV 58 (oktober).
66.	1923	[Correspondentie van Koffiekamp.] We 15 juli.
*67.	1924	Naar de Boschnegers in de binnenlanden van Suriname. Tweede uitgave. [Met voorwoord door P. Hopmans.] Uitgave van de Zusters Penitenten-Recollectinen. Roosendaal: J. van Poll Suykerbuyk. [O/KTLV/□]
68.	1924/25	Een interessante beschikking van den Gouverneur van Suriname. WIG 6:238-40.
*69.	1925	Boschnegers op bezoek. BHW (5):79.

*70.   1925   Geneeskunde der Boschnegers. GG 11 september.

*72.   1926   Afkodree (zwarte kunst). Pe 65:2.

*73.   1927   De Redemptoristen in de heidenmissies: Suriname
                en zijn bewoners. Vo 15 nov:377-381.

*74.   1928[?]   Aan de grenzen van Cayenne. [See item 1142.]

75.   1930   Bespreking van H. Bielke. Een reis naar de Surinaamse
               Bosnegers, voordracht. Ne 4:61.

*76.   1930   Hoe de boschlandzending begon. OS december.

*77.   1930   De roepstem uit het boschland. OS dec.

*79.   1931   De boschlandzending op de Kerkconferentie te
                Paramaribo. OS december.

*80.   1931   Suriname: de ontvangst der eerste zendelingen
                [24 dec. 1765] in het boschland. NZ feb.

*81.   1932   Grepen uit het verslag van een inspectiereis naar de
                Boven-Marowijne. OS (dec.):187-193.

81a.   1932-38   Suriname: Bevolking. *In* J. de Vries (ed.), Winkler
                   Prins Algemeene Encyclopedie, 5^e geheel nieuwe druk,
                   pp. 488-89. [DLC/KB/□]

*82.   1933   Bij de bewoners van het Surinaamsche Hoogland:
                Boschnegers en Indianen. Pri 15 juli.

*83.   1933   Boschnegers en Indianen. KW 24 augustus.

*84.   1933   Boschnegers of Marrons. *In* Oosthoek's
                Encyclopaedie, 3de druk. Utrecht: N.V. A. Oosthoek's
                Uitgevers Mij. [O/KB/□]

*85.   1933   Op Bambey, Boven Suriname. He 28 mei, 11 juni.

*86.   1933   Donker boschland. (Een en ander uit den
                zendingsarbeid onder de Boschnegers in Suriname:

de booze geesten; de groote moreele nood van de
Boschnegers; de strijders in het oerwoud; lichtpunten).
OS mei.

*87.   1933   Op vacantie (een 8-daagsche vacantietocht op en
langs de Saramacca-rivier). PD mei.

*88.   1933   Waar zijn zij gebleven? (teekeningen, miniatuur-woning,
wassen poppen, alles vervaardigd door Kapitein
Stedman, die van 1772-1777 de tochten tegen de
Marrons meemaakte). KW 27 april, 4 mei.

*89.   1933   De wraak van Tonné [Boschnegerverhaal; Tonné is de
watergod der Saramaccaners]. NRC, 5 Nov., Ochtenblad
B.

90.   1933   De Suriname-Zending der Evangelische
Broedergemeente in kaart. Zeist: Zendingsgenootschap
der E.B.G. [O/□/□]

*91.   1933   Zeden en gebruiken in het Boschland. He 18 juni,
16 juli.

*92.   1934   Bij de Saramaccaners te Ligori-Kondre (Gran-Rio).
PD maart (no. 4).

*93.   1934   Black lords of the bush: Dutch Guiana, the only place
where a nation of whites is subservient to a nation of
blacks. TS, Thursday, June 7. [Cited, apparently
incorrectly, in WIG 16:271(1933/34).]

*94.   1934   Feest bij de Saramaccaners. PD nov.

*95.   1934   Hoe men in de Boschlandgemeenten zendingsfeest
viert (door een deelnemer). OS maart (no. 3).

*96.   1934   De Surinaamsche staatsinrichting, boschnegers en
immigranten. NRC 28 Dec. Avondblad C.

*97.   1934   Suriname. Uitgeven door de Vereeniging ter Bevordering
van het Vreemdelingenverkeer en Toerisme in
Suriname te Paramaribo. Amsterdam: N.V. Drukkerij
Plantijn. [Also in an English translation (Netherlands
Guiana), same publisher]. [O/□/□]

*98.	1934	Suriname's oerwoud in levend beeld. OS nov. (no. 11).
*99.	1935	Die op onze hulp Wachten in 1935. Het werk onder de Awana-negers op Nw. Goejaba. OS Feb. (no. 2).
100.	1935	Gedenkboek ter herdenking van twee eeuwen Suriname-zending, 1735-1935. Zeist. [O/KTLV/□]
*101.	1935	Een verdrag met boschnegers in Suriname. NRC 29 April. Avondblad B.
*102.	1935	Verslag over de Boven-Saramacca. OS nov. (no. 11).
103.	1936	Bij de voorposten in het boschland. OS aug. (no. 8): 113-26.
*104.	1936	Boschnegerkwestie. Su 4 en 11 juli(nrs. 4359 en 4360).
105.	1936	Een merkwaardige beweging onder de Boschnegers. OS mei (no. 5):75-77.
*106.	1936	Zuster Nelly de Borst schrijft in haar driemaandelijk rapport uit Ganzee. MN no. 2.
*107.	1936	Zuster Nelly de Borst op reis in het binnenland. OS Sept. (no. 7):131-135.
*108.	1937	Hoe Ganzee het huwelijkfeest van Prinses Juliana met Prins Bernhard vierde. OS juni (no. 6).
*109.	1939	Het nieuwe woonhuis van Zr. Nelly op Ganzee. OS nov. (no. 11).
*110.	1940	Bericht van prof. dr. N. H. Swellengrebel over zijn bezoek aan Ganzee. OS feb. (no. 2).
*111.	1940	Geneeskunde bij de Bosnegers. EM 25 nov. (no. 12).
*112.	1940	Medische hulp aan de Boschnegers. OS maart (no. 3).
*113.	1941	Het zendingswerk in het boschland. OS januari (no. 1).

*114.   1946   Over twee flinke Djoeka-meisjes. EM 25 dec. (no. 1).

115.   1946   Uit de West: wetenswaardigheden van Suriname.
               InN 2(18):14.

*116.   1951   De installatie der Bosneger-granmans. V 1, 12 april.

117.   c.1955 Jaarverslagen van de Medische Zending der Evangelische
               Broedergemeente in Suriname. Mimeo. [Appears
               yearly.] [O/AHZ/AHP]

118.   1959   Boslandcreolen. *In* Oosthoek's Encyclopedie. Utrecht:
               N.V. A. Oosthoek's Uitgeversmaatschappij. [5de druk]
               Vol. 2, pp. 550-60. [O/KTLV/□]

119.   1959   De transmigratie van de bosnegers in Suriname: een
               ingewikkeld en lastig probleem. ACu 1 april.

*120.   1959   Enorm stuwmeer in Surinaams oerwoud zal 5000
               negers verdrijven. NA 15 mei.

*121.   1959   Enorm stuwmeer in Suriname zal 5000 negers
               verdrijven. NTC 30 mei.

*122.   1959   Het water verdrijft het volk van de Saramaccaners.
               Lim 20 juni.
        ___ [J.E.V.]
123.   1960   De vuurdans (Naar een artikel in het Engels in
               Bauxco Nieuws van Aug. 1960.) Dj 3(2):12-13.

124.   1961   Er bestaat een schrijfwijze van de Aucanertaal. Sch
               9(6):1-2.

*125.   1961   Miljoenen project verjaagt Boslandcreolen van
               geboortegrond. Bi augustus (?).

126.   1961   Onze oude banden met Afrika. Surinames culturele
               achtergronden 1. Paramaribo: Bureau Volkslectuur.
               [DLC/□/BCC]

*127.   1961   Opleving van houtsnijkunst, Boslandcreolen in
               Suriname. Bi 6 oktober.

*128.   1961   25 Bosnegerdorpen zullen verzwolgen worden door water. BD 17 augustus.

*129.   1962   De Saramaccaners en de Transmigratie. We 11 november.

*130.   1962   Politie patrouilleert in Suralcokondre. WT 16 februari.

131.   1963   Dí kéíki kó taánga. Amsterdam: Het Nederlandsch Bijbelgenootschap. [O/□/BCC]

131a.   1963   Suriname fotoboek: uitgegeven ter gelegenheid van het 100-jarig Emancipatiefeest, 1 juli 1963. Paramaribo: Leo Victor. [O/KITC/□]

132.   1964   Dam in Surinam near completion. NYT December 25:36.

*133.   1964   Duizenden dieren bedreigd door stijgend water. Va 14 november.

134.   1964   In de dierenriem. PoD 39(10):5.

135.   1964   Nieuws van Marowijne. Drs. J. Michels pionier van het binnenland. We 6 februari.

*136.   1964   Suriname: beknopte beschrijving van het land, de bevolking, de staatkundige, sociale en economische structuur. Paramaribo. [O/□/□]

136a.   1964   Suriname 1964, Paramaribo: H. van der Boomen. [O/KITC/□]

137.   1964   Two try to save Surinam animals. NYT Nov. 29:23.

*138.   1965   "Operation Gwamba" to rescue the animals. LI 38(5).

*139.   1965   10000 Tiere vor dem Ertrinken gerettet. HS 4 Dezember.

140.   1969   France's pad in South America. Tm 93(11):42.

141.   1970   De Nederlandse vertaling van Sebe Saamaka oto (zeven Saramaccaanse verhalen). Paramaribo: Summer

Institute of Linguistics/Ministerie van Onderwijs en Volksontwikkeling. [See item 145.] [DLC/□/BCC]

142. 1970 Dí fósu bedáki. Paramaribo: Summer Institute of Linguistics met medewerking van het Taalbureau. [See item 149.] [DLC/□/BCC]

143. 1970 Price list for the antique Bushnegro items included in the private collection of Madame Bolwerk-Lavant, wife of the Curator of the Surinam Museum, Paramaribo, Surinam. Hodge Podge Annex, 206 East Anapamu Street, Santa Barbara, California 93104. Mimeo. [O/□/□]

*144. 1970 Rapport van de commissie ter bestudering van de problematiek rondom de opvangcentra der boslandbewoners. Paramaribo, 19 December. Notities van een toespraak van Gazon voor de Nederlandsche parlementaire delegatie. MS. [O/□/LP]

145. 1970 Sebe Saamaka oto. Paramaribo: Summer Institute of Linguistics/Ministerie van Onderwijs en Volksontwikkeling. [See item 141.] [DLC/□/BCC]

146. 1970 Suriname: het werk van de fraters van Tilburg onder de vijfsterrinvlag. [Special issue.] Intercom-Fraters, Nr. 7. Tilburg: Fraters van O. L. Vrouw, Moeder van Barmhartigheid. [O/KTLV/□]

147. 1971 Bosnegers. In Grote Winkler Prins, Amsterdam: Uitgeverij Elsevier Nederland N.V., vol. 4, p. 348. [DLC/KTLV/□]

148. 1971 De ellende van Bosnegers en Indianen in de Opvangcentra. SB 2(5):12-13.

149. 1971 De nederlandse vertaling van Di fosu bedaki (de eerste kerstmis). Paramaribo: Instituut voor Taalwetenschap in Suriname met medewerking van het Taalbureau. [See item 142.] [DLC/□/BCC]

150. 1971 De strijd van de Bosnegers voor lotsverbetering. SB 2(5):8-10.

151.   1971   Di bunu buka u Gaangadu di Maaku bi sikifi.
                   Paramaribo: Instituut voor Taalwetenschap in
                   Suriname met medewerking van het Taalbureau.
                   [DLC/□/BCC]

152.   1971   Dii nongo toli di Jesoesoe koti. Paramaribo: Instituut
                   voor Taalwetenschap. [DLC/□/BCC]

153.   1971   Hogere toelagen voor bosland-functionarissen.
                   SN 21(21):10.

154.   1971   Kwintiers een kleine Bosnegerstam. SN 21(20):2.

155.   1971   Lezing over winti cultus in Suriname. SN 21(2):4.

156.   1971   Machten en magie in het oerwoud. SZ 4:10-13.

157.   1971   Wan toli foe Saanan anga Afrikan. Paramaribo:
                   Instituut voor Taalwetenschap. [DLC/□/BCC]

158.   1972   Bosneger jeugd voor onafhankelijkheid. Go 1(2):3.

159.   1972   Bosnegerhut voor Prins Maurits. SN 22(16):1.

160.   1972   Bosnegerjongeren eisen 4 September als nationale
                   feestdag. SN 22(29):6.

161.   1972   Di woto fu Masa Jesusu: fa libi sembe kij ēn ku fa a weki
                   baka. Paramaribo: Instituut voor Taalwetenschap.
                   [DLC/□/BCC]

162.   1972   Gadden leider PBP. SN 22(3):3.

163.   1972   Grootopperhoofd Gazon in Paramaribo. SN 22(32):2.

164.   1972   Hoofdkapitein voor Matuariērs. SN 22(33):5.

165.   1972   Indianen en Bosnegers demonstreerden. SN 22(23):3.

166.   1972   Ore ships and jungle scenes. SS 8(2):1-3.

167.   1972   The art of the Djukas. SS 8(2):3-4.

168.   1972   The Two-girl mission. HH 7(11):17.

169.   1972   Waka buku fu Saamaka sembe. Paramaribo: Instituut
                voor Taalwetenschap in Suriname met medewerking
                van het Taalbureau. Mimeo. [DLC/☐/BCC]

170.   1972   Wan toli fu fa Jesusu be meke. Paramaribo: Instituut
                voor Taalwetenschap. [DLC/☐/BCC]

171.   1973   Bosland Zending. SZ no. 3:2-4.

172.   1973   De vuurdans. Ha 1(2):8.

173.   1973   Granmans legden grensgeschil bij. SN 23(26):4.

*173a. 1973   Ondi na a moo koni man?/Wan toli fu Baa Leu.
                Paramaribo: Instituut voor Taalwetenschap.
                [DLC/☐/BCC]

174.   1973   Rebel village in French Guiana: a captive's description.
                [Translation of the document published in item 894.]
                In Maroon societies: rebel slave communities in the
                Americas. Richard Price (ed.) Garden City. N.Y.:
                Anchor Press, pp. 312-19. [DLC/KTLV/☐]

175.   1973   Waka buku fu Ndjuka sama. Paramaribo: Instituut
                voor Taalwetenschap. [DLC/☐/BCC]

175a.   1974   Bosland in het nauw. SZ (3). [Special issue on Bush
                Negroes.]

176.   1974   Boslandkind. SZ no. 1:1-7.

176a.   1974   Bosnegers van Brokopondo ontevreden over
                Commissaris Bottse. We 2 Nov.:2.

177.   1974   Bruynzeel en de ondergang van de Bosnegers. SB
                5(4):5-6.

177a.   1974   De strijd van de marrons. SM (3-4):21.

177b.   1974   Geen kunst, wel Bosnegers voor Nederland. We 20 Aug.

*177c. 1974   Granman. Or 1(1):24.

177d.   1974   In het spoor der Surinaamse Marrons. Mevrouw Silvia
              de Groot vervulde een opdracht in het binnenland. We
              August [?].

178.   1974   Initieel ontwikkelingsplan binnenland. Paramaribo:
              Ministerie van Districtsbestuur en Decentralisatie.
              Mimeo. [Prepared for internal circulation.]
              [□/□/SM]

178a.   1974   Italiaanse reportage over Suriname. We 15 Aug.

179.   1974   Padfinderij in Bosland. SZ no. 2.

180.   1974   Registratie van boslandbewoners. SN 24(10).

181.   1974   Top figuren van Harvard naar het binnenland. We
              24 juni:2.

181a.   1974   Wanlö pampia di Paulu bi mbei manda da sĕmbĕ; zes
              brieven van de apostel Paulus uit de Bijbel. Paramaribo:
              Instituut voor Taalwetenschap. [DLC/□/BCC]

181b.   1974   Wan toli fa fu solugu i seefi bun anga i kondee.
              Paramaribo: Instituut voor Taalwetenschap.
              [DLC/□/BCC]

*182.   1974   Wat gebeurt er in Suriname? De rol van de kerken.
              Utrecht: Suriname aktie '73, Werkgroep Kerken.
              [O/KTLV/□]

182a.   1975   Groot gevecht te Langatabbetje om een
              vrouwenkwestie. We 10 Januari: 2, 5.

182b.   1975   Initieel ontwikkelingsplan binnenland Suriname.
              SN 25(2):3.

182c.   1975   De kwestie Manto. We 14 Januari:2.

182d.   1975   Soni miti Seema. Paramaribo: Instituut voor
              Taalwetenschap/Ministerie van Onderwijs.
              [DLC/□/BCC]

182e.   1975   Suriname: van slavernij naar onafhankelijkheid.
              Wetenschappelijke Publicatie no. 3, Organisatie van

Studenten in de Geschiedenis in Nederland.
Amsterdam: Stichting ter bevordering van de studie
der Geschiedenis in Nederland. [O/KTLV/BCC]

183.   n.d.   A bun toli fu Jeisusu di Maaka sikifi. Paramaribo:
                   Instituut voor Taalwetenschap. In press.

184.   n.d.   A toli fu fa Gadu sete goontapu. Paramaribo:
                   Instituut voor Taalwetenschap. In press.

*185. n.d.   Aucanische woorden. MS. [20th century]
                   [O/□/AHP].

186.   n.d.   Boschnegers. MS. [O/□/SM]

187.   n.d.   Curious adventures of Captain Stedman, during an
                   expedition to Surinam . . . London: Thomas Tegg.
                   [A pirated edition of Stedman 1796.] [Y/□/□]

*188. n.d.   Koenoe (Kunu). Paramaribo: Surinam Government
                   Information Service. Mimeo. [O/□/□]

*189. n.d.   Kort, doch waarachtig verhaal van de rebellie en
       [1760s?]   opstand der negers in de colonie de Berbice en de
                   ysselyke wreedheden aan deszelfs inwoners gepleegt
                   van den 21 February tot den 14 Juni, ingesloten.
                   Middleburg: P. Gillessen. [O/KB/□]

190.   n.d.   Transmigratie der Bosneger-dorpen aan de
                   Boven-Suriname. MS. [O/□/Bi]

191.   n.d.   Wi e wooko nanga G.M.D. Paramaribo: Instituut voor
                   Taalwetenschap. In press.

APTHORP, GEORGE HENRY
192.   1792   A topographical description of the Dutch colony of
                   Surrinam (in a letter to his father James Apthorp,
                   Esq. of Braintree). Boston: Collections of the
                   Massachusetts Historical Society. Vol. 1 (first series).
                   pp. 61-66 [BrU/□/□]

ARKIEMAN, TJ.
193.   1945   Suriname, het vergeten land. Amsterdam: W. L.
                   Salm. [NYP/KTLV/SM]

ARMSTRONG, ROBERT PLANT
*194. 1957   Patterns in the stories of the Dakota Indians and the
                   Negroes of Paramaribo, Dutch Guiana. Unpublished

Ph.D. dissertation. Northwestern University.
Evanston, Ill. [NU/☐/☐]

ASIN, HUMPHRY REINIER GEORGE

195.   1962   De invloed van het contact tussen stads- en
boslandbevolking op de epidemiologie van parasitaire
darminfecties: een prognose bij de bouw van een
stuwdam in de Suriname-rivier. Leiden: Luctor et
Emergo. [O/KTLV/SM]

ASIN, H. R. G. en P. H. VAN THIEL

196.   1963   An intestinal protozoa in the urban and bushland
population in Surinam. DMGT 15:108-20.

197.   1963   On the distribution of intestinal helminths in the
urban and bushland population in Surinam. DMGT
15:257-67.

ASINEI, KALINOO

198.   1974   Hafu pasa; hafu an pasa 1. Paramaribo: Instituut voor
Taalwetenschap/Ministerie van Onderwijs. [DLC/☐/BCC]

199.   1974   Hafu pasa; hafu an pasa 2. Paramaribo: Instituut voor
Taalwetenschap/Ministerie van Onderwijs. [DLC/☐/BCC]

ASSID

200.   1946   De eeuwige cirkel: leven en strijd van de Indianen en
Marrons in Suriname. The Hague: van der Laan.
[DLC/KTLV/SM]

v. B., M.

*201.   1934   Bij de boschnegers van Suriname. OH juli.

BAËZA, CH.

*202.   1904   Ingezonden [Letter to the editor]. MW 10(42),
Jan. 16:550-51.

BAKHUIS, L. A.

203.   1902   Verslag der Coppename-expeditie. TKNAG (2^e serie)
19:695-852.

204.   1908   De 5de wetenschappelijke expeditie naar het
binnenland van Suriname. TKNAG (2^e serie)
25:94-112.

BAKKER, J. P.

205.   1955   Over onstaan en vervorming van de laaggelegen
landbouwgronden der bosnegers langs de grote rivieren
van Suriname. *In* De wereld der mensen. Sociaal-
wetenschappelijke opstellen aangeboden aan Prof. Dr.
J. J. Fahrenfort ter gelegenheid van zijn afscheid als
hoogleraar in de Volkenkunde aan de Universiteit
van Amsterdam. Groningen: J. B. Wolters.
[DLC/UBU/☐]

BAKKER, PIET

206.   n.d.   Naar "de West." Joure-Utrecht: Douwe Egberts.
[1949?]   [O/KTLV/☐]

van BALEN, JAN HENDRIK

*207. n.d. De commandant van de negerjagers. Historisch verhaal van de krijgstochten tegen de boschnegers in Suriname 1772-1778. *In* J. H. van Balen, De Nederlanders in Oost en West, te Water en te Land. II, 3. Amsterdam: Jan Leendertz & Zoon, 1883-84. [CrU/BM/SM]

van BALEN, WILLEM JULIUS

208. 1935 Antilia: een gids door de Caraibische wereld (Uw reismakker naar West-Indië). Amsterdam: Van Holkema & Warendorf N.V. [DLC/KTLV/□]

209. 1941 Kennismaking met Suriname, proeve ener schets van Nederlands Guyana. Deventer: W. van Hoeve. [DLC/KTLV/SM]

210. 1949 Zoeklicht op Zuid-Amerika. Haarlem: Boom-Ruygrok. [2^e druk.] [Y/KITC/□]

BANEKE, ED.

211. 1964 Transmigratie van Bosnegers. Sc 58:22-25.

BARNETT, A. C.

212. 1931/32 Colonial survivals in Bush Negro speech. AS 7:393-97.

BARTH, H.

213. 1925 Overzicht van de Boschlandzending. BHW (1):11-16.

214. 1930 Iets over de Boschland-Zending der Evangelische Broeder-Gem. EC 1 juli.

BASTIDE, ROGER

215. 1965 Nègres marrons et nègres libres. AESC 20:169-74.

216. 1967 Les Amériques noires. Paris: Payot. [DLC/KTLV/□]

216a. 1972 African civilizations in the New World. New York: Harper and Row. [Translation of item 216]. [DLC/KTLV/□]

217. 1968 La divination chez les Afro-Américains. *In* La divination, A. Caquot and M. Leibovici, (eds.). Paris: Presses Universitaires de France, pp. 393-427. [NYP/BM/□]

BECHLER, TH.

218. 1904 Paka Paka. *In* In alle Welt. Missionsstunden aus der Brudergemein 4. Herrnhut: Missionsbuchhandlung der Missionsanstalt der Evangelische Brüder-Unität, pp. 19-32. [Y/BHZ/□]

219. 1906 Mengen zur Beute und die starken zum Raube. Zwei bilder aus der Buschlandmission in Suriname. *In* In Alle Welt, Missionsstunden aus der Brüdergemein 5. Herrnhut: Missionbuchhandlung der Missionsanstalt der Evang. Brüder-Unität, pp. 57-74. [Y/BHZ/□]

*220. 1930 Rudolf oder: Wie ein Surinamer Bursch ein Evangelist wurde. Herrnhut: Verlag der Missionsbuchhandlung. [O/BHZ/□]

BECK, SIEGFRIED

221.   1914   Die wirtschaftlich-soziale Arbeit der Missionsgeschäfte der Brüdergemeine in Suriname . . . Herrnhut. [NYP/KTLV/□]

222.   1924   Lezingen over Surinaamsche problemen. Paramaribo: C. Kersten & Co. [UF/KTLV/SM]

*223.   1925   Die Wegläufer von Rac à Rac: Ein Stück Surinamer Kolonial- und Missions geschichte aus dem 19. Jahhrundert. MMBS februari.

*224.   1925   Een tocht over de Suriname-rivier. NZ 8:136-38.

225.   1926   De wegloopers van Rac à Rac. Een stuk koloniale- en zendingsgeschiedenis van de 19e eeuw. BHW (1):3-13. [Translation of item 223].

de BEET, CHRIS and MIRIAM STERMAN

225a.   n.d.   People in between: the Matawai maroons of Surinam. Ph.D. dissertation in preparation, University of Utrecht.

de BEET-STERMAN, MIRIAM

226.   1974   Review of Jean Hurault 1970. BTLV 130:165-67.

BEHN, APHRA

227.   1688   Oroonoko or the royal slave: a true history. London: W. Canning. [Y/BM/SM]

BENJAMINS, H. D.

228.   1920/21   Review of W. F. van Lier 1919, WIG 2:163-72.

229.   1923/24   Bevolkingscijfers van Britisch-Guiana en Suriname. WIG 5:197-215.

230.   1924/25   Emigratie uit Oost-Indië naar Suriname in 1714? WIG 6:479-80

231.   1929/30   Een Amerikaansche professor over Surinaamsche Boschnegers. WIG 11:483-87. [For Kahn's response, see item 635.]

232.   1929/30,   "Sneki-Koti": inenting tegen den beet van vergiftige
        1931/32   slangen. WIG 11:497-512 and WIG 13:3-24, 317-24.

233.   1929/30   Treef en lepra in Suriname. WIG 11:187-216.

234.   1930/31   [Comment on items 634 and 635.] WIG 12:452.

BENJAMINS, H. D. and JOH. F. SNELLEMAN (eds.)

235.   1917   Encyclopaedie van Nederlandsch West-Indië. The Hague: Martinus Nijhoff. [See, in particular, sections s.v. afgoderijdans, akra, amuletten, anansitori, bakrôe, boschnegers, boschpatrouilles, broedergemeente, dansen, kandoe, musea, muziek-instrumenten en muziek, naamgeving, onderzoekingstochten en onderzoek, ostagiers, slangenvereering, winti, zee- en landkaarten.] [DLC/KTLV/SM]

BENOIT, P. J.

236.   1839   Voyage à Surinam: description des possessions néerlandaises dans la Guyane. Bruxelles: Société

des Beaux-Arts. [Facsimile reprint, with summary and annotations in English by Silvia W. de Groot, 1967. Amsterdam: S. Emmering.] [DLC/KTLV/SM]

van BERK, LAMBERT HENDRIK

*237. 1930 Bijdrage tot de kennis der West-Indische volksgeneeskruiden. Doctoral dissertation, Utrecht. [DLC/UBU/□]

van BERKEL, ADRIAAN

238. 1695 Amerikaansche voijagien, behelzende een reis na Rio-de-Berbice, enz., en na de colonie van Suriname. Amsterdam: Johan ten Hoorn. [DLC/KTLV/SM]

*239. 1789 Beschreibung seiner Reisen nach Rio-de-Berbice und Surinam. Memmingen: Seijler. [Translation of item 238.] [O/BM/SM]

240. 1941 Travels in South America, between the Berbice and Essequibo Rivers, and in Surinam, 1670-1689. Translated and edited [from item 238] by Walter Edmund Roth, 1925. [Second impression 1942.] Georgetown, British Guiana: The "Daily Chronicle" Ltd. [DLC/KITC/SM]

BERVOETS, J. A. A.

240a. 1974 Inventarissen van het archief "Kabinet Geheim" van de gouverneur van Suriname 1885-1962 en van de beheerder van het Surinaams Welvaartsfonds 1947-1960. Tweede Afdeling. The Hague: Algemeen Rijksarchief. [O/KTLV/□]

BEX, A.

241. 1926 Uit het geestenrijk van Suriname. Paramaribo: G. Randag. [O/KTLV/□]

BIELKE, H. M.

*242. 1930 In Suriname's Boschland. Kan de Boschneger heden ten dage medische hulp ontvangen? MeN no. 2.

BIELKE, H., P. M. Legêne *et al.*

*243. 1938[?] Menschen in Nood. Suriname-nummer der vereeniging "Simavi," ten bate van een Suriname's boschland te stichten ziekenhuis. [O/□/□]

BIJLSMA, R.

244. 1921 Alexander de Lavaux en zijne Generale Kaart van Suriname 1737. WIG 2:397-406.

van BLANKENSTEIJN, M.

245. 1923 Suriname. Rotterdam: Nijgh en van Ditmar's. [DLC/KTLV/SM]

BLANKESTEIJN, G.

246. 1959 Rijksdelen overzee. De Nederlandse Antillen. Suriname. Nieuw Guinea. Leerboek voor Mulo-scholen tevens

voor andere vormen van voortgezet onderwijs. Meppel:
N. V. Uitgeverij A. Roelofs van Goor. [O/KTLV/□]

BLOM, ANTHONY

247.   1786   Verhandeling over den landbouw, in de Colonie
Suriname, volgens eene negentien-jaarige
ondervinding zamengesteld door ___: in orde gebragt;
en met de noodige ophelderingen en bewysredenen
voorzien, door Fl. V. Heshuysen, Haarlem: Cornelis
van der Aa. [DLC/KTLV/SM]

248.   1787   Verhandeling van den landbouw in de colonie
Suriname. Amsteldam: J. W. Smit. [USDA/KTLV/SM]

BLUMBERG, B., J. McGIFF, and I. GUICHERIT

249.   1951   Filariasis in Moengo (Surinam) in 1950. DMGT
3:368-72.

250.   1952   Malaria survey among the Bush Negroes of Marowyne
District, Surinam, S.A. in 1950. DMGT 4:2-4.

251.   1953   A survey of intestinal parasites in the school children of
Moengo, Surinam, 1950. DMGT 5:137-40.

BOLKESTEIN, G.

252.   1927   Buitenlandse zaken. [Djankuso's letter to the League of
Nations.] O 9:943-45.

BONAPARTE, PRINCE ROLAND

*253.   1884   Ethnographie de la Guyane et de Suriname. BSGP ___:
612-16. [Cited in E. Abonnenc *et al.*, Bibliographie de
la Guyane Française, Paris, Larose, 1957, but it is not
in 1884 volume.]

254.   1884   Les habitants de Suriname, notes recueillies à l'exposition
coloniale d'Amsterdam en 1883. Paris: A. Quantin.
[DLC/KTLV/SM]

255.   1886   Exploration du Dr. néerlandais ten Kate dans
l'Amérique du Sud. CRSG 1886:106-9.

256.   1886   Le Dr. Ten-Kate à la Guyane Hollandaise. RGI
11(123):4-5.

*257.   1898   Suriname. Paris: Plon. [DLC/KITC/□]

*258.   [?]   La Guyane Hollandaise, Paris: Bibliothèque Illustrée de
Voyages. [O/□/□]

BONNE, C.

259.   1919   De maatschappelijke beteekenis der Surinaamsche
ziekten. WIG 1:291-310.

260.   1920   Het Boschnegerschrift van Afaka. WIG 2:391-96.

BONNE-WEPSTER, J.

*261.   1927   Schetsen van de Marowyne. AHV 63:135-40, 158-60,
204-9.

de BORST, NELLY

*262.   1935   Brief [uit Ganzee.] OS nov. (no. 11).

263.	1936	Bericht . . . [uit Ganzee]. OS dec. (no. 12):186-88.
*264.	1936	Vreugde en teleurstellingen in Ganzee (Boven-Suriname). OS maart (no. 3):34-38.
265.	1937	Bericht . . . [uit Ganzee]. OS sept (no. 9):134-38.
*266.	1937	Een kreet uit Suriname's boschland. MeN no. 4.
267.	1938	Ärztliche Arbeit im Surinamer Buschland MBB 102:89-90.

BOSCH, G. B.

| 269. | 1829-43 | Reizen in West-Indië, en door een gedeelte van Zuid- en Noord-Amerika. Utrecht: N. van der Monde. [O/KTLV/SM] |

van den BOSCH, JOHANNES

| 270. | 1818 | Nederlandsche bezittingen in Azië, Amerika en Afrika. The Hague and Amsterdam: Gebr. van Cleef. [DLC/KTLV/SM] |

BOSSERS, A.

| 271. | 1884 | Beknopte geschiedenis der Katholieke Missie in Suriname. Gulpen: M. Alberts. [Y/KTLV/□] |

BOUSSENARD, LOUIS

| 272. | 1892 | Les mystères de la Guyane. Paris: Librairie Illustrée. [CaU/□/□] |

BOUYER, FRÉDÉRIC

| 273. | 1866 | Voyage dans la Guyane Française. TM 13:273-352. |
| 274. | 1867 | La Guyane Française. Notes et souvenirs d'un voyage exécuté en 1862-63. Paris: Hachette. [DLC/KTLV/□] |

BRAUER, JOHANN HARTWIG

| 275. | 1847 | Das Missionswesen der evangelischen Kirche, Hamburg. [Y/□/□] |

BRETT, REV. W. H.

| 276. | 1881 | Mission work among the Indian tribes in the forests of Guiana. London: Society for Promoting Christian Knowledge. [DLC/UBL/□] |

BRONS, J. C.

| 277. | 1952 | Het rijksdeel Suriname. Haarlem: De Erven F. Bohn. [UCB/KTLV/SM] |

BROUWN, CHARLES

| 278. | 1796 | Historie der orlogen met de Marrons of Surinaamsche Boschnegers. In Surinaamsche Staatkundige Almanach voor den Jaare 1796. Paramaribo: W. P. Wilkens, pp. 87-130. [DLC/□/SM] |

BRUIJNING, C. F. A.

| 279. | 1957 | Man-biting sandflies (Phlebotomus) in the endemic Leishmaniasis area of Surinam. DMGT 9:229-36. |

BRUMMER, A. F. J.
280.   1941   Suriname: een vluchtige schets van land en volk. NMa
1:31-49

BRUNETTI, R. P. JULES
*281.   1887   Deux peuplades africaines sur les bords du Maroni.
MC 19:5-9, 17-21, 29-33, 41-46, 52-56, 65-69, 77-80,
92-95, 104-7, 113-17.
282.   1890   La Guyane Française. Souvenirs et impressions de voyage.
Tours: Alfred Mame et Fils. [DLC/□/□]

BUBBERMAN, F. C., A. H. LOOR *et al.,* and C. KOEMAN (ed.)
282a.   1973   Links with the past: the history of cartography in
Suriname 1500-1971. Amsterdam: Theatrum Orbis
Terrarum. [JHU/KTLV/SM]

BUCK, G.
*282b.   1892/93   Tagebuch des Bruder Buck in Wanhatti (Cottica).
MS. [O/ABU/□]
*282c.   1893   Suriname. MBB 57:179-86.
*282d.   1895   Missionsbilder aus Suriname. MMBS:45-54.

BUISKOOL, J. A. E.
283.   1946   Suriname nu en straks. Amsterdam: W. L. Salm.
[DLC/KTLV/SM]

BUREAU, CAPITAINE GABRIEL
284.   1936   La Guyane méconnue. Paris: Fasquelle Éditeurs.
[DLC/BM/□]

BURKHARDT, G.
285.   1858   Die evangelische Mission unter den Negern in Westindien
und Südamerika. Bielefield: Verlag von Belhage und
Klasing. [DLC/□/□]
286.   1898   Die Mission der Brüdergemeine in Missionsstunden.
Zweites Heft: Suriname. Leipzig: F. Jansa.
[Y/KTLV/□]

BURKHARDT, W.
*288.   1925   Een bezoek aan de Boschnegers. NA 8:71-73.
289.   1925   Reis naar het Saramacca-gebied. BHW (2):26-31;
(3):35-43. [Translation of item 290.]
290.   1925   Reise an die Saramakka. MBB 89:15-20, 38-40.
[Also in MMBS (6), 1925.]
*291.   1926   Adventstage in Ganzee. MMBS 1 März.
*292.   1926   Suriname. Samuel Adabikolina (Boschneger). NZ juli.
293.   1927   Surinam. IRM 16(63):415-24.
*294.   1929   Reisebilder von der oberen Suriname. MMBS nos. 1, 2.
*295.   1930   Begint het te dagen onder de Aukaner- Boschnegers?
OS dec.

BUSCHKENS, W. F. L.
*296.   1963   Bosnegerrechtspraak. MS. [O/□/□]

BUTTS, DONALD C. A.
297.   1955   Blood groups of the Bush Negroes of Surinam.
                DMGT 7(1):43-9.
BUVE, R.
298.   1963   Surinaamse slaven en vrije negers in Amsterdam
                gedurende de achttiende eeuw. BTLV 119:8-17.
299.   1966   Gouverneur Johannes Heinsius: de rol van van Aerssen's
                voorganger in de Surinaamse Indianenoorlog,
                1678-1680. NWIG 45:14-26.
299a.   1975   Governor Johannes Heinsius: the role of van Aerssen's
                predecessor in the Surinam Indian war, 1678-1680.
                [Translation of item 299.] In Current anthropology
                in the Netherlands, Peter Kloos and Henri J. M.
                Claessen (eds.). Rotterdam: Anthropological Branch of
                the Netherlands Sociological and Anthropological
                Society, pp. 39-47. [JHU/KTLV/□]
van CALKER
300.   1865   [Letter of August 4 from Br. van Calker.] BHW
                (10):229.
CAMERON, NORMAN EUSTACE
301.   1929-34 The evolution of the Negro. Georgetown: Argosy.
                [Facsimile reprint, 1970, Westport, Conn: Greenwood
                Press.] [DLC/□/□]
van CAPPELLE, H.
302.   1902   Bij de Indianen en Boschnegers van Suriname. EGM
                23:240-51. 310-23, 370-83.
303.   1903   De binnenlanden van het Distrikt Nickerie. Lotgevallen
                en algemeene uitkomsten van eene expeditie door het
                westelijk deel der Kolonie Suriname in September en
                October van het jaar 1900. Baarn: Hollandia
                Drukkerij. [HU/KTLV/SM]
*304.   1904   Surinaamsche negervertellingen. EGM 28:314-27.
*305.   1905   De kankantrie, de boschgouverneur den Surinaamschen
                neger. EGM 29:181-84.
306.   1916   Surinaamsche negervertellingen. BTLV 72:233-379.
*307.   1926   Mythen en sagen uit West-Indië. Zutphen: W. J. Thieme.
                [NYP/KTLV/□]
308.   1931   Van slavenstaat naar Boschneger-maatschappij. TN
                3:373-77, 387-93, 405-12.
CARPENTER, JOHN ALLEN and JEAN CURRENS LYONS
309.   1970   Surinam. Chicago: Childrens Press. [DLC/□/BCC]
CATEAU van ROSEVELT, J. F. A.
310.   c. 1862? Verslag van de reis ter opname van de Beneden en de
                Boven Suriname Rivier. MS. In Beschrijvingen der
                tochten . . . [O/KITC/□]

CATEAU van ROSEVELT, J. [F.] A. and H. W. van HEERDT
*311.   1862   Rapport van het Nederlandsch gedeelte der commissie
                      belast met de exploratie van de rivier de Marowijne.
                      MS. [O/□/SM]

CATEAU van ROSEVELT, J. F. A. and J. F. A. E. van LANSBERGE
312.   1873   Verslag van de reis ter opname van de Rivier Suriname.
                      MS [Later published in item 877, pp. 183-92, 289-99,
                      321-42.]

CERFBERR [de MÉDELSHEIM], AUGUSTE EDOUARD
313.   1854   La Guyane, civilisation et barbarie; coutumes et
                      paysages. Paris: D. Giraud. [UP/BM/□]

CHARPENTIER, S. and G.
314.   1954   An Indianist experiment in French Guiana. BI 14(2):
                      133-40.

CHARRIÈRE, ARISTIDE
315.   1856   Notice sur l'existence de l'or à la Guyane Française.
                      RC 16:274-83.
316.   1856   Notice sur le Maroni. RC 16:373-88.
317.   1856   Sur l'origine des Boss et des Bonis. RC 16:388-97.

CLARKE, JOHN HENRIK
318.   1973   Slave revolt in the Caribbean. BW 22(4):12-25.

CLAUSEN, J. and H. ENGEL
*319.   1931   In het boschland aan de Boven Suriname. OS dec.

van COLL, C.
*320.   1894-96   Grepen in de land- en volkenkunde van Suriname. Su
                      6 jan. 1894-28 juni 1896.
321.   1903   Gegevens over land en volk van Suriname. BTLV
                      55:451-635. [Revised and expanded version of item
                      320.]

COLLIS, LOUISE
322.   1966   Soldier in Paradise; the life of Captain John Stedman,
                      1744-1797. New York: Harcourt, Brace and World.
                      [DLC/KTLV/□]

COMITÉ SPECIAL DE LA GUYANE NÉERLANDAISE
323.   1931   Surinam: aperçu général de la Guyane Néerlandaise.
                      Publié par Comité Exécutif pour la Participation
                      Néerlandaise à l'Exposition Coloniale Internationale,
                      Paris, Amsterdam: J. H. de Bussy. [O/KTLV/□]

COMMISSIE TER BESTUDERING VAN HET ONDERWIJS IN HET
BINNENLAND
324.   1969   Rapport inzake materiële en personele voorzieningen.
                      Paramaribo: Ministerie van Onderwijs. Mimeo.
                      [O/□/□]

COMVALIUS, THEOD, A. C.

324a. 1907 Kort overzicht van de Surinaamse geschiedenis voor de lagere school. Paramaribo: Schefferdrukkerij Dordrecht. [2nd edition.] [O/UBA/SM]

*325. 1935 De Aucaners en de vrachtvaart in het Marowynegebeid. Va 20 juli, Avondblad D.

CONSEN, H.

326. 1964 Het stuwmeer. Sc 58:7-11.

COPIJN, A.

327. 1858 Bijdrage tot de kennis van Suriname's binnenland; bijzonder die van eenen inlandschen volksstam. Uit het journaal van een pleziertochtje naar de Opper-Saramacca, gedaan oct. 1847. WI 2:3-17.

COSTER, A. M.

328. 1866 De Boschnegers in de kolonie Suriname, hun leven, zeden, en gewoonten. BTLV 13:1-36. [English translation HRAF]

COUDREAU, HENRI

329. 1888 La Haute-Guyane. RE 7:454-81.

330. 1891 Dix ans de Guyane. BSGP (sér. 7) 12:447-80.

331. 1893 Chez nos Indiens: quatre années dans la Guyane Française (1887-1891). Paris: Hachette. [DLC/KTLV/□]

COUNTER, S. ALLEN and DAVID L. EVANS

331a. 1974 Djuka counterpoint. New 84 (19):4, 8.

COVARRUBIAS, MIGUEL

332. 1946 Los Djukas: Bush Negroes de la Guyana Holandesa. Af 2(3):121-22.

CRANZ, DAVID

333. 1771 Alte und Neue Brüder-Historie. Barby: H. D. Ebers [See item 517.] [DLC/UBA/□]

334. 1780 The ancient and modern history of the brethren. London: W. and A. Strahan. [Translated from the 1771 German edition by Benjamin La Trobe.] [NYP/BM/□]

CREVAUX, JULES

335. 1875 Mémoire sur les Nègres Bosh ou Nègres Marrons des Guyanes. BMSA 2:259-80.

336. 1878 Voyage en Guyane (1877). BSGP 16:385-417 [plus maps].

337. 1879 Voyage d'exploration dans l'intérieur des Guyanes, 1876-77. TM 20:337-416.

338. 1879 Voyage d'exploration en Guyane. RMC 60:706-26.

339. 1880 Erste Reise im Innern von Guyana (1876 bis 1877). Gl 37:1-7, 17-23, 33-38, 49-55, 65-72, 81-83.

340.   1883   Voyages dans l'Amérique du Sud, 1878-1881, Paris:
                    Hachette. [DLC/KTLV/SM]
    CRISPINE, SR. M.
*341.   1925   Van Djoeka's en van hun nieuw dorp. EM 25 april.
    CROWLEY, DANIEL J.
342.   1956   Bush Negro combs: a structural analysis VG 2:145-61.
    CURRIE, A.
*343.   1948   Nota inzake bestuurszorg voor Boschnegers en
                    Indianen. MS. [O/□/□]
    CURRIER, REV. CHARLES WARREN
344.   1899   The Bush Negroes of Dutch Guiana. CW 70(416):
                    227-38.

    DAELEMAN, JAN
345.   1971   Kongo words in Saramacca Tongo. *In* Pidginization and
                    creolization of languages, Dell Hymes (ed.). Cambridge:
                    Cambridge University Press, pp. 281-83. [DLC/KTLV/□]
346.   1972   Kongo elements in Saramacca Tongo. JAL 11(1):1-44.
    DALBY, DAVID
347.   1968   The indigenous scripts of West Africa and Surinam:
                    their inspiration and design. ALS 9:156-97.
348.   1969   Further indigenous scripts of West Africa: Manding,
                    Wolof and Fula alphabets and Yoruba "holy"
                    writing. ALS 10:161-81.
349.   1970   Black through white: patterns of communication in
                    Africa and the New World. Bloomington: African
                    Studies Program, Indiana University. [DLC/□/□]
    DALTON, HENRY G.
349a.   1885   The history of British Guiana . . . London: Longman, Brown,
                    Green, and Longmans. [DLC/UBL/□]
    DAMAS, LÉON GONTRAN
349b.   1938   Retour de Guyane. Paris: José Corti. [O/□/□]
    DANCE, CHARLES DANIEL
349c.   1881   Chapters from a Guianese log-book; or, the folk-lore and
                    scenes of sea-coast and river life in British Guiana.
                    Comprising sketches of Indian, Boviander and Negro
                    life, habits, customs, and legendary tales, with historic
                    notes, political and natural . . . Georgetown, Demerara:
                    The Royal Gazette Establishment. [CPL/KTLV/□]
    van DANTZIG, A.
350.   1968   Het Nederlandse aandeel in de slavenhandel. Bussum:
                    Fibula-van Dishoek. [DLC/KITC/SM]
    DARK, PHILIP J. C.
351.   1950   Bush Negro art: an African art in the Americas.
                    Unpublished M.Phil. thesis, Department of
                    Anthropology, Yale University. [Y/□/□]

352. 1951 Some notes on the carving of calabashes by the Bush negroes of Surinam. Ma 51:57-61.
353. 1952 Bush Negro calabash-carving. Ma 52:126. [Reply to Herskovits 1951.]
354. 1954 Bush Negro art: an African art in the Americas. London: Tiranti. [Second edition 1970.] [DLC/KTLV/SM]

DARNOUD, TH. A.
*355. 1971 Afrikaanse mensen en mochten, een overzicht en een beoordeling van de ontmoeting tussen Afrikaanse religie en Christelijk geloof. Paramaribo. [O/□/□]

DAVIS, HASSOLDT
356. 1949 On the flowing highway in Guiana forests. Tr 92(6): 4-9, 31.
357. 1952 The jungle and the damned. New York: Duell, Sloan and Pearce. [DLC/BTHD/□]
358. n.d. La jungle et les damnés. Paris: La Toison d'Or [Translation of item 357.] [O/□/□]

DEBBASCH, YVAN
359. 1961/62 Le marronnage. Essai sur la désertion de l'esclave antillais. ASo 1961:1-112 and 1962:117-95.

DEBIEN, GABRIEL
360. 1966 Le marronage aux Antilles Françaises au XVIIIe siècle. CS 6 (3):3-43.

DEBIEN, GABRIEL and JOHANNA FELHOEN KRAAL
361. 1955 Esclaves et plantations de Surinam vus par Malouet, 1777. WIG 36:53-60.

DECKER, STEPHEN E.
361a. 1972 Man's niche in the tropical rain forest. AF 78(2):52-55, 60-63.

DELAFOSSE, MAURICE
362. 1912 De quelques persistances d'ordre ethnographique chez les descendants des nègres transplantés aux Antilles et à la Guyane. RES 3:234-37.
363. 1925 Survivances africaines chez les nègres "Bosch" de la Guyane. An 35:475-94.

DENIS, FERDINAND
364. 1823 La Guyane, ou historie, moeurs, usages et costumes des habitans de cette partie de l'Amérique. Paris: Nepveu. [DLC/□/□]

DENNISON, I. D. [pseud.]
365. 1972 A very different vacation. SA 4(12):6-7.

DEROLLE, G.
366. 1944 Surinam, o Guyana Holandesa. RGA 21:163-68.

DEVÈZE, MICHEL
367.   1968   Les Guyanes. Paris: Presses Universitaires de la France.
             [DLC/UBL/□]
DEW, EDWARD
368.   1974   Elections: Surinam style. CR 6 (2):20-22, 24, 26.
van DIJK, W. and C. F. G. GETROUW
369.   1951   De ontwikkeling van de Surinaamse geschiedenis.
             Paramaribo: N.V. Ed Corona. [O/KTLV/SM]
DIJKMANS, M. A. F.
370.   1949   Rapport over de activering van het Surinaamse bos.
             Paramaribo. Mimeo. [O/KITC/□]
DIJKSTRA, JAN
371.   1973   Suriname-gegevens: informatie over Suriname voor een
             beter begrip omtrent de gebeurtenissen van februari
             1973. Voorburg: Protestantse Stichting tot Bevordering
             van het Bibliotheekwezen en de Lectuurvoorlichting in
             Nederland. [O/KTLV/□]
DOMERGUE, AD.
*372. 1890/91 Mission au Maroni Jusqu'au saut Hermina. BSGP ___:
             478, 515;___:250-. [Cited in E. Abonnenc et al.,
             Bibliographie de la Guyane Française, Paris, Larose,
             1957, but it is not in these volumes.]
DOMPIG, J.
*372a. n.d.   Amba de vrouw van Boni. [O/□/SM]
DONICIE, ANTOON
373.   1948   Sterfhuis en begrafenis bij de Saramakkanen. WIG 29
             175-182.
374.   1952   Iets over de taal en de sprookjes van Suriname. WIG
             33:153-73.
375.   1958   De vorm (n)a in het Negerengels en Saramaccaans.
             VG 3:87-93.
DONICIE, ANTOON C.ssR. and JAN VOORHOEVE
376.   1963   De Saramakaanse woordenschat. Amsterdam: Bureau
             voor Taalonderzoek in Suriname van de Universiteit
             van Amsterdam. Mimeo. [DLC/KTLV/SM]
DOORNBOS, LIEUWE
*377. 1966   Kinderjaren aan de Tapanahony. Groningen: Van
             Denderen. [CrU/UBU/□]
DOORNBOS, L. and R. ALBITROUW
378.   1962   Medische zending in Suriname. SZ 9:62-66.
DOORNBOS, L., J. H. P. JONXIS and H. K. A. VISSER
379.   1968   Growth of Bushnegro children on the Tapanahoni
             River in Dutch Guiana. HB 40:396-415.

van DOORNINCK, A.
380. 1968 De onrust onder de blanken van Suriname in de achttiende eeuw. OW 61(3):9-11, 16.

te DORSTHORST, T.
381. 1973 Trainingscursus voor Boslanddorpen. St 3 (5):3-4.

DOTH, R. E. C. *et al.*
382. n.d. Kondre sa jere. Zeist: Seminarie der Evangelische
      [1965?] Broedergemeente. [O/□/SM]

DOUGLAS, CHARLES
383. 1930 Een blik in het verleden van Suriname. Beknopt verhaal omtrent gebeurtenissen met de slaven en toestanden in Suriname gedurende de jaren 1630-1863. Paramaribo: J. H. Oliviera. [DLC/KTLV/SM]
384. 1934 Encyclopaedie der Guyana's van 1492-1933. Paramaribo: Drukkerij Eben Haëzer. [O/KTLV/□]
385. 1936 Eenige eigenaardigheden en typische merkwaardigheden uit de geschiedenis van de planterij in Suriname, gedurende de vorige eeuwen tot heden. Paramaribo: Drukkerij "De Tijd" O. C. Marcus. [O/KTLV/SM]

van DRIMMELEN, C.
386. 1925/26 De Neger in zijn cultuurgeschiedenis. WIG 7:385-97.

DUBELAAR, C. N.
387. 1970 Het Afakaschrift in de Afrikanistiek. NWIG 47:294-303.
387a. 1972 Negersprookjes uit Suriname. NV 22 (3/4).
*387b. 1973 Surinam Negro folktales, I. Groningen. [Translation of item 387a.] [O/□/SM]

DUBELAAR, C. N. and J. W. GONGGRYP
388. 1968 Het Afakaschrift: een nadere beschouwing. NWIG 46:232-60.

van DUSSELDORP, D. B. W. M.
389. 1962 Een classificatie van de occupatievormen in Suriname. TKNAG (2^e serie) 79:128-47.

EASTON, DAVID K.
390. 1957 The Guyanas. Fo 8:3.

EDMUNDA, SR. M.
*391. 1934 Bezoek van twee heeren Djoeka's. EM juni (no. 7).

EERSEL, CHRISTIAN H.
392. 1969 De Surinaamse taalsituatie. Paramaribo: Taalbureau Suriname, Ministerie van Onderwijs en Volksontwikkeling. [O/KTLV/BCC]
393. 1970 Houtsnijkunst. Sc 74:13-14.
394. 1971 Prestige in choice of language and linguistic form. *In* Pidginization and creolization of languages, Dell

Hymes (ed.). Cambridge: Cambridge University Press,
pp. 317-22. [DLC/KTLV/□]

EILERTS de HAAN, J. G. W. J.

395.   1910   Verslag van de expeditie naar de Suriname-Rivier.
TKNAG (2^e serie) 27:403-68, 641-701.

EINAAR, JOHAN FRIEDERICH EGBERT

396.   1934   Bijdrage tot de kennis van het engelsch tussenbestuur
van Suriname, 1804-1816. Leiden: M. Dubbeldeman.
[DLC/KTLV/SM]

ELLIS, H. W. R.

397.   1853   Chronologie der geschiedenis van Suriname.
Paramaribo: J. Morpurgo. [DLC/□/SM]

EMERITUS

*398.   1935   Schatting aan Boschnegers en Boschneger beschaving.
Ri 10 april.

ESSED, F. E.

398a.   1973   Een volk op weg naar zelfstandigheid. Paramaribo:
Stichting Planbureau Suriname. [O/□/□]

ESSED, W. F. R.

399.   1930/31   Eenige opmerkingen naar aanleiding van de artikelen
over treef en lepra in dit tijdschrift verschenen.
WIG 12:257-67.

VAN EYCK, J. W. S.

*400.   1828   Algemeen verslag van den tegenwoordigen staat en de
huisselijke inrigtingen, benevens de levenswijs der
bevredigde Boschnegers binnen deze kolonie, door
den Heer Jacob Willem Stockelaar van Eyck,
Posthouder en Resident bij de Saramaccaner- en
Sarakreker Boschnegers, den 5 junij 1828 aan Z. Exc.
den Kommissaris- Generaal Joh. van den Bosch. MS.
[Cited in Teenstra 1835, II: 172. Location unknown.]
[O/□/□]

401.   1830   Beschouwing van den tegenwoordigen staat, zeden en
gewoonten van de Saramaccaner bevredigde Boschnegers,
in deze kolonie. *In* Surinaamsche almanak voor het
jaar 1830. Amsterdam: C. G. Sulpke, pp. 260-77.
[DLC/KTLV/SM]

FAGG, WILLIAM

402.   1952   Notes on some West African Americana. Ma 52:119-22.

FAUQUE, le père

403.   1751   Lettre du père Fauque, de la Compagnie de Jésus,
au père Allart, de la même Compagnie. *In* Lettres
édifiantes et curieuses, écrites des missions étrangères.
Lyon: J. Vernarel and É. Cabin (1819), vol. 5, pp. 1-16.
[HU/KTLV/□]

FERMIN, PHILLIPPE

404.   1769   Déscription générale, historique, géographique et physique de la colonie de Surinam . . . Amsterdam: E. van Harrevelt. [DLC/KTLV/SM]

405.   1770   Nieuwe algemeene beschrijving van de colonie van Suriname. Harlingen: V. van der Plaats, Jr. [Translation of item 404.] [DLC/KTLV/□]

406.   1778   Tableau historique et politique de l'état ancien et actuel de la Colonie de Surinam, et des causes de sa décadence. Maestricht: J. E. Dufour & Ph. Roux. [DLC/KTLV/SM]

407.   1781   An historical and political view of the present and ancient state of the colony of Surinam, in South America, with the settlements of Demerary and Issequibo, together with an account of its produce for 25 years past. By a person who lived there 10 years. London: W. Nicoll. [Abridged translation of item 406.] [DLC/BM/□]

FISCHER, H.

408.   1935   Verslag over de Boven-Saramacca. OS dec (11):173-76.

*409.   1936   Medisch werk aan de Bovenste Suriname. MeN no. 4.

FLETCHER, ALAN MARK

410.   1966   The land and people of the Guianas. Philadelphia: J. B. Lippincott. [DLC/□/SM]

FLOETHE, LOUISE LEE and RICHARD FLOETHE

411.   1971   Jungle people: story of the brave blacks of Surinam. New York: Scribner. [DLC/□/□]

FLU, P. C.

412.   1912   Rapport over het wetenschappelijk onderzoek naar het voorkomen der malaria in de bovenlanden der kolonie Suriname en de bestudering van die ziekte. The Hague: Algemeene Landsdrukkerij. [DLC/KTLV/SM]

FOCKE, H. C.

413.   1858   De Surinaamsche negermuzijk. WI 2:93-107.

414.   1855   Neger-Engelsch woordenboek. Leiden: P. H. van den Heuvell. [DLC/KTLV/□]

FONTAINE, OCTAVE

415.   1885   La Guyane Néerlandaise. BSRB 9:347-65.

416.   1891   La Guyane néerlandaise ou colonie de Surinam. BSRB 15:589-637.

FORBES, ROSITA

417.   1936   Women of the flame. CLA 70 (5):57-60, 82, 86.

FOURGEOUD

418.   1775   Missive van den Collonel Fourgeoud, commandeerende de troupen van den Staat in Suriname. *In* item 6a, vol. II, pp. 164-67.

FRANCO, JOSÉ L.
419.   1961   Afroamérica. Havana: Publicaciones de la Junta
                    Nacional de Arqueología y Etnología. [Cu/□/□]
FRANKE, RICHARD
420.   1971   Economic circuits in a Surinam village. NWIG
                    48:158-72.
FRANKE, S.
421.   1957   Bij de Surinaamse bosnegers. Hoorn: West-Friesland.
                    [O/KB/BCC]
FRANSSEN HERDERSCHEE, A.
422.   1905   Verslag van de Gonini-expeditie. TKNAG (2^e serie)
                    22:1-174.
423.   1905   Verslag van de Tapanahoni-expeditie. TKNAG
                    (2^e serie) 22:847-1032.
FRANSZOON, ADIANTE
423a.   n.d.   A preliminary investigation of social conditions in
                    Suriname's "transmigration villages." MS.
                    [O/KTLV/SM]
FREY, J.
*424.   1928   Naar de Marowijne. BHW juli-augustus: 52-58;
                    september-oktober:67-72.
FREYTAG, GOTTFRIED A.
425.   1921   Albina (Suriname). MBB 85:66-69, 76-79.
426.   1925   Geschichte der Paramakkaner-Gemeine am
                    Marowijnestrom. MBB 89:172-79.
427.   1926   De Paramakkanergemeente aan de Marowijne. BHW
                    (4):56-61; (5):77-78.
428.   1927   Johannes King der Buschland-Prophet. Ein Lebensbild
                    aus der Mission der Brüdergemeine in Suriname. Nach
                    seinen eigenen Aufzeichnungen dargestellt. Herrnhut:
                    Missionsbuchhandlung. [Y/RPU/SM]
FRIEDMANN, Dr.
429.   1861   Zustände von Niederländisch-Guiana im Jahre 1858.
                    ZAE (N.S.) 11:134-55.
FURLONG, CHARLES WELLINGTON
430.   1914   Through the heart of the Surinam jungle. HMa 128
                    (February):327-39.
GAANDER, C. F.
*431.   1934   Medische hulp aan het boschland in Suriname. MeN
                    no. 2.
*432.   1952   Goden, geesten en mensen in het bosland van Suriname.
                    Gem (1):2-16.
GAFFARD, PAUL
433.   1877   La Guyane Française. RG 1:104-18, 198-208, 262-73.

[GALARD de TERRAUBE, VICOMTE]
434.   An VII   Tableau de Cayenne ou de la Guiane
       (1799)   Française. Paris: Tilliard. [DLC/□/□]
       GALLAGHER, BILL
435.   1972   Pingo. SS 8 (3):4-6; (4):2-5.
       GEIJSKES, D. C.
436.   1954   Het dierlijk voedsel van de Bosnegers aan de Marowijne.
                   VG 1 (2):61-83.
437.   1954   De landbouw bij de Bosnegers van de Marowijne. WIG
                   35:135-53. [English translation HRAF.]
438.   1957   Met de Oajana's op stap. Verslag van een reis naar de
                   Litani (Boven Marowijne). VG 2 (5, 6):193-200.
439.   1959   De expeditie naar de Tafelberg in 1958. VG 3 (4):1-52.
440.   1961   Expeditie naar de Tafelberg in 1958. I. Sc 45:2-7.
       GETROUW, C. F. G.
441.   1953   De stemming van de bevolking vóór, tijdens en na de
                   emancipatie van de slaven in Suriname. WIG 34:3-12.
       GETROUW, C. F. G. and A. J. MORPURGO
*441a. 1966   Honderd jaar woord en daad: gedenkboek bij het
                   eeuwfeest der Redemptoristen in Suriname. [O/□/□]
       GILBERT, W. G.
*442.   1939   Gewijde trommen op Haïti en in Suriname. NRC 31
                   december.
443.   1940   Een en ander over de Negroide muziek van Suriname.
                   Amsterdam: Koninklijke Vereeniging Koloniaal
                   Instituut, Mededeling 55. [Y/KTLV/SM]
*444.   1940   Negermusiek uit de Nederlandsche West. NRC 10
                   februari.
*445.   1942(?)   Muziek uit oost en west; inleiding tot de inheemsche
                   musiek van Nederlandsch Oost- en West-Indië. The
                   Hague: J. Philip Kruseman. [DLC/KITC/□]
       van GINNEKEN, JAC.
*446.   1913   Handboek der Nederlandsche taal. Deel 1: De
                   sociologische structuur der Nederlandsche taal 1.
                   Nijmegen. [Second edition 's-Hertogenbosch: L. G. G.
                   Malmberg, 1928.] [DLC/UBU/□]
       GLOCK, NAOMI
447.   1972   Clause and sentence in Saramaccan. JAL 11(1):45-61.
448.   1972   Role structure in Saramaccan verbs. *In* Languages of
                   the Guianas, Joseph E. Grimes (ed.), Norman: Summer
                   Institute of Linguistics of the University of Oklahoma,
                   pp. 28-34. [JHU/SOAS/SM]
       GLOCK, NAOMI and STEPHEN H. LEVINSOHN
448a.   n.d.   Structure of the Saramaccan folktale. MS.

DE GOEJE, C. H.

449.   1906   Bijdrage tot de ethnographie der Surinaamsche
                    Indianen. IAE 17, supplement, 118 pp.

450.   1907   Review of Stuart of Dromana 1891. TKNAG (2^e serie)
                    24:471-73.

451.   1908   Verslag der Toemoekhoemak-expeditie. TKNAG
                    (2^e serie) 25:943-1169.

452.   1910   Beiträge zur Völkerkunde von Surinam: IAE 19:1-34.

453.   1934   Suriname ontdekt. TKNAG (2e serie) 51:51-89.

454.   1939   Bij primitieve volken. Gi 103:343-73.

455.   1946   Primitieve volkjes, gespiegeld aan den modernen mens
                    (en omgekeerd). The Hague: Martinus Nijhoff.
                    [DLC/KTLV/SM]

456.   1947   Anasi, l'araignée rusée. RMP 1:125-26.

457.   1947   Negers in Amerika. WIG 28:217-21.

457a.   1950   Bouwsteentje. WIG 31:196.

GÖHL, T.

458.   1927   Nederzettingen van boschnegers in Suriname [naar het
                    Duits]. Paramaribo: Kersten. [O/□/□]

GONGGRIJP, J. W.

*459.   1955   Some remarks on the Brokopondo project. VG
                    1:145-48.

460.   1958   De geschiedenis van het Djoeka-schrift van Afaka.
                    Op december: 24-29.

461.   1960   The evolution of a Djuka-script in Surinam. NWIG
                    40:63-72.

GONGGRYP, J. W. and C. DUBELAAR

462.   1960   Pater Morsink en Afaka. Op december: 1-11.

463.   1963   De geschriften van Afaka in zijn Djoeka-schrift.
                    NWIG 42:213-54.

GONGGRIJP, J. W. and GEROLD STAHEL

464.   1923/24   Verslag van een reis naar den Hendriktop
                    (Boven-Saramacca). WIG 5:1-20, 77-94, 129-50.

van GORKUM, J. A. J.

465.   1961   Het distrikt Brokopondo. Sc 41:33-40.

GOSLINGS, B. M.

466.   1935   De Indianen en Bosnegers van Suriname. Gids in het
                    Volkenkundig Museum, Koninklijke Vereeniging,
                    Koloniaal Instituut, Amsterdam, deel 13.
                    [O/KTLV/SM]

GOUKA, Ir. A.

467.   1948   In het Surinaamse oerwoud: het leven in de
                    goudvelden. The Hague: W. van Hoeve.
                    [DLC/KTLV/BCC]

GRAFF van LIMBURG STIRUM, O. E. G.

468.   1923/24   De Surinaamsche mijnwetgeving. WIG 5:385-94.

GREAT BRITAIN, FOREIGN OFFICE.
469.　1920　Dutch Guiana. London: H. M. Stationery Office.
[DLC/BM/□]
470.　1920　French Guiana. London: H. M. Stationery Office.
[DLC/BM/□]

GREEN, EDWARD
471.　1972　Living with the Matawai Bushnegroes. SA 4(12):17.
472.　1974　The Matawai maroons: an acculturating Afro-American
society. Unpublished Ph.D. dissertation, The Catholic
University of America, Washington, D.C.
[CaU/□/SM]

GRIGOROVICH, I. R. i kolliegiia
*473.　1969　Gviana-Guiana, Frantsuzkaia Gviana, Surinam.
Moscow: Izdatel'stovo "Nauka." [O/□/□]

GRIMES, JOSEPH E.
474.　1972　Languages of the Guianas, ed. by Joseph E. Grimes.
Norman: Summer Institute of Linguistics of the
University of Oklahoma. [JIIU/SOAS/SM]
475.　1972　Writing systems for the interior of Surinam. *In*
Languages of the Guianas, Joseph E. Grimes (ed.),
Norman: Summer Institute of Linguistics of the
University of Oklahoma, pp. 85-91.
[JHU/SOAS/SM]

GRIMES, JOSEPH E. and NAOMI GLOCK
476.　1970　A Saramaccan narrative pattern. La 46:408-25.

de GROOT, P. A.
*477.　1947　Welkom te Ganzee. OS maart (no. 3).
*478.　1948　Het eerste half-jaarverslag van het Prinses Juliana
Zendings-Hospitaal. ZEBG 7(8/9).
*479.　1950　Verslag van een medische expeditie naar de
Saramaccanerbosnegers. SZ pp. 100-9.
480.　1953　Dokter in het oerwoud. Nijkerk: G. F. Callenbach.
[NYP/UBU/BCC]

de GROOT, SILVIA W.
481.　1963　Van isolatie naar integratie: de Surinaamse Marrons
en hun afstammelingen. Officiële documenten
betreffende de Djoeka's (1845-1863). Verhandelingen
van het Koninklijk Instituut voor Taal-, Land- en
Volkenkunde 41. The Hague: Martinus Nijhoff.
[DLC/KTLV/SM]
482.　1965　A short history of the Djukas. Paramaribo: Surinam
Government Information Service, Mimeo. [O/□/□]
483.　1965　Migratiebewegingen der Djoeka's in Suriname van
1845 tot 1863. NWIG 44:133-151.
484.　1967　Summary of the description by P. J. Benoit [item 236],
with annotations, Amsterdam: S. Emmering.
[O/□/□]

485. 1968   Naar aanleiding van het herdrukken van Benoit's
             Voyage à Surinam. NWIG 46:292-96.
486. 1969   Djuka society and social change: history of an attempt
             to develop a Bush Negro community in Surinam
             1917-1926. Assen: Van Gorcum. [JHU/KTLV/SM]
487. 1970   Rebellie der zwarte jagers. Gi 133:291-304.
488. 1970/71 Vier Surinaamse Groot-Opperhoofden op zoek naar
             hun oorsprongen. VN 31, December 26, 1970:1, 19,
             27; January 2, 1971: 1, 17, 18.
489. 1971   Hoe Suriname bevolkt werd en hoe de grootopperhoofden
             Aboikoni, Abone, Forster en Gazon de weg terug
             gingen. Av (juli):111-114.
490. 1971   210 jaar zelfstandigheid; het verdrag van 10 oktober
             1760. Gi 134:410-13.
491. 1973   The Bush Negro chiefs visit Africa: diary of an
             historic trip. *In* Maroon societies: rebel slave communities
             in the Americas, Richard Price (ed.), Garden City, N.Y.:
             Doubleday Anchor, pp. 389-98. [DLC/KTLV/SM]
492. 1974   Surinaamse granmans in Afrika: vier
             groot-opperhoofden bezoeken het land van hun
             voorouders. Aula-paperback 28. Utrecht/Antwerp: Het
             Spectrum. [JHU/KTLV/SM]
492a. 1974   De Surinaamse marrons. Historisch overzicht. *In*
             Geschiedenis Suriname 1674-1974.
             Wetenschappelijke Publicatie no. 2, Organisatie van
             Studenten in de Geschiedenis in Nederland, pp. 11-19,
             [O/□/BCC]
492b. 1975   A short history of the Djuka's. SM March:12-17.
492c. 1975   The Boni maroon war 1765-1793, Surinam and French
             Guiana. Bo 18:30-48.
492d. 1975   Conflictsituaties. De marrons in Suriname (sedert de
             18e eeuw). *In* Suriname: van slavernij naar
             onafhankelijkheid. Wetenschappelijke Publicatie no. 3,
             Organisatie van Studenten in de Geschiedenis in
             Nederland, pp. 27-39. [O/KTLV/BCC]
*492e. 1975 History of an opposition to social change in a maroon
             society. *In* Rule and reality: essays in honour of André
             J. F. Köbben, Peter Kloos and Klaas W. van der Veen
             (eds.). Amsterdam: Universiteit van Amsterdam,
             Afdeling Culturele Antropologie,
             Antropologisch-Sociologisch Centrum, Uitgave 8,
             pp. 66-78. [JHU/KTLV/□]
493. n.d.   Black revolt in Surinam, 1788-1809: the aftermath of
             the Boni wars and the rebellion of the Black
             Chasseurs. CS. (In press)

GRUNEWALD, J.
*494.   Apensa, der Buschnegerhäuptling. Eine Taufreise im Urwald. [Cited in this form in Weiss 1911:87.] [O/RPU/□]

GUDA, G. M.
495.   1967   De transmigratie van de bosnegers uit het Brokopondomeer-gebied in Suriname. Doctoraal scriptie, Instituut voor Culturele Antropologie, Utrecht. [O/UBU/□]

GUFFROY, M.
*496.   1901   Note sur les peuples autochtones des Guyanes et sur les tribus noirs du Maroni et ses affluents, l'Awa et le Tapanahony. Revue Coloniale [?] (1):160-85. [Original source of this reference was lost, through an error, and it has not been possible to confirm reference in its present form.]

de HAAN, J. H.
497.   1954   Nomadische landbouw. SL 2:4-8.

van HAAREN, F. L. J.
*498.   1932   Een tocht naar Suriname's binnenland. TN 5:11-13, 21-29, 51-55, 73-77, 87-91, 125-28, 141-44, 175-76, 189-92, 203-8.

HALL, ROBERT A., Jr.
499.   1966   Pidgin and creole languages. Ithaca, N.Y.: Cornell University Press. [DLC/LSE/□]

HAMBLY, W. D.
500.   1935   Negro culture in Guiana. FMN 6 (9):3.

HAMILTON, J. TAYLOR
501.   1900   Dutch Guiana, or Surinam. *In* Protestant missions in South America, Harlan P. Beach, J. Taylor Hamilton, *et al.* New York: Student Volunteer Movement for Foreign Missions, pp. 45-55. [DLC/□/□]

HANCOCK, IAN F.
502.   1969   A provisional comparison of the English-based Atlantic creoles. ALR 8:7-72.
503.   1970   Some Dutch-derived items in Papia Kristang. BTLV 126:352-356.
504.   1971   West Africa and the Atlantic creoles. *In* The English language in West Africa, John Spencer (ed.), London: Longman, pp. 113-22. [DLC/□/□]

HANRATH, J. J.
505.   1952   Het binnenlandse verkeer in Suriname. TESG 43:158-66.
506.   1952   "Planning" met betrekking tot het binnenlandse verkeer van Suriname. TESG 43:233-42.

HARDENBROOK, FRED G.
507.   1950   Exploring Dutch Guiana jungles. MS 23:38.

HARRER, HEINRICH
508.   1969   Geister und Dämonen. Magische Abenteuer in fernen
                     Ländern. Berlin: Ullstein. [DLC/□/□]
509.   1971   Geesten en demonen: magische avonturen in verre
                     landen. The Hague: La Riviere en Voorhoeve.
                     [Translation of item 508.] [O/□/□]

HARRIS, SIR CHARLES ALEXANDER, and J. A. J. de VILLIERS
(eds.)
509a.   1911   Storm van 's Gravesande: the rise of British Guiana.
                     London: Hakluyt Society, Second Series, Nos.
                     xxvi and xxvii. [DLC/KTLV/□]

HARTSINCK, JAN JACOB
510.   1770   Beschrijving van Guyana of de Wilde Kust in
                     Zuid-Amerika. Amsterdam: Gerrit Tielenburg.
                     [Facsimile reprint, 1974. Amsterdam: S. Emmering.]
                     [DLC/KTLV/SM]

HAUGER, J.
511.   1957   La population de la Guyane Française. AG 66:509-18.

ten HAVE, J. J.
*512.   1892   Oost en West: land en volk onzer koloniën. The Hague:
                     J. Ijkema. [DLC/UBU/□]

HAYES, CHARLES F., III
513.   1964   Bush Negro art of Dutch Guiana. MS 37:78-81.

HECKERS, A. A.
514.   1923   Het district Nickerie. Geografische aanteekeningen en
                     geschiedkundig overzicht. Paramaribo:
                     Stoomdrukkerij H. van Ommeren. [NU/KTLV/SM]

van HEECKEREN [van WALIËN, E. L.] GODARD P. C.
515.   1826   Aanteekeningen betrekkelijk de kolonie Suriname.
                     Arnhem: C. A. Thieme. [DLC/KTLV/SM]

van HEEMSTRA, M. J. BARONES
516.   1944   Op de markt te Paramaribo. CI 6:163-73.

HEGNER, JOHANN KONRAD
517.   1791-   Fortsetzung von David Cranzens Brüderhistorie.
         1816   Barby: Conrad Schilling: Gnadau. [See item 333.]
                     [NYP/UBA/□]

HELSTONE, S. F.
*518.   1912   Herleving van een Aucaansche wonderman als de
                     oppergodheid. MS. [O/□/AHP]

HENRY, A.
519.   1950   La Guyane Française: son histoire 1604-1946.
                     Cayenne: Paul Laporte. [DLC/□/□]

HERING, C. J.
*520.   1901   Verhandeling over de voedingsmiddelen der kolonie
                    Suriname . . . Paramaribo. [DLC/UBL/SM]
HERLEIN, J. D. [pseud. J. D. HL.]
521.   1718   Beschryvinge van de Volk-plantinge Zuriname.
                    Leeuwarden: Meindert Injema. [Tweede druk.]
                    [DLC/KTLV/SM]
HERMANS, WILLEM FREDERIK
522.   1969   De laatste resten tropisch Nederland. The Hague:
                    Mouton. [DLC/KTLV/SM]
HERRENBERG, J. E.
522a.   1935,   De spoorweg naar het binnenland van Suriname van
         1936   Paramaribo naar Dam. ST 8(nos. 22, 23, 24, 26, 27);
                    9(nos. 1, 2).
HERSKOVITS, MELVILLE J.
523.   1928/29   Preliminary report of an ethnological expedition to
                    Suriname, 1928. WIG 10:385-90.
523a.   1929   A trip to "Africa" in the New World. NUAN 8(6):10-12.
524.   1929   Adjiboto, an African game of the Bush-Negroes of
                    Dutch Guiana. Ma 29:122-27.
524a.   1929/30   The second Northwestern University Expedition for
                    the study of the Suriname Bush Negroes. WIG
                    11:393-402.
525.   1930   Bush Negro art. Ar 17 (51):25-37, 48-49. [Reprinted
                    in The New World Negro, Frances S. Herskovits (ed.),
                    Indiana University Press 1966, pp. 157-67.]
                    [DLC/UBU/BCC]
526.   1930   The Negro in the New World: the statement of a
                    problem. AA 32:145-55.
527.   1930   The social organization of the Bush-Negroes of
                    Suriname. PICA 23:713-27.
528.   1930/31   On the provenience of the Portuguese in Saramacca
                    Tongo. WIG 12:545-57.
529.   1931   The New World Negro as an anthropological problem.
                    Ma 31:68-69.
530.   1932   Wari in the New World. JRAI 62:23-38.
531.   1933   Man, the speaking animal. SXQ 21 (2):67-83.
532.   1933   On the provenience of New World Negroes. SF
                    12:247-62.
533.   1934   Freudian mechanisms in primitive Negro psychology.
                    In Essays presented to C. S. Seligman, E. E.
                    Evans-Pritchard, R. Firth, B. Malinowski, and I.
                    Schapera (eds.). London: Kegan Paul, Trench,
                    Trubner and Co., pp. 75-84. [DLC/BM/□]
534.   1938   African ethnology and the New World Negro. Ma
                    38:9-10.

535.   1941   The myth of the Negro past. New York: Harper.
[Second edition 1958, with a new preface by the
author. Boston: Beacon.] [DLC/UBA/□]
536.   1945   Problem, method and theory in Afroamerican Studies.
Af 1:5-24. [Also published in Ph .7:337-54 (1946).]
537.   1949   Afro-American art. *In* Studies in Latin American art,
Elizabeth Wilder (ed.). Proceedings of a conference
held in the Museum of Modern Art, New York,
28-31 May 1945. Washington, D.C.: American Council
of Learned Societies, pp. 58-64. [Y/□/□]
538.   1950   The hypothetical situation: a technique of field
research. SWJA 6:32-40.
539.   1951   Bush Negro calabash carving. Ma 51:163-64.
540.   1952   Note sur la divination judiciaire par le cadavre en
Guyane Hollandaise. *In* Les Afro-Américains.
Mémoires de l'Institut Français d'Afrique Noire
(Dakar) 27, pp. 187-92. [DLC/□/□]
541.   1952   Some psychological implications of Afroamerican
studies. *In* Acculturation in the Americas, Sol Tax
(ed.), Chicago: University of Chicago Press, pp. 152-60.
[DLC/BM/□]
542.   1959   Art and value. *In* Aspects of primitive art; the Museum
of Primitive Art Lecture Series Number One. New
York: The Museum of Primitive Art, pp. 41-68,
95-97. [Y/BM/□]
543.   1966   The New World Negro: selected papers in Afroamerican
studies, edited by Frances S. Herskovits. Bloomington:
Indiana University Press. [First paperbound edition,
New York, Minerva Press, 1969.] [DLC/UBU/BCC]

HERSKOVITS, MELVILLE J. and FRANCES S. HERSKOVITS
543a.   1928-29   Collection of field recordings from Haiti and Surinam.
On deposit in the Archives of Traditional Music, the
Folklore Institute, Indiana University, Bloomington,
Indiana.
544.   1934   Rebel destiny: among the Bush Negroes of Dutch
Guiana. New York: McGraw-Hill. [Facsimile reprint,
1974. Amsterdam: S. Emmering.] [DLC/UBL/SM]
545.   1936   Suriname folk-lore. Columbia University Contributions
to Anthropology 27. New York: Columbia University
Press. [Facsimile reprint 1969, New York: AMS
Press.] [DLC/UBA/SM]

HESSELINK, GERRIT
546.   1974   De maatschappijstad Moengo en haar omgeving.
Bijdragen tot de sociale geografie, nr. 6. Amsterdam:
Vrije Universiteit. [O/UBA/□]

HEYDE, H.
547.   n.d.   Surinaamse planten als volkmedicijn: nengre oso
       (1971?)   dresi. Amsterdam: Schrijvers Collectief Granma.
                 [O/KITC/□]

HIGGINSON, THOMAS WENTWORTH
548.   1889   Travellers and outlaws: episodes in American history.
                 Boston: Lee and Shepard. [DLC/BM/□]
549.   1969   Black rebellion. New York: Arno Press and the New
                 York Times. [Facsimile reprint of pp. 116-335 of item
                 548, with a new preface by James M. McPherson.]
                 [DLC/KITC/□]

HIGHTOWER, MARVIN
550.   1974   Africa in the New World: The Djuka uphold traditions
                 with pride, poetry, defiance. HUG 69(25):6.

HISS, PHILIP HANSON
551.   1943   Netherlands America: the Dutch territories in the West.
                 New York: Duell, Sloan and Pearce. [DLC/KTLV/SM]

HOETINK, H.
552.   1961   Diferencias en relaciones raciales entre Curazao y
                 Surinam. RCS 5:499-514.
553.   1965   Review of Silvia W. de Groot 1963. CS 5 (1):55-56.
554.   1972   Suriname and Curaçao. *In* The freedman in the slave
                 societies of the New World, David Cohen and Jack
                 P. Greene (eds.). Baltimore: Johns Hopkins University
                 Press. [DLC/□/□]

VAN HÖEVELL, W. R.
555.   1855   Slaven en vrijen onder de Nederlandsche wet.
                 Zaltbommel: J. Noman & Zoon. [O/□/SM]

HOLDRIDGE, DESMOND
556.   1937   Escape to the tropics. New York: Harcourt, Brace
                 and Company. [DLC/BM/□]

HOLMES, JOHN
557.   1818   Historical sketches of the missions of the United
                 Brethren . . . Dublin: R. Napper. [NYP/BM/□]

de HOOG, J.
558.   1958   Suriname: een land in opkomst. Delft: Etnografisch
                 Museum te Delft, Serie Monografieën No. 1.
                 [DLC/KTLV/□]

van der HORST, HERMAN
559.   1964   Faja lobbi; impressies van het binnenland van Suriname.
                 Haarlem: De Spaarnestad. [NYP/KTLV/SM]

HOSTMANN, F. W.
561.   1850   Over de beschaving van negers in Amerika door
                 kolonisatie met Europeanen. Amsterdam: J. C. A.
                 Sulpke. [Y/UBA/SM]

HOUSTON, HILL
562.   1941   Surinam. FCW 5, November 8:4-5, 36-37.
van den HOVEN van GENDEREN, H. A.
563.   1930   Het land van den dood [Zuid-Suriname]. WH 3:122-24.
HOWARD, JOSEPH H.
564.   1967   Drums in the Americas. New York: Oak Publications.
                    [DLC/UBA/□]
HOWE, MARVINE
564a.   1975   Blacks in Surinam's interior wary of independence.
                    NYT, June 9:12.
HUE, FERNAND
565.   1886   La Guyane Française. Paris: H. Lecène and H. Oudin.
                    [Y/BM/□]
HUE, FERNAND and GEORGES HAURIGOT
566.   1886   Nos grandes colonies; Amérique, les Antilles et la
                    Guyane. Paris: H. Lecène and H. Oudin. [UI/BM/□]
HULK, J. F.
567.   1911   Brieven over de Corantijn-Expeditie. TKNAG
                    (2e serie) 28:299-310.
van HULZEN, J.
*568.   1946   Onze Westindische geschiedenis. The Hague: W. van
                    Hoeve. [CU/KTLV/□]
HUMMELEN, J. A.
569.   1968   Commewijne en Saramacca. Sc 68:35-44.
570.   1968   Marowijne en Brokopondo. Sc 68:19-27.
571.   1969   Levenspatroon van de bosnegers. Sc 70:2-9.
HURAULT, JEAN
572.   1950   Note sur la conduite d'une mission de reconnaissance
                    dans l'intérieur de la Guyane. Paris: Imprimerie de
                    l'Institut Géographique National. [NYP/□/□]
573.   1959   Étude démographique comparée des Indiens Oayana
                    et des Noirs Réfugiés Boni du Haut-Maroni (Guyane
                    Française). Po 14:509-34. [English translation
                    HRAF.]
574.   1960   Histoire des Noirs Réfugiés Boni de la Guyane Française.
                    RFHO 47:76-137.
575.   1961   Canots africains en Guyane. BFT 78:45-55.
576.   1961   Les Noirs Réfugiés Boni de la Guyane Française.
                    Mémoires de l'Institut Français d'Afrique Noire
                    (Dakar) 63. [English translation HRAF.]
                    [DLC/KTLV/SM]
577.   1963   Chasse et pêche chez les populations d'origine
                    Africaine en Guyane. BFT 87:3-8.
578.   1964   A propos de la recension par A. Trouwborst du livre de
                    J. Hurault sur "les Noirs Réfugiés Boni de la Guyane
                    française." Anth 6:236-37.

579. 1965 La vie matérielle des Noirs Réfugiés Boni et des
             Indiens Wayana du Haut-Maroni. Paris: Office de la
             Recherche Scientifique et Technique Outre-Mer.
             [DLC/LSE/□]
580. 1968 Comment on Köbben's review of item 576. CS
             7(4):65-67. [See items 683 and 686.]
581. 1970 Africains de Guyane: la vie matérielle et l'art des Noirs
             Réfugiés de Guyane. Paris-The Hague: Mouton.
             [DLC/KTLV/SM]
582. 1972 Français et indiens en Guyane 1604-1972. Paris:
             Union Générale d'Editions. [DLC/KTLV/□]
583. 1972 The Indians of French Guiana and the policy of
             assimilation. I: The "Francization" of the Indians.
             In The situation of the Indian in South America:
             contributions to the study of inter-ethnic conflict
             in the non-Andean regions of South America, W.
             Dostal (ed.). Geneva: World Council of Churches,
             pp. 358-70. [Y/KTLV/□]
584. 1973 Réponse à "The Guiana maroons: changing perspectives
             in 'Bush Negro' society." CS 12 (4):117-21. [See items
             1023 and 1026.]
585. n.d. Eléments de vocabulaire de la langue Boni (Aluku).
             MS. [O/KITA/□]
*585a. n.d. Les funérailles de Kotoïda. [16 mm. color film with
             sound, 19 min., available through SCET Productions,
             66 rue de la Fontaine au Roi, Paris 11e.]

         HURAULT, JEAN and ANDRÉ FRIBOURG-BLANC
*586. 1949 Mission astro-géodésique de l'Oyapoc (Guyane
             Française), juillet à novembre 1947. Paris: Institut
             Géographique National. [O/□/□]

         HUTTAR, GEORGE L.
587. 1972 A comparative word list for Djuka. *In* Languages of the
             Guianas, Joseph E. Grimes (ed.). Norman: Summer
             Institute of Linguistics of the University of Oklahoma,
             pp. 12-21. [JHU/SOAS/SM]
587a. 1974 Some Kwa-like features of Djuka syntax. Summer
             Institute of Linguistics. MS.
587b. 1975 Sources of creole semantic structures. La 51(3).

         HUTTAR, GEORGE L. and MARY L. HUTTAR
588. 1972 Notes on Djuka phonology. *In* Languages of the
             Guianas, Joseph E. Grimes, (ed.). Norman: Summer
             Institute of Linguistics of the University of Oklahoma,
             pp. 1-11. [JHU/SOAS/SM]

         HUTTAR, G. L. and P. PAWIROREDJO
589. 1972 A toli fu malalia sautu di abi obia (Het verhaal over
             gemedicineerd malariazout). Paramaribo: Geologisch

Mijnbouwkundige Dienst/Instituut voor
Taalwetenschap. [DLC/□/BCC]

HUTTAR-LARSEN, M. E. and G. L. HUTTAR

590.   1972   Instruktieboekje voor instrukteurs in de Ndjuka Taal,
delen 1 en 2. (Behorend bij: Leisi buku fu Ndjuka
Tongo.) Paramaribo: Geologisch Mijnbouwkundige
Dienst/Instituut voor Taalwetenschap. [DLC/□/BCC]

HUTTAR-LARSEN, M. E., G. L. HUTTAR, A. DEEL and
P. PAWIROREDJO

591.   1972   Leisi buku fu Ndjuka Tongo (Aukaans Leesboek,
Delen 1, 2 en 3). Paramaribo: Geologisch
Mijnbouwkundige Dienst/Instituut voor
Taalwetenschap. [DLC/□/BCC]

HUTTON, J. E.

592.   1922   History of the Moravian missions. London: Moravian
Publication Office. [Y/□/□]

IJZERMAN, ROBERT

593.   1931   Outline of the geology and petrology of Surinam
(Dutch Guiana). Utrecht: Kemink en Zoon.
[NYP/KTLV/SM]

INTELLECTUS [pseud.]

593a.   1965   Waarom heet ik Kwami? Dj 7(3):11-12.

JACOBS, H. J.

594.   1955   Reizen en pleisteren. Een serie aardrijkskundige
leesboeken voor het onderwijs. Zutphen: N. V. W.
J. Thieme & Cie [O/KTLV/□]

JACQUEMIN, [Mgr. NICOLAS]

595.   1782   Journal de mon voyage chez les indiens et les nègres
réfugiés sur nos terres, fait en decembre 1782, par
l'abbé Jacquemin, curé de Sinnamary. [O/AN/□]

596.   An VII [1799] Mémoire sur la Guyane Française.
Paris: Baudelot et Eberhart. [DLC/□/□]

JANSEN, P.

597.   1971   Noodtoestand onder de bosnegers in Suriname.
"Houtassociatie" wapen in de strijd tegen woekeraars.
GA 31 juli.

JANSSEN, J. F.

598.   1961   The health of maroon children in Surinam. JTP
7:91-99.

JEAN-LOUIS, PAUL and JEAN HAUGER

599.   1962   La Guyane Française: présentation géographique.
Besançon: Imprimerie Jacques et Demontrond.
[DLC/LSE/□]

599a.   1962   La Guyane Française, historique. Besançon:
Imprimerie Jacques et Demontrond. [DLC/□/□]

JOEST, WILHELM
600. 1891 Guayana im Jahre 1890. VGE 17 (7):386-403.
601. 1892 Der Siedenwollenbaum in Geistesleben der Neger. G1
61:350-51.
*602. 1892 Über ein angebliches Mittel gegen Schlangengift aus
Surinam. G1 61:61-63.
603. 1893 Ethnographisches und Verwandtes aus Guyana. IAE 5,
supplement.
*604. 1895 Guyana. Wf 1:53-.
JOHNSON, EDWIN D.
605. 1925 Aphra Behn's "Oronooko." JNH 10 (3):334-42.
JOHNSTON, Sir HARRY H.
606. 1910 The Negro in the New World. London: Methuen.
[DLC/UBL/□]
JONES, JOHAN FRITS
607. 1966 De ontmoeting van het Christelijk geloof en de
West-Afrikaanse religie in Suriname. Unpublished thesis.
Brussels: Protestantse Theologische Faculteit.
[O/□/BCC]
JOSEPH, W.
608. 1961 Het distrikt Suriname. Sc 41:16-21.
609. 1961 Marowijne. Sc 41:22-26.
*610. 1964 De granman is dood leve de granman. GA 16 mei.
JOSEPHZOON, E.
611. 1970 Bosnegers en politiek. Gi 133:305-8.
de JOSSELIN de JONG, J. P. B.
*612. 1919 Boschnegers in Suriname. In 2 (3):339, 371, 419, 531.
JOZEFZOON, E. O. I.
613. 1963 Enige opmerkingen t.a.v. de Boslandcreoolse woningen
in Suriname. Sc 51:40-41.
614. 1969 Bosnegercultuur. Sc 70:10-16.
JOZEFZOON, O. J. R.
615. 1959 De Saramaccaanse wereld. Paramaribo: N.V. Varekamp
and Co. [O/KTLV/SM]
JUNKER, L.
616. 1922/23 Eenige mededeelingen over de Saramakkaner-
Boschnegers. WIG 4:449-80.
617. 1923/24 Over de afstamming der Boschnegers. WIG 5:310-17.
618. 1924/25 Godsdienst, zeden, en gebruiken der Boschnegers.
WIG 6:73-81.
619. 1925/26 De godsdienst der Boschnegers. WIG 7:85-95, 127-37,
153-64.
620. 1932/33 Het einde van een dynastie: de dood van Jankosoe.
WIG 14:49-58.
621. 1932/33 Een staat in den staat. WIG 14:267-80, 321-36.

622.	1933/34	Herinneringen aan het oerwoud; Uit mijn dagboek van 1921. WIG 15:177-90, 209-26.
*623.	1934	De godsdienst der Boschnegers. OA 7:331-36.
*624.	1935	De geheimzinnige wreker in het Surinaamsche oerwoud. NRC 1 Juli, Avondblad A.
625.	1940	Primitief communisme. WIG 22:277-83.
626.	1941	Herinneringen aan het oerwoud: jacht en jachtwild in Suriname. WIG 23:302-16, 330-39, 353-64.
627.	1941	Herinneringen aan het oerwoud: reizen en trekken in Suriname; tooverkunst in de wildernis; wegen der ellende. WIG 23:234-52.
628.	1941	Malaria in Suriname. WIG 23:23-30.
629.	1942	Herinneringen aan het oerwoud: vischvangst in Suriname. WIG 24:143-58.
630.	1944/45	Herinneringen aan het oerwoud: uit mijn dagboek van 1923 en 1924. WIG 26:111-27, 129-46.
631.	1947	De benoeming van een grootopperhoofd der Boschnegers. WIG 28:107-18.

KAHN, MORTON CHARLES

632.	1927	Where black men look down on civilized whites. LD 95 (October):57-58.
633.	1928	The Bush Negroes of Dutch Guiana. NH 28:243-52.
634.	1929	Notes on the Saramaccaner Bush Negroes of Dutch Guiana. AA 31:468-90. [See item 231.]
635.	1930/31	An American professor responds to Dr. Benjamins' criticism of certain remarks on the Bush Negroes. WIG 12:449-52. [See item 234.]
636.	1931	Art of the Dutch Guiana Bush Negro. NH 31 (2):155-68.
637.	1931	Djuka: The Bush Negroes of Dutch Guiana. New York: The Viking Press. [DLC/KTLV/SM]
638.	1936	Blood grouping of 336 Upper Aucaner Bush Negroes . . . in Dutch Guiana. JI 31:377-85.
639.	1936	A tuberculin survey of Upper Aucaner Bush Negroes in Dutch Guiana. AJH 24:456-78.
640.	1936	Where black man meets red; adventures in medical research among two strange tribes of Dutch Guiana; notes on the possible whereabouts of the aviator Redfern. NH 37:382-99.
641.	1939	Africa's lost tribes in South America; an on-the-spot account of blood-chilling African rites of 200 years ago preserved intact in the jungles of South America by a tribe of runaway slaves. NH 43:209-15, 232.
642.	1954	Little Africa in America: the Bush Negroes. Am 6 (10):6-8, 41-43.
643.	1959	The Djukas of Surinam. EJ 37 (1):12-18.

KALFF, S.
644.   1925/26   Een Westindische Gouverneur uit de 18de eeuw.
WIG 7:507-27.

van KAMPEN, N. G.
645.   1831-33   Geschiedenis der Nederlanders buiten Europa. Haarlem:
de Erven François Bohn. [DLC/KTLV/□]

KAPPLER, AUGUST
646.   1854   Sechs Jahre in Surinam oder, Bilder aus dem
militärischen Leben dieser Colonie, und Skissen zur
Kenntniss seiner socialen und naturwissenschaftlichen
Verhältnisse. Stuttgart: E. Schweizerbart.
[DLC/UBL/SM]
647.   1854   Zes jaren in Suriname; schetsen en tafereelen uit het
maatschappelijke en militaire leven in deze kolonie.
Utrecht: W. F. Dannenfelser. [NYP/KTLV/SM]
648.   1862   Holländisch-Französische Expedition ins Innere von
Guiana, September bis November 1861. PM 8:173-79,
246-54.
649.   1880   Eine Reise zu den Auca-Buschnegern in Holländisch Guiana.
Gl 38:121-25, 139-43.
650.   1881   Holländisch-Guiana: Erlebnisse und Erfahrungen während
eines 43 jährigen Aufenthalts in der Kolonie Surinam.
Stuttgart: W. Kohlhammer. [DLC/KTLV/□]
651.   1883   Nederlandsch-Guyana. Winterswijk: Albrecht.
[Translation by F. L. Postel of item 650.]
[DLC/KTLV/SM]
652.   1887   Surinam: sein Land, seine Natur, Bevölkerung und seine
Kultur-Verhältnisse mit Bezug auf Kolonisation.
Stuttgart: J. G. Cotta'sche Verlagsbuchhandlung.
[DLC/BM/SM]

KARBAAT, J.
653.   1962   Slangenbeten. NMGT 15:218-40.

ten KATE, H. F. C.
654.   1885   Het werk van Prins Roland Bonaparte voor de
inboorlingen van Suriname. TKNAG (2e serie) 2:58-61.
655.   1886   Note sur un voyage dans l'Amérique du Sud. CRSG
1886:518-22.
656.   1886   Travels in Guiana and Venezuela. RCI 2:537-40.
657.   1887   Observations anthropologiques recueillies dans la Guyane
et le Venezuela. RA 2:45-68.
658.   1888   Beitrag zur Ethnographie von Surinam. IAE 1:223-26.
659.   1888   Een en ander over Suriname. Gi 52 (2):181-221.
660.   1929/30   Versieringskunst der Boschnegers. WIG 11:437-42.
[Review of L. C. van Panhuys 1928, "Quelques
ornements . . ."]

KÄYSER, C. D.

661. 1912 Verslag der Corantijn-expeditie, TKNAG (2^e serie) 29:442-514.

KESLER, C. K.

662. 1927/8, Een conflict tusschen Amsterdam en de
      1928/9 Staten-Generaal over Suriname in 1774 en '75. WIG 9:575-82; 10:11-16.

663. 1932/33 Na 100 jaar: branden in Paramaribo. WIG 14:164-74.

*664. 1935 Een Afrikaansche samenleving in het binnenland van Suriname. Bu nos. 1 and 2.

665. 1936 Zwarte en roode bewoners der binnenlanden van Suriname. TN 9:232-37, 247-51.

666. 1939 Een Moravische zuster uit de 18e eeuw: Anna Maria Kersten. geb. Tonn, 1723-1807. WIG 21:206-17.

667. 1940 Slavenopstanden in de West. WIG 22:257-70, 289-302.

VAN KEULEN, J.

668. 1929 Van een neger uit het bosch, die Boschneger werd. WH 2:98-100, 110-12, 121-23.

KING, JOHANNES

*669. 1864- Tagebücher von Johannes King. MSS.
      1894 [O/AHZ/□]

669a. 1865 Suriname [excerpt from King's Diary]. BHW (11): 239-48.

*670. 1882 Maripastoon, Den 23. Juni, 1882. MS. [O/ABU/□]

*671. 1886 Johannes King, den 3. Augustus, 1886. mi ben kisi da boekoe na Gran leriman na foto. Paramaribo. MS. [O/ABU/□]

*672. 1888 Johannes King. vo. Maripastoon, 1888. MS. [O/ABU/□]

673. 1958 Selection from Skrekiboekoe. *In* Suriname: spiegel der vaderlandse kooplieden, Ursy M. Lichtveld and Jan Voorhoeve (eds.). Zwolle: W. E. J. Tjeenk Willink, pp. 92-119. [NYP/KTLV/SM]

674. 1958 Het eerste visioen van Johannes King (naar het handschrift uit Herrnhut meegedeeld [door Jan Voorhoeve] in moderne spelling). VG 3 (1):41-45.

675. 1973 Guerrilla warfare: a Bush Negro's view [translation by Richard and Sally Price of portions of item 673]. *In* Maroon societies: rebel slave communities in the Americas, Richard Price (ed.). Garden City, N.Y.: Doubleday Anchor, pp. 298-304. [DLC/KTLV/SM]

676. 1973 Koiri ini hemel [selection from Het eerste visioen van Johannes King—see item 674]. *In* Kri, kra! proza van Suriname, Thea Doelwijt (ed.). Paramaribo: Bureau Volkslectuur, pp. 25-28. [O/KTLV/SM]

677.　1973　Life at Maripaston (edited by H. F. de Ziel).
　　　　　　Verhandelingen van het Koninklijk Instituut voor Taal-,
　　　　　　Land- en Volkenkunde 64, The Hague: Martinus
　　　　　　Nijhoff. [DLC/KTLV/BCC]

*678.　n.d.　Johannes King's Tagebuch, enthaltend Traumgesichte,
　　　　　　Geschichtliches, Verschiedenis. Übersetzung des
　　　　　　negerenglischen Originals von Freytag und Renkeevitz.
　　　　　　MS. [O/ABU/□]

*679.　n.d.　Traumgesichte und Erzählungen aus dem Buschland.
　　　　　　MS. [O/AHZ/□]

de KLERK, JOOST
680.　n.d.　Grietjebie, schoonheid van Suriname. Haarlem:
　　　[1966?]　Uitgeverij de Toorts. [DLC/KTLV/SM]

KLINCKOWSTRÖM, A.
681.　1891　Fem månader i Suriname. Ym 11:230-45.

KLUGE, H. C.
682.　1923　Curious loggers of the world, the Boschneger of
　　　　　　Suriname: descendants of escaped slaves fill important
　　　　　　place in South American logging. HR 55 (10):18-20, 22.

KNICKERBOCKER, BRAD
682a.　1974　Tracing a lost black colony. CSM 66 (149):1, 8.

KÖBBEN, A. J. F.
683.　1965　Review of Jean Hurault 1961, Les Noirs Réfugiés
　　　　　　Boni de la Guyane Française. CS 5 (3):63-65.

684.　1967　Participation and quantification; field work among the
　　　　　　Djuka (Bush Negroes of Surinam). *In* Anthropologists
　　　　　　in the field, D. G. Jongmans and P. C. W. Gutkind
　　　　　　(eds.). Assen: Van Gorcum, pp. 35-55.
　　　　　　[DLC/KTLV/SM]

685.　1967　Unity and disunity: Cottica Djuka society as a kinship
　　　　　　system. BTLV 123:10-52. [Reprinted in Maroon
　　　　　　societies, Richard Price (ed.). Garden City, N.Y.:
　　　　　　Doubleday Anchor. 1973, pp. 320-69.]

686.　1968　A reply [to Hurault 1968]. CS 7 (4):67-68.

687.　1968　Continuity in change: Cottica Djuka society as a
　　　　　　changing system. BTLV 124:56-90.

688.　1969　Classificatory kinship and classificatory status: the
　　　　　　Cottica Djuka of Surinam. Ma (N.S.) 4:236-49.

689.　1969　Law at the village level: the Cottica Djuka of Surinam.
　　　　　　In Law in culture and society, Laura Nader (ed.).
　　　　　　Chicago: Aldine, pp. 117-40. [HU/ASC/□]

689a.　1975　Opportunism in religious behavior. *In* Explorations in
　　　　　　the anthropology of religion, W. E. A. van Beek and
　　　　　　J. H. Sherer (eds.). Verhandelingen van het Instituut
　　　　　　voor Taal-, Land- en Volkenkunde 74. The Hague:
　　　　　　Martinus Nijhoff, pp. 46-54. [DLC/KTLV/□]

689b.   1975   The periphery of a political system: the Cottica Djuka
                   of Surinam. PoA 1(3-4).
*690.   n.d.   Of freedom and bondage: the Cottica Djuka of
                   Suriname. MS. In preparation.

KOHLER, JOSEF
691.   1912   Zum Negerrecht in Surinam. ZVR 27 (3):392-403.

KÖLBING, FRIEDRICH LUDWIG
*692.   1832   Die Übersicht der Missions-Geschichte der evang.
                   Brudergeschichte in ihrem ersten Jahrhundert.
                   [SU/□/□]

KOM, A. de
693.   1934   Wij slaven van Suriname. Amsterdam: Contact N.V.
                   [Tweede druk 1971.] [DLC/KTLV/SM]

KONINKLIJK INSTITUUT VOOR DE TROPEN
*693a. 1962   Catalogus van de tentoonstelling Suriname. Amsterdam.
                   [O/KITC/□]
694.   1969   Suriname. Landendocumentatie no. 118/119.
                   Amsterdam: Advies- en Documentatiebureau, afd.
                   Agrarisch Onderzoek, Koninklijk Instituut voor de
                   Tropen. [DLC/KTLV/SM]

KOORNDIJK, E. M.
695.   1952   Een blik in het leven der Bosnegers. Gem no. 2:4-11.
696.   1954   Een geopende deur voor het evangelie aan de Suriname
                   rivier. Gem 2(1):11-19.
*697.   1959   Mission im Buschland von Suriname. HM 108 (22 Juni).

KOORNDIJK, E. R.
698.   1939   Uit de zendingsarbeid aan de Tapanahony. OS no.
                   2:20-24.

KOPPERS, JAKOB
699.   1911   Niederländisch Guyana oder Surinam. Bonn: Paul Rost.
                   [NYP/KTLV/SM]

KOULEN, PAUL
700.   1973   Schets van de historische ontwikkeling van de
                   manumissie in Suriname (1733-1863). SSMM 12:8-36.

KRETSCHMER, HERBERT
701.   1952   Der Gaddo-Tikki: Eine Erzählung nach Missionsberichten
                   frei gestaltet. Lahr: Ernst Kaufman. [O/BHZ/□]

KROENNER, Le R. P.
702.   1868   Correspondance: Guyane Française (Amérique
                   méridionale). [Mission des Paramakas.] LMC 1:162-65.

KROLIS, H. J.
*703.   1927   Pimba doti. Pe 146.
*704.   1934   Donker boschland. OS juni (6):88-91.

KRUIJER, G. J.
705. 1953   Suriname en zijn buurlanden. Meppel: J. A. Boom en
                zoon. [2e herziene druk.] [DLC/KTLV/SM]
706. 1968   Suriname en zijn buren: landen in ontwikkeling.
                Meppel: J. A. Boom en zoon. [DLC/KTLV/SM]
KUHN, F. A.
707. 1828   Beschouwing van den toestand der Surinaamsche
                plantagieslaven. Amsterdam: C. G. Sulpke.
                [DLC/KTLV/SM]
KUIJPERS, A.
*708. 1929   Uittreksel uit een brief: de Boschnegers timmeren niet
                hoog. Vo 15 dec.
*709. 1931/32   Wisi (tovermiddel Boschnegers). PD 12:68-71, 131, 140.
KUNITZ, J. D.
710. 1805   Surinam und seine Bewohner oder Nachrichten über die
                geographischen, physischen, statistischen, moralischen
                und politischen Verhältnisse dieser Insel während eines
                Zwanzigjährigen Aufenthalts daselbst. Erfurt: Beyer
                und Maring. [DLC/UBA/□]
van der KUYP, EDWIN
*711. 1939   Verslag van een dienstreis naar de omgeving van
                Koffiekamp en Ganzee van 4-20 juli 1939. MS.
                [O/□/DV]
712. 1950   Contribution to the study of the malarial epidemiology
                in Surinam. Amsterdam: Koninklijk Vereeniging
                Indisch Instituut Mededeling No. 89, Afdeling
                Tropische Hygiëne No. 18. [AGS/KTLV/SM]
713. 1950   Iets over de malaria in Suriname. WIG 31:181-92.
714. 1962   Literatuuroverzicht betreffende de voeding en de
                voedingsgewoonten van de Boslandcreool in Suriname.
                NWIG 41 (3):205-71.
715. 1970   Voedingsgewoonten in Suriname. Voe 31:407-33.
716. 1973   Medisch-wetenschappelijk onderzoek. *In* 100 jaar
                Suriname: gedenkboek i.v.m. één eeuw immigratie
                (1873-5 juni-1973), J. H. Adhin (ed.). Paramaribo:
                Nationale Stichting Hindostaanse Immigratie, pp.
                129-40. [O/KTLV/SM]
KUYPERS, MGR. ST.
717. n.d.   Transmigratie der Bosnegers i.v.m. Brokopondoplan.
                MS. [O/□/Bi]
ter LAAG, A. A.
*718. 1912   De zending in Suriname van de Evangelische
                Brüder-unität in het bijzonder in betrekking tot hare
                bezittingen in die kolonie. The Hague: Luctor et
                Emergo. [O/UBU/□]

LABORIA, JOSEPH EMMANUEL
719.   1843   De la Guyane Française et de ses colonisations. Paris: J. Corréard. [DLC/BM/□]

de LAMBERTERIE, R.
720.   1947   Notes sur les Boni de la Guyane Française. JSAP 35:123-47.

LAMMENS, ADRIAAN FRANÇOIS
*721.   n.d.   Mémoires en onuitgegeven werken met de daartoe
        [1788-   relatieve stukken. MS. [O/□/SM]
        1836]

LAMPE, P. H. J.
722.   1928/29   Het Surinaamsche treefgeloof, WIG 10:545-68.

LAMUR, H. E.
723.   1965   De levensomstandigheden van de in Paramaribo werkende Aukaner arbeiders. NWIG 44:119-32.

van der LAND, SIPKE
724.   1970   Open oog voor Suriname. Zeist: Uitgeverij N.I.B. [DLC/KTLV/SM]

LARSEN, HENRY and MAY PELLATON
725.   1956   Pirogues sous les lianes: expédition Maroni-Oyapoc. Neuchâtel: Editions de la Baconnière. [NYP/□/□]

726.   1958   Behind the lianas: exploration in French Guiana. Edinburgh and London: Oliver and Boyd. [Translation, by A. and G. Reid, of item 725.] [NYP/KTLV/□]

LASERRE, GUY
727.   1950   En Guyane Française: les pays de l'Oyapoc. CO 3:77-83.

728.   1952   Noirs et indiens des pays du Maroni (Guyane Française). CO 5:84-89. [Review of André Sausse, 1951, Populations primitives . . .]

LAURIERS, L. A.
729.   1967   Zending, missie, onderwijs en volksontwikkeling. Sc 66:29-36.

LA VARRE, WILLIAM
730.   1936   The kingdom of the black rebels of Surinam. Tr 66 (4):29-31.

*731.   1937   Auf der suche nach dem "Weissen Gott." BIZ 26 Aug. en 2 Sept.

732.   1948   My black friend's thumbprint. RD (March):83-102.

LA VARRE, WILLIAM and ALICE LA VARRE
*733.   1937,   Ontdekkingsreis onder de Djukajs [sic]. StL 3 and 4.
        1938?

LAWTON, J. S.
733a.   1975   Awari banje. SM march:22-23.

LEDDERHOSE, KARL FRIEDRICH
734.   1847   Die Mission unter den freien Buschnegern in Surinam
                    und Rasmus Schmidt. Heidelberg: Universitäts
                    Buchhandlungen von Karl Winter. [Dritte Ausgabe,
                    1876] [Y/KTLV/SM]

LEERDAM, H.
735.   1932   De strijd om het oerwoud van Suriname. Verslag van
                    het werk onder de Aukaners aan de Tapanahonij over
                    het jaar 1931. OS mei (5):67-77.
*736.   1935   Ons werk in Botopasi (Boven-Suriname). MeN no. 4.
737.   1935   Verslag over het medisch werk aan de Boven-Suriname.
                    OS april (4):67-71.
*738.   1938   Van den medischen arbeid in het oerwoud. OS dec. (12).
739.   1955-57   Onze bosbewoners. We 1955: 30 Dec; 1956: 31 Jan,
                    3 April, 4 April, 8 May, 31 May, 26 June, 10 July,
                    11 Aug, 17 Sept, 25 Sept, 9 Oct, 10 Nov, 23 Nov,
                    3 Dec, 20 Dec, 29 Dec; 1957: 21 Jan, 14 Feb, 19 Mar,
                    22 Mar, 23 Mar, 1 April, 2 April, 13 April, 23 April,
                    7 May, 9 May, 18 May, 25 May, 8 June, 26 June.

LEERDAM, H. and J. LEERDAM
740.   1939   De nood der Saramaccanen. OS sept (9):135-6.

LEERDAM, J. M.
*741.   1934   Hoe men in Nieuw-Goejaba het Kerstfeest viert. OS
                    maart (4).
*742.   1934   Uit het boschland. OS jan. (1):4-10.
743.   1935   Het nieuwe zendingshuis te Nw. Goejaba. OS juni
                    (6):93-96.
744.   1935   Het werk onder de Awana-negers op Nw. Goejaba.
                    OS (2):34-39.
745.   1936   Het licht breekt door in het donkere boschland. OS nov.
                    (11):165-170.
746.   1936   Uit de boschlandzending: iets over de reis van Brs.
                    Steinberg en Fischer aan de Boven-Suriname. OS juli
                    (7):97-103.
*747.   1937   In fellen strijd met de machten der duisternis. OS april
                    (4).
*748.   1938   Medisch werk onder de Boschnegers. MeN no. 3.
749.   1939   Hoe de Boschnegers handelen met hun zickten en
                    dooden. OS nov.(12):175-79.
*750.   1946   De zendingspost te Poese Groenoe, Suriname. MMo
                    Feb. (no. 582). [Cited in WIG 27:319.]

de LEEUW, HENDRIK
751.   1937   Onze West. Amsterdam: Wereldbibliotheek.
                    [NYP/KTLV/SM]
752.   1938   Crossroads of the Caribbean Sea. Garden City: Garden
                    City Publishing Co. [DLC/□/SM]

[LEFROY, CHRISTOPHER EDWARD]
752a.   1826   Outalissi; a tale of Dutch Guiana. London: J. Hatchard
                     and Son. [DLC/BM/□]
LEGÊNE, J. J.
*752b. 1960   225 jaar Suriname-zending: herdenkingsnummer van het
                     Zeister Zendingsgenootschap. Zeist. [O/RPU/□]
LEGÊNE, P. M.
753.   1930   Zending en werkelijkheid, of de moeilijkheden bij de
                     verkondiging van het Evangelie aan de volken. Zeist: Het
                     Zendingsgenootschap der Evangelische Broedergemeente.
                     [CrU/RPU/□]
*753a. 1931   De symphonie van het oerwoud, II. (In de Surinaamsche
                     bosschen.) NZ juni.
754.   1932   Van Boschnegers en Roodhuiden . . . . The Hague: J. N.
                     Voorhoeve. [Y/KTLV/□]
*755.   1933   Met den dokter per sneltrein door het oerwoud van
                     Suriname. AP 6 sept. (no. 36).
*756.   1933   Met den dokter per sneltrein door het oerwoud van
                     Suriname. MeN no. 4.
757.   1935   Herdenking Suriname zending, twee eeuwen
                     1735-1935. Gendenkboek uitgegeven door Zeister
                     Zendingsgenootschap. Zeist. [O/BHZ/□]
*758.   1935   Surinaamsche schetsen. De kruisen in het oerwoud.
                     AWC 27 juli(no. 39).
*759.   1936   Wat het bosch mij vertelde. AWC 29 mei (no. 31).
760.   1938   Waar demonen regeeren. Zeist: Het
                     Zendingsgenootschap der Evangelische
                     Broedergemeente. [Y/KTLV/□]
761.   1941   Waar is uw broeder? Een verhaal uit het donkere
                     oerwoud van Suriname. Zeister Tracktaten No. 4.
                     Zeist: Het Zendingsgenootschap der Evangelische
                     Broedergemeente. [O/RPU/□]
*762.   1947   Een volk in nood. OS maart (no. 3).
763.   1948   Suriname: land mijner dromen! The Hague: J. N.
                     Voorhoeve. [DLC/KTLV/SM]
764.   1948   Van strijd en overwinning in Suriname: 1735-1948.
                     Zeist: Het Zendingsgenootschap der Evangelische
                     Broedergemeente. [O/KTLV/□]
765.   1949   Het leven en sterven der Bosnegers in de binnenlanden
                     van Suriname. Serie Licht in Duisternis No. 1. Zeist:
                     E.B.G. [Y/UBL/□]
766.   1949   Tani het godenkind: een roman uit de wereld der
                     demonen. The Hague: J. N. Voorhoeve.
                     [NYP/KTLV/□]
767.   1950   Swititaki: een verhaal uit het donkere oerwoud van
                     Suriname. Licht in duisternis. Zeister Tractaten, no. 1.

		Zeist; Zendingsgenootschap der Evangelische Broeder Gem. [O/KTLV/□]
768.	1952	Kinderen van het oerwoud. Zeist: Zendingsgenootschap der Evangelische Broedergemeente. [O/KTLV/□]
768a.	1954	Onder de Paramaccaners. SZ april: **43-45.**
769.	n.d.	Akoeba: een noodkreet om medische hulp uit het donkere boschland van Suriname. Zeist(?). [O/RPU/SM]
770.	n.d.	Laat de kinderkens tot mij komen! Zeist: Het Zendingsgenootschap der Evangelische Broedergemeente. [O/□/□]
771.	n.d.	Vrienden van den heere Jezus. Zeist: Het Zendingsgenootschap der Evangelische Broedergemeente. [O/RPU/□]
772.	n.d.	De wereldzending der Broedergemeente in woord en beeld. Zeist: Het Zendingsgenootschap der Evangelische Broedergemeente. [Y/□/□]
773.	n.d.	De zwarte profeet uit het oerwoud. Zeist: Zendingsgenootschap der Evangelische Broedergemeente. [Y/RPU/□]

LEJEAN, G.

774.	1856	L'intérieur de la Guyane Française. BSGP 11:246-64.

van LELYVELD, TH. B.

775.	1919/20	De kleeding der Surinaamsche bevolkingsgroepen in verband met aard en gewoonten. WIG 1:249-68, 458-70; WIG 2:20-34, 125-43.
776.	1933/34	Uit een oud dagboek. WIG 16:369-92.

LENOIR, J. D.

777.	1973	The Paramaka maroons: a study in religious acculturation. Unpublished Ph.D. dissertation, The New School for Social Research, New York. [NSSR/□/SM]
777a.	1974	Politics of Christianity and obia in a Surinam maroon society. Paper presented to the 73rd Annual Meeting of the American Anthropological Association, Mexico. MS.
777b.	1975	Surinam national development and Maroon cultural autonomy. SES 24:308-19.

LEPRIEUR

778.	1837	Exploration de la Guyane. BSGP 7:174-77.

LESCALLIER, DANIEL

779.	An VI [1798]	Exposé des moyens de mettre en valeur et d'administrer la Guyane. Paris: Du Pont. [DLC/BM/□]

LEVAT, DAVID

780.	1902	La Guyane Française en 1902. Paris: Imprimerie Universelle. [DLC/KTLV/□]

LIACHOWITZ, CLAIRE *et al.*

781.   1958   Abnormal hemoglobins in the Negroes of Surinam.
                 AJM 24 (1):19-24.

LICHTVELD, LOU

782.   1928/29,   Afrikaansche resten in de creolentaal van Suriname.
       1929/30   WIG 10:391-402, 507-26; WIG 11:72-84, 251-62.
783.   1930/31   Op zoek naar de spin. WIG 12:209-30, 305-24.
784.   1930/31   Een Afrikaansch bijgeloof: sneki-koti. WIG 13:49-52.
785.   1954   Enerlei Creools? WIG 35:59-71.
786.   1958   Van Bosnegers en Indianen. *In* Suriname in
                 stroomlijnen, J. van de Walle and H. de Wit (eds.).
                 Amsterdam: Wereld Bibliotheek, pp. 59-75.
                 [DLC/KTLV/☐]

LICHTVELD, LOU and C. F. A. BRUIJNING

787.   1957   Suriname: geboorte van een nieuw volk. Amsterdam:
                 N.V. Amsterdamsche Boek- en Courant Mij.
                 [NYP/KTLV/SM]
*788. 1957   Surinam. Neues Leben auf alter Erde. Amsterdam:
                 Wetenschappelijke Uitgeverij. [Translation of item 787.]
                 [DLC/BM/☐]
789.   1959   Suriname: a new nation in South America. Paramaribo:
                 Radhakishun. [Translation by James J. Healy of item
                 787.] [HU/BM/☐]

LICHTVELD, URSY M. and JAN VOORHOEVE

790.   1958   Suriname: spiegel der vaderlandse kooplieden. Een
                 historisch leesboek. Zwolle: W. E. J. Tjeenk Willink.
                 [NYP/KTLV/SM]

van LIER, R. A. J.

791.   1947   Cultureel leven van Indianen en Bosnegers. *In* Ons
                 Koninkrijk in Amerika, West-Indië, B. J. O. Schrieke &
                 M. J. van Heemstra, eds. The Hague: W. van Hoeve,
                 pp. 206-18. [DLC/KTLV/SM]
792.   1949   Samenleving in een grensgebied: een sociaal- historische
                 studie van Suriname. The Hague: Martinus Nijhoff.
                 [Second edition 1971. Deventer: van Loghum Slaterus.]
                 [DLC/KTLV/SM]
793.   1971   Frontier society: a social analysis of the history of
                 Surinam. Koninklijk Instituut voor Taal-, Land- en
                 Volkenkunde Translation Series 14. The Hague:
                 Martinus Nijhoff. [Translation of item 792, 1971
                 edition.] [DLC/KTLV/BCC]

van LIER, W. F.

794.   1918/19   Iets over de Boschnegers in de Boven Marowijne. Sur
                 5 feb. 1918 - 7 jan. 1919.
795.   1919   Iets over de Boschnegers in de Boven Marowijne.

		Paramaribo: H. van Ommeren. [Reprint, with additions, of item 794.] [O/ASC/□]
796.	1921/22, 1922/23	Bij de Aucaners. WIG 3:1-30; WIG 4:205-30, 597-612.
*797.	1926	Hoe Boni aan zijn einde kwam. Pe 93.
*798.	1927	De invloed van het Christendom op de Matuariërs. He 14, 15, 16. [Revised version of item 799.]
*799.	1927	Iets over de invloed van het Christendom op de Matuariers. [Lecture, 13 January, to Christelijke Jongelieden Vereeniging Paulus.] MS. [O/CvL/□]
*800.	1927	Land- en volkenkunde. Pe 165.
*801.	1930	Een en ander over het wisibegrip bij de Boshnegers. Su (October).
*802.	1930	Iets over de Rechtsbegrippen bij de Aucaners. EC, 1 Juli, no. 5.
803.	1938	Kandoe. EC 1 juli.
804.	1938	Symbolen bij de Boschnegers. [Text of a lecture delivered to the Masonic Lodge "Concordia".] MS. [O/KITA/□]
*805.	1938-40	Kina. SP nos. 4, 11, 13 and ?.
806.	1940	Aanteekeningen over het geestelijk leven en de samenleving der Djoeka's (Aukaner Boschnegers) in Suriname [met een inleiding en gegevens van C. H. de Goeje]. BTLV 99 (2):131-294.
807.	1940	Notes sur la vie spirituelle et sociale des Djuka (Noirs Réfugiés Auca) au Surinam. Avec introduction et données de C. H. de Goeje. MS. [Translation by H. R. Kousbroek of item 806.] [O/KITC/□]
808.	1943	Een aanvulling van moela. Su 18 sept.
809.	1943	Kandoe, kina, moela, drie Boschnegerbegrippen. Paramaribo: Oliviera. [Reprint of items 803, 810, and 808.] [O/KTLV/SM]
*810.	1943	Kina. EC.
811.	1943	Symbolen bij de Boschnegers. SZ nos. 3, 4/5.
812.	1944	Een en ander over het wisi-begrip bij de Boschnegers. SZ nos. 3, 4, and 5/6. [Reprint with additions of item 801.]
813.	1944	Missie werk. SZ no. 8.
814.	1945	Een en ander over het wisi-begrip bij de Boschnegers. Paramaribo: Oliviera. [Offprint of item 812.] [O/KTLV/□]
815.	1945	Nieuwjaarsviering bij de Aucaners. N 31 december.
816.	1947	Iets over koenoe (het noodlot), N 4 januari.
817.	1948	Iets over de godsdienst bij de Aucaners en de Matoeariërs. Radiolezing voor de Avros op 30 september. MS. [O/CvL/BCC]
818.	1949	Iets over het animisme bij de Bosnegers. E1 1:370-75.

819. 1949   Kantamasi. MS. [O/CvL/☐]
820. 1950   Iets over het leven in het binnenland (zoals het voorheen
                 was). We 6 juli.
821. 1951   Boesi-mama. We 13 april.
822. 1951   Iets over afkodrai. We 4 mei.
823. 1951   Symbolen bij de Boschnegers. Pr 10 februari.
824. n.d.   Hoe een Djoka [sic] sterft en begraven wordt. MS.
      [1920?]   [O/CvL/☐]
825. n.d.   't Een en ander over afkôdrai, wisi, bakroe, jorka, enz.
                 [O/KITC/☐]

      van LIER, W. F. and D. MULDER
826. 1944   Orthodoxie en modernisme bij de Aucaner-Boschnegers.
                 Pr 26 augustus en 2 september.

      LINDBLOM, GERHARD
827. 1924   Afrikanische Relikte und Indianische Entlehnungen in
                 der Kultur der Busch-Neger Surinams. Gothenburg:
                 Elanders Boktryckeri Aktiebolag. [Y/KTLV/☐]
*828. 1926   Einige Details in der Ornamentik der Buschneger.
                 Riksmuseets Etnografiska Avdelning, Stockholm,
                 Smårre Meddelanden I. [DLC/BM/☐]

      van der LINDE, JAN MARINUS
*829. 1952   Introduction [to Gaander 1952]. Gem (1):1-2.
*830. 1953   Kroniek. Gem (1-2):37-40.
831. 1956   Het visioen van Herrnhut en het apostolaat der
                 Moravische Broeders in Suriname, 1735-1863.
                 Paramaribo: C. Kersten en Co. [HU/KTLV/SM]
832. 1956   Johannes King, ca. 1830-1898. [Reprinted from item
                 831.] We 9 april.
833. 1966   Surinaamse suikerheren en hun kerk. Plantagekolonie
                 en handelskerk ten tijde van Johannes Basseliers,
                 predikant en planter in Suriname, 1667-1689.
                 Wageningen: H. Veenman en Zonen.
                 [NYP/KTLV/SM]

      LISMAN, J. AEGIDIUS
834. 1849   Verslag van eene reis naar de rivier Marowijne en naar
                 het etablissement Mana, in Fransch- Guyana, uitgebragt
                 aan Zijne Excellentie den Gouverneur der Kolonie
                 Suriname, op den 16n. maart. Paramaribo: J. C. Muller.
                 [DLC/KTLV/SM]

      LOHIER, MICHEL
835. 1969   Les grandes étapes de l'histoire de la Guyane Française:
                 aperçu chronologique (1498-1968). Clamency:
                 Laballery and Co. [DLC/KTLV/☐]

      LOTH, J. E.
836. 1910   Aanteekeningen over de Djoeka's (Aucaner Boschnegers)
                 in Suriname. TKNAG (2e serie) 27:339-45.

LOTH, W. L.

837.   1879   Verslag van de expeditie tot het traceeren van een weg van Brokopondo in de Rivier Boven-Suriname tot de hoogte van het Awara-Eiland in de Rivier Boven-Saramacca. TKNAG 3:332-35 [plus map].

838.   1879   Verslag van de tweede expeditie tot het traceeren van een weg van Brokopondo aan de Rivier Suriname tot de Pedrosoengoe-vallen aan de Marowijne. TKNAG 3:159-66 [plus 2 maps].

839.   1880   Verslag van eene expeditie tot het traceeren van een weg van de Tempatiekreek naar de Rivier Suriname. TKNAG 4:250-55.

840.   1881   Verslag van een reis, gedaan in de maanden Augustus en September 1879, tot het opnemen van een gedeelte der Boven-Saramacca, de Kleine Saramacca, Moeroe Moeroe- en Mindrineti-Kreeken, alsmede het traceeren en opmeten van een lijn van af de Mindrineti Kreek naar de Rivier Suriname. TKNAG 5:10-16 [plus 1 map].

*841.   1892   Verslag van een reis naar de Lawa tot het verkennen van het terrein tusschen die rivier en de Tapanahoni en dat tusschen de Toso- en de Sarakreek, gedaan van januari tot mei 1892. Handelingen der Staten Generaal. Bijlage C. Koloniaal Verslag van 1892. Suriname, Bijlage A (5.2). [O/KTLV/SM]

842.   1893   Verslag van eene reis naar de Lawa . . . TKNAG (2^e serie) 10:73-87.

LOWENTHAL, DAVID

843.   1960   Population contrasts in the Guianas. GR 50:41-58.

844.   1972   West Indian societies. London: Oxford University Press. [DLC/KTLV/□]

LUCIENNE, Sr. M.

*845.   1934   Hoog bezoek van Granman Antindende [sic]. EM juli.

LUDWIG, JOHANN FRIEDRICH

845a.   1789   Neueste nachrichten von Surinam. Jena: Academischen Buchhandlung. [DLC/KITC/SM]

LUEDERS, CYNTHIA

846.   1973   "Lost" tribe preserves African cultural heritage: Evans and Counter visit S. America. HI March 8-14:6-7.

van LUMMEL, H. B.

*847.   1900   Suriname en de Boschnegers en andere verhalen. Rotterdam: J. M. Bredée. [O/KTLV/□]

*848.   1901   Suriname en de Boschnegers. Li 5-6. [Reprint of item 847.]

LUQUET, G. H.
849.   1933   Exposition d'ethnographie guyanaise au Trocadéro. Na
61 (2896):30-32.

LUYKEN, R.
850.   1961   Nutrient-behoefte van enkele Surinaamse
bevolkingsgroepen. SL 9:129-39.
851.   1963   Voedingsfysiologisch onderzoek in Suriname. NWIG
42:190-200.

LUYKEN, R., F. W. M. LUYKEN-KONING, *et al.*
852.   1960/61   Studies on the physiology of nutrition in Surinam.
DMGT 12:229-42, 303-14; and 13:42-54, 123-30.

LUYKX, P.
*853.   n.d.   Eerste apostolische expeditie naar de Boven-Suriname
[c. 1908]   NBC. [Cited in Morssink n.d.: 145.]

van LYNDEN, A. J. H., *et al.*
854.   1939   Op zoek naar Suriname's zuidgrens. De grens bepaling
tussen Suriname en Brazilië, 1935-1938. TKNAG
(2^e serie) 56:793-882.

van LYNDEN, J. W.
854a.   n.d.   In het oerwoud van Suriname. Zeist:
[1946]   Zendingsgenootschap der Evangelische Broedergemeente.
[O/RPU/BCC]

MAIDENBERG, H. J.
855.   1967   Surinam's proud Bush Negroes retain old customs from
Africa. NYT, December 25:17.
856.   1970   "Originals" of Surinam go their own way, NYT, March
29, section XX:3.

MALMBERG, M. G. and H. LABADIE
*857.   1944   Onderzoek van de Bosnegers aan de Marowijne. MS.
[O/□/DV]

MALOUET, V. P. [sic]
858.   An X   Collection de mémoires et correspondances
[1802]   officielles sur l'administration des colonies, et
notamment sur la Guyane française et hollandaise.
Paris: Baudouin. [DLC/KTLV/SM]

MARTIN, K.
859.   1886   Bericht über eine Reise ins Gebiet des Oberen Surinam.
BTLV 35:1-76 [plus 4 plates].
860.   1887   Westindische Skizzen: Reise-Erinnerungen. Leiden: E. J.
Brill. [HU/KTLV/SM]
861.   1888   Bericht über eine Reise nach Niederländisch West-Indien
und darauf gegründete Studien. Leiden: E. J. Brill.
[CPL/KTLV/SM]

MASTENBROEK, F. B.
862.   1962   Verschrivingen van cultuur. Sc 46:24-28.

MASTENBROEK, F. M.
863. 1953 Evangelieprediking in het bosland van Suriname. Gem (1-2):17-27.

MATHEWS, GERTRUDE S.
864. 1917 Treasure. New York: Henry Holt. [DLC/□/□]

MATHEWS, THOMAS G.
865. 1966 The three Guianas. CHi 51:333-37, 365-66.

MAUFRAIS, RAYMOND
866. 1949 Les rois des rivières de Guyane sont des africains déscendants d'esclaves revoltés. SV 31 (47):352-56, 358.
867. 1952 Aventures en Guyane; carnets. Paris: Julliard. [NYP/□/□]

MAURITIUS, JAN JACOB
*868. 1749 Aanspraak van den Herre Gouverneur van Suriname aan de Burger Officieren wegens de geapprobeerde conventie met haar Ed. Gr. Achtb. en haar advys in het maken van de vreede met de wegloopers. 13 May. [O/KB/□]

van MAZIJK, J.
869. 1967 Het medisch werk onder de Trio's, Wayana's en Aloekoe's van de Stichting Medische Zending voor Suriname in het tweede halfjaar van 1966. Paramaribo. [O/□/SM]

van der MEIDEN, J. A.
870. 1959 Suriname: materie en geest. Sc 34:16-19.

MEIJER, J.
871. 1956 Van Corantijn tot Marowijne: beknopt overzicht van de geschiedenis van Suriname. Paramaribo: Kersten. [UF/BKH/SM]
872. 1957 Sleutels tot Sranan: wegwijzer in de Surinaamse geschiedenis. Amsterdam: Meulenhoff. [NYP/BM/SM]

MEIJER, J. en F. FERRARI
873. 1955 Suriname volk en geschiedenis. Cultuur-historisch leesboek voor het Mulo en de lagere klassen van A. M. S. en kweekschool. (Tweede druk). Paramaribo: C. Kersten. [UF/□/SM]

MEISSNER, S.
873a. 1848 Verhal van den zendingspost der Evangelische Broedergemeente in het Boschnegerland van Suriname. Uit het hoogduitsch. Amsterdam: H. Höveker. [□/□/SM]
*873b. 1850 Bericht von dem Entstehen der Brüder-Mission zu Bambey. Verm. gem. R. Schmidt. Schreiberhau. [O/□/□]

MENKMAN, W. R.

*874.   1935   Boschnegers, reclamekunst en nog wat. OW jan.
                     (no. 1).
875.   1938   Moderne ontdekkingsreizen in het Surinaamsche
                     binnenland. [Review of item 733.] WIG 20:342-45.
876.   1944/45   Suriname in Willoughby's tijd. WIG 26:1-18.
877.   1946   Uit de geschiedenis der opening van het Surinaamsche
                     binnenland. WIG 27:182-92, 289-99, 321-43.
                     [Includes item 312.]
878.   1953   Slavernij-slavenhandel-emancipatie. WIG 34:103-12.

MERWE, H. te

*879.   n.d.   Zendingstocht. Delft: Meinema. [O/KTLV/□]

MICHELS, JAN

*880.   1948   Reisverslag Boven-Suriname. Mimeo. [O/□/□]
*881.   1954   Brokopondo-raad, subcommissie voor bestudering van
                     de verplaatsing van de bevolking uit het stuwmeergebied.
                     Verplaatsing bevolking. Stuk no. 54-59. MS. [O/□/□]
882.   1955   Suriname's binnenlands bestuur. VG 1:73-78.
883.   1958   Transmigratie Saramakkaners en Aukaners
                     Boven-Suriname. Paramaribo. Mimeo. [O/□/□]
*884.   1964   Transmigratie van Saramakkaners en Aukaners in de
                     Boven-Suriname. We 21, 22, 24, en 25 februari.
*885.   1965   Iets over rechtspleging en traditie bij de Bosnegers.
                     Roundtable. Mimeo. [O/□/□]
886.   1965   Operation Gwamba. Sc 60:18-24.
*887.   1969   Toelinga en Manto. Granman bij de Aloekoe. Mimeo.
                     [O/□/□]
*888.   1970   Regionale occupatievormen in Suriname. Rotary
                     Paramaribo. Mimeo. [O/□/□]
889.   1971   Tembe. Er 23 (1):43-44.
890.   1973   Transmigratie in recente tijden. *In* 100 jaar Suriname:
                     gedenkboek i. v. m. één eeuw immigratie (1873-5
                     juni-1973), J. H. Adhin (ed.). Paramaribo: Nationale
                     Stichting Hindostaanse Immigratie, pp. 31-35.
                     [O/□/SM]

MINTZ, SIDNEY W.

891.   1970   Review of Silvia W. de Groot 1969. CS 10 (2):135-36.
892.   1974   The Caribbean region. D 103 (2):45-71. [Reprinted in
                     Slavery, colonialism, and racism, Sidney W. Mintz (ed.).
                     New York: Norton, 1974, pp. 45-71.] [DLC/KTLV/□]

MINTZ, SIDNEY W. and RICHARD PRICE

893.   n.d.   An anthropological approach to the Afro-American
                     past: a Caribbean perspective. Philadelphia: ISHI
                     Publications. (In press)

MIROT, SYLVIE

894.   1954   Un document inédit sur le marronnage à la Guyane
                     Française au XVIIIe siècle. RHC 41:245-56.

[An edited, annotated English translation of the document appears as Rebel village in French Guiana: a captive's description. *In* Maroon societies, Richard Price (ed.). Garden City, N.Y.: Doubleday Anchor, 1973, pp. 312-19.] [DLC/KTLV/SM]

MOLS, J.

895. 1916 Missietochten naar de Boschnegers. *In* Een halve eeuw in Suriname, 1866-1916. Ten dankbare herinnering aan het gouden jubilé van de aankomst der eerste Redemptoristen in de missie van Suriname, samengesteld door eenige missionarissen. Paramaribo, pp. 45-47. [O/KTLV/□]

MONSELS, H. J.

896. 1952 Iets over de gemeente Botopasi. Gem (2):11-15.

MORPURGO, A. J.

897. 1932/33 Eenige opmerkingen over de Surinaamsche Negertaal. WIG 14:397-408.

898. 1935/36 Folklore in Suriname. WIG 17:116-25.

899. 1959 Brokopondo. Sc 36:3-11.

MORRISON, J. D.

900. 1912 The land of the Dutch Blacks, Dutch Guiana, where Eastern and Western customs are strangely mingled—the bush-Negroes and their "Taki-Taki"—Paramaribo, the city of mixed races—jewelry by the pound. Tr 18:40-42, 55-56.

MORSSINK, F.

*901. 1917/18 Reis van Mgr. van Roosmalen over de watervallen naar de Boschnegers. OM 1:200-12.

902. 1918 Iets over de Boschnegers in de Boven-Marowijne. [Review of W. F. van Lier 1918/19.] Su, 22 December.

903. 1918/19 Eerste reis naar de Tapanahoni (26 juli-20 aug. 1918). Vo 40:91-96, 122-28, 141-44, 155-58.

904. 1919/20 Missie in Suriname. Bezoek aan den zwarten koning der wouden. Vo 41:312-20, 346-52.

905. n.d. Boschnegeriana (misschien beter: [1934?] Silvae-nigritiana?). Eenige gegevens omtrent geschiedenis en missioneering onzer Surinaamsche Boschnegers. MS. [A typescript copy is located at Secretariaat der Surinaamse Missie, Keizersgracht 218, Amsterdam.] [O/□/Bi]

906. 1934/35 Nogmaals: de dood van Jankoeso en: nog niet het einde van een dynastie. WIG 16:91-105. [Commentary on item 620.]

MÜLLER, KARL

907. 1931/32 200 Jahre Brüdermission in Herrnhut. Herrnhut: Verlag Missionsbuchhandlung. [O/BHZ/□]

MÜLLER, BR. TH.
*908.   1922   Uit het jaarverslag van 1921 over Suriname. BHW (4).

MÜLLER, VICTOR
909.   n.d.   Surinamer Buschlandreise. [O/BHZ/☐]
        [1956?]

MUNGRA, M.
910.   1970   Toerisme. Sc 74:1-7.

de MUNNICK, O. M.
911.   1946   Het rijke ertsland Suriname en zijn problemen.
                   Hengelo: H. L. Smit. [Y/KTLV/SM]

MUNTSLAG, F. H. J.
912.   1966   Tembe: Surinaamse houtsnijkunst. Amsterdam:
                   Prins Bernhard Fonds. [Y/KTLV/SM]

NAIPAUL, V. S.
913.   1962   The middle passage. London: André Deutsch.
                   [Penguin edition 1969.] [DLC/KTLV/☐]

NASSY, DAVID de ISHAK COHEN, *et al.*
914.   1788   Essai historique sur la colonie de Surinam . . . Le tout
                   redigé sur des pieces authentiques y jointes, et mis en
                   ordre par les Régens et Réprésentans de ladite Nation
                   Juive Portugaise. [Facsimile reprint, 1968. Amsterdam:
                   S. Emmering.] [DLC/KTLV/SM]

915.   1791   Geschiedenis der kolonie van Suriname . . . . Geheel
                   op nieuw samengesteld door een gezelschap van
                   geleerde Joodsche mannen aldaar. Amsterdam en
                   Harlingen: Allart en van der Plaats. [Translation of item
                   914.] [Facsimile reprint, 1974. Amsterdam: S.
                   Emmering.] [DLC/KTLV/SM]

915a.   1974   Historical essay on the colony of Surinam 1788.
                   Translated [from item 914] by Simon Cohen; edited
                   by Jacob R. Marcus and Stanley F. Chyet. Publications
                   of the American Jewish Archives No. 8. Cincinnati and
                   New York: American Jewish Archives and KTAV
                   Publishing House. [JHU/☐/☐]

NEER, KEES
916.   1949   Viottoe. Paramaribo: van der Boomen.
                   [O/KTLV/SM]

NELSON, E.
917.   1922   Iets over de Boschnegers aan de Boven-Saramacca
                   (Suriname). BHW (1):17-19.

NETSCHER, P. M.
918.   1888   Geschiedenis van de koloniën Essequebo, Demerary,
                   en Berbice, van de vestiging der Nederlanders aldaar
                   tot op onzen tijd. [Uitgegeven door het Provinciaal
                   Utrechtsch Genootschap van Kunsten en
                   Wetenschappen.] The Hague: M. Nijhoff.
                   [Y/KTLV/SM]

NEUMANN, PETER
919.	1961	Eine verzierte Kalebassenschüssel aus Suriname. VMVL 11:481-98.
*920.	1965	Bermerkungen zu einigen Rechtsauffassungen der Buschneger Surinames. AMVD 25:1-15.
921.	1965	Zur Funktion des Bassia der Gesellschaftlichen Organisation der Buschneger Surinames. AMVD 24:61-72.
922.	1967	Wirtschaft und materielle Kultur der Buschneger Surinames: Ein Beitrag sur Erforschung afroamerikanischer Probleme. AMVD 26.

NEWMAN, THELMA
923.	1972	The wood carvers of Surinam. CH 32 (1):28-29, 57-58.

NIDA, EUGENE A.
924.	1966	African influence in the religious life of Latin America. PA 13 (4):133-38.

OLENSKI, H. E.
*924a.	1974	Het volksdeliktrecht der Saramaccaners in Suriname. Doctoraalscriptie, Leiden. [O/KI/□]

OOFT, C.
*925.	1964	Rechten van Saramaccaners. Sur 1 feb.

OOSTBURG-COP, M. J. P., M. F. ABBENHUIS, and Mrs. NICOLE SMITH
*926.	1941	Notes to accompany recordings 4731-4756, Archives of Folksong. [DLC/□/□]

ORGEAS, J.
927.	1886	La pathologie des races humaines et le problème de la colonisation; étude anthropologique et économique faite à la Guyane Française. Paris: Octave Doin. [DLC/□/□]

OSTENDORF, F. W.
928.	1962	Nuttige planten en sierplanten in Suriname. Landbouwproefstation in Suriname Bulletin No. 79. Amsterdam: Van Leeuwen. [DLC/KTLV/SM]

OTTEVANGERS, J. H.
929.	1959	Bij Suriname's vuurdansers. Sc 34:24-27.

OUDSCHANS DENTZ, FRED.
930.	1917	De boschnegers in Suriname. Bu 11 (47):563.
931.	1917/18	De bevolking van Suriname. In 1:214-19.
932.	1919	De boschnegers in Suriname. KW 19 (13 februari):2-3.
933.	1927	De kolonisatie van de Portugeesch Joodsche natie in Suriname en de geschiedenis van de Joden Savanne. Amsterdam: Menno Hertzberger. [Y/KTLV/SM]
934.	1928/29	Het einde van de legende Dahlberg-Baron. WIG 10:165-67.
935.	1929/30	Sneki-koti. WIG 11:581.
*936.	1935	Tam-tam. Ri 8 mei.

937.   1935/36   Het Boschnegerdeurslot: zijn oorsprong en toepassing.
                   WIG 17:228-30.
938.   1938   Cornelis van Aerssen van Sommelsdijck. Amsterdam:
                   P. N. van Kampen. [O/KTLV/SM]
939.   1946   Zijn de Boschnegers een gevaar voor Suriname? InN
                   23:10-11.
940.   1947   De bevolking van Suriname. WIG 29:9-10.
941.   1948   De afzetting van het Groot-Opperhoofd der
                   Saramaccaners Koffy in 1835 en de politieke
                   contracten met de Boschnegers in Suriname. BTLV
                   104:33-43.
942.   1949   Geschiedkundige tijdtafel van Suriname. Amsterdam:
                   J. H. de Bussy. [New edition of Oudschens Dentz and
                   Bueno de Mesquita 1925.] [DLC/KTLV/SM]
943.   1954   Een welvaartsplan voor Suriname in 1770, voorgesteld
                   door Gouverneur Jan Nepveu. WIG 35:91-94.
943a.   1972   Geschiedkundige aanteekeningen over Suriname en
                   Paramaribo. (Overdrukken uit De West). Paramaribo:
                   De West. [O/KTLV/BCC]

OUDSCHANS DENTZ, F. and J. A. BUENO de MESQUITA
944.   1925   Geschiedkundige tijdtafel van Suriname. Paramaribo:
                   van Ommeren. [See item 942.] [O/KTLV/BCC]

OUDSCHANS DENTZ, FRED. and HERM. J. JACOBS
945.   1917   Onze West in beeld en woord. Amsterdam: J. H. de
                   Bussy. [2^e druk, 1929.] [DLC/KTLV/SM]

van OUWERKERK de VRIES, J.
*946.   1841   Het godsdienstig onderwijs der negerslaven en de bloei
                   der kolonie Suriname in groot gevaar . . . Amsterdam:
                   ten Brink en de Vries. [O/KTLV/SM]

PAËRL, ERIC
947.   1972   Klassentrijd in Suriname. Sunschrift 59. Nijmegen:
                   Socialistische Uitgeverij. [DLC/KTLV/BCC]

PAKÓSIE, ANDRÉ R. M.
948.   1972   De dood van Boni. Paramaribo: [Available through the
                   author: Bolletriestraat 10, Paramaribo.]
                   [JHU/KTLV/□]
949.   n.d.   De bevrijding van mijn volk (a fri fu mi pipel). Mimeo.
        [1973?]   [O/□/□]
949a.   n.d.   Mijn Suriname/mi Saanan. Paramaribo. [O/□/BCC]
        [1974?]

PALGRAVE, W. G.
950.   1876   Bush Negroes. In Dutch Guiana. FR 19:536-41.
                   [Reprinted in LA 14:409-12, 1876.]
951.   1876   Dutch Guiana. London: Macmillan and Company.
                   [DLC/KTLV/SM]

PALLOTTELI, DUILIO

*951a. 1974 [Series of articles on Bush Negroes.] E July 11, 18, 25.

van PANHUYS, L. C.

952. 1896 Iets over de Marowijne-Rivier en hare geschiedenis. BKM 12:14-30.
953. 1898 Proeve eener verklaring van de ornamentiek van de Indianen in Guyana. IAE 11:51-72.
954. 1899 Boschnegers. TB (Nieuwe Reeks) 3:29-30.
955. 1899 Toelichting betreffende de voorwerpen verzameld bij de Aucaner Boschnegers. *In* Catalogus der Nederlandsche West-Indische tentoonstelling te Haarlem, pp. 74-82. [O/KTLV/□]
956. 1902 Are there pygmies in French Guiana. PICA 13:131-33.
957. 1902 Neger-Engelsche liederen en Surinaamsche folklore. Het gebruik van de Nederlandsche taal in Suriname. Suriname-lezingen gehouden voor het Koloniaal Museum te Haarlem en de Vereeniging Oost en West te 's-Gravenhage, IV. IM 25 (6):101-102.
*958. 1902 Surinaamsche versieringskunst en ornamentiek. Suriname-lezingen gehouden voor het Koloniaal Museum te Haarlem en de Vereeniging Oost en West te 's-Gravenhage, III [reported by L. Lacomblé]. IM 25 (1):1.
959. 1904 About the ornamentation in use by savage tribes in Dutch Guiana and its meaning. BTLV 56:618-21.
*960. 1904 Beiträge zur Ethnographie, Linguistik und Entdeckungsgeschichte Amerikas, dem XIII ten Amerikanisten Kongress in New York vorgelegt. The Hague. [DLC/KTLV/□]
961. 1904 Review of C. van Coll 1903. TKNAG (2^e serie) 21:164-72, 412-19.
962. 1905 About the ornamentation in use by savage tribes in Dutch Guiana and its meaning. PICA 13:209-12.
963. 1905 Verslag omtrent de door de Gonini-expeditie medegebrachte afdrukken van ornamenten. TKNAG (2^e serie) 22:168-74.
964. 1905 Verslag omtrent de door de Tapanahoni-expeditie medegebrachte afdrukken van ornamenten. TKNAG (2^e serie) 22:1022-32.
965. 1906 Näheres über die Ornamente der Naturvölker Surinams. PICA 14 (2):437-39.
966. 1908 Iets over de Marowijne rivier en hare geschiedenis. BKM 12:15-66. [Reprint, with additions, of item 952.]
967. 1908 Mitteilungen über Surinamische Ethnographie und Kolonisationsgeschichte: Trommelsprache; Tätowieren;

Zauber- und Heilmittel; Kurze Bemerkungen über
Zahlmittel und ein merkwürdiges Buch über das
Geistesleben der Indianer. PICA 16:521-40.

*967a.   1911   Une conférence musicale et scientifique (sur les chansons
et la musique de la Guyane néerlandaise). MV 23
décembre.

968.   1912   Development of ornament amongst the Bush-Negroes in
Suriname. PICA 18:380-81.

969.   1912   Les chansons et la musique de la Guyane Néerlandaise.
JSAP 9:27-39.

970.   1913   The heathen religion of Bush-Negroes in Dutch Guiana.
ACIHR 4 (Leiden):53-57.

971.   1913   Recent discoveries in Dutch Guiana. PICA 18:376-79.

972.   1917   Boschnegers. *In* Encyclopaedie van Nederlandsch
West-Indië, H. D. Benjamins and J. F. Snelleman (eds.).
The Hague: Martinus Nijhoff, pp. 152-65.
[DLC/KTLV/SM]

973.   1917   Naamgeving . . . . *In* Encyclopaedie van Nederlandsch
West-Indië, H. D. Benjamins and J. F. Snelleman (eds.).
The Hague: Martinus Nijhoff, pp. 500-2.
[DLC/KTLV/SM]

974.   1919   Een adres over Boschnegers en Indianen. WIG 1:71-72.

975.   1919   Invloeden die rassen op elkander uitoefenen,
waargenomen aan de Marowijne rivier. BNA april:3-6.

976.   1921/22   Het aantal en de woonplaatsen van de Boschnegers en
Indianen in Suriname. WIG 3:83-99.

977.   1924   About the "trafe" superstition in the colony of
Surinam. Ja 28:357-68.

978.   1924   The trafe-superstition in Suriname. PICA 21:182-85.

979.   1924/25   Review of Gerhard Lindblom 1924. WIG 6:419-26.

980.   1925   Contribution à l'étude de la distribution de la serrure
à chevilles. JSAP 17:271-74.

*981.   1928   [On the 1928 Herskovits-Kahn expedition.] NRC 7
Augustus, Avondblad B; 26 October, Avondblad B.

982.   1928   Quelques ornements des nègres des bois de la Guyane
Néerlandaise. PICA 22:231-74.

983.   1930   Ornaments of the Bush-Negroes in Dutch Guiana; a
further contribution to research in Bush-Negro art.
PICA 23:728-35.

984.   1931/32   Boschnegerkunst. WIG 13:153-62.

985.   1931/32   Surinaamsche onderwerpen op het Amerikanisten-
Congres te Hamburg. WIG 13:203-16, 310-16.

986.   1932   A propos de similitudes remarquables entre ornements
d'origine différente. RIE 2:139-44.

987.   1932/33   Folk-lore in Nederlandsch West-Indië. WIG 14:124-30.

988.   1933/34   Folklore in Suriname. WIG 16:17-32.

989.   1933/34   Suriname bekroond! WIG 16:294-301. [Review of
                   Melville J. and Frances S. Herskovits 1934.]
990.   1934   African customs and beliefs preserved for two
                   centuries in the interior of Dutch Guiana. PICAES
                   1:247-48.
991.   1934   Die Bedeutung einiger ornamente der Buschneger von
                   Niederländisch Guyana. PICA 24:196-206.
992.   1934   Quelques chansons et quelques danses dans la Guyane
                   Néerlandaise. PICA 24:207-11.
993.   1936/37   Aard en karakter van Surinaamsche liederen. WIG 18:1-12.
994.   1943   Malaria het beletsel voor Suriname's bloei. WIG 25:303-19.
995.   1943   'Sneki-koti,' inenting tegen den bijt van vergiftige
                   slangen. WIG 25:122-28.
996.   1947   A most remarkable obeah from Suriname. Et 12:93-94.

        PAREAU, A. H.
997.   1898   Onze West: Reisschetsen. The Hague: W. P. van
                   Stockum en Zoon. [O/KTLV/SM]

        PARIS, L. M. B.
*998.   An VI   Voyage à la Guiane et à Cayenne, fait en 1789
        [1798]   et années suivantes. [Cited in item 321, p. 531.]
                   [O/□/□]

        PARK, JAMES F.
998a.   n.d.   Paragraph in Djuka deliberative discourse. MS.

        PARSER, A. C.
*999.   1934   Op reis naar Zuid-Amerika. X: Boschnegers. HA 12 aug.
                   (no. 220).

        PAULME, DENISE
1000.   1967   Two themes on the origin of death in West Africa.
                   Ma 2:48-61.

        PEDRICK, HOWARD A.
1001.   1930   Jungle gold: Dad Pedrick's story. Indianapolis:
                   Bobbs-Merrill. [DLC/BM/□]

        PEOTTER, E. J. G.
1002.   1926   The runaway slaves of Dutch Guiana. The strange
                   descendants of runaway slaves—the house of the
                   magician—curious customs at birth. Tr 47 (3):17-19, 46.

        PETZOLDT, T. R.
1003.   1970   Bosnegers en Indianen. Sc 73:10-20.
1004.   1970   Cultuur en Folklore. Sc 77:34-41.

        PFAFF-GIESBERG, R.
*1005. 1931/32   Über die Verbreitung der Neger in Südamerika.
                   JWVH 50:151-58.

        PIERCE, B. E.
1006.   1971   Kinship and residence among the urban *Nengre* of
                   Surinam: a re-evaluation of concepts and theories of

the Afro-American family. Unpublished Ph.D. dissertation, Tulane University, New Orleans. [TU/□/□]

PINCKARD, G.

1006a. 1806   Notes on the West Indies. London: Longman, Hurst, Rees and Orme. [DLC/BM/SM]

PISTORIUS, THOMAS

1007. 1763   Korte en zakelyke beschryvinge van de colonie van Zuriname . . . Amsterdam: Theodorus Craijenschot. [Y/KTLV/SM]

PLEYTE, C. M.

1008. 1896   Die kwakwabank der Buschneger Surinams. G1 69:370-71.

van de POLL, WILLEM

1009. 1949   Suriname: een fotoreportage van land en volk. The Hague: W. van Hoeve. [2^e druk, 1951]. [NYP/KTLV/SM]

1010. 1951   Surinam, the country and its people. The Hague: W. van Hoeve. [Translation of item 1009. Later editions 1959, 1960.] [DLC/KTLV/□]

1011. 1954   Surinam. GM 26:654-61.

1012. 1959   Suriname. Paramaribo: Varekamp, The Hague: W. van Hoeve. [DLC/KTLV/SM]

POLLAK-ELTZ, ANGELINA

1013. 1970   Afro-Amerikaanse godsdiensten en culten. Roermond: J. J. Romen. [DLC/KTLV/□]

1014. 1971   Review of Jean Hurault 1970. MAG 101:134.

1015. 1971   Review of Silvia W. de Groot 1969. MAG 101:134-35.

1016. 1972   Cultos Afroamericanos. Caracas: Instituto de Investigaciones Históricas, Universidad Católica "Andrés Bello." [Translation, with revisions, of item 1013.] [HU/UL/□]

1017. 1972   Panorama de estudios afroamericanos. Mo 1:259-317.

1018. 1974   El concepto de múltiples almas y algunos ritos fúnebres entre los negros americanos. Caracas: Instituto de Investigaciones Históricas, Universidad Católica "Andrés Bello." [□/KTLV/□]

POOL, J. F.

1018a. 1898   De oorspronkelijke bewoners van Suriname. Nat 18:281-83, 291-95, 340-46.

PRICE, RICHARD

1019. 1969   Saramaka social structure. Unpublished Ph.D. dissertation, Harvard University, Cambridge, Massachusetts. [HU/□/□]

1020.   1970   Review of Silvia W. de Groot 1969. Ma (N.S.)
5:155.

1021.   1970   Saramaka emigration and marriage: a case study of
social change. SJA 26:157-89.

1022.   1970   Saramaka woodcarving: the development of an
Afroamerican art. Ma (N.S.) 5:363-78 [plus plates].

1023.   1972   The Guiana Maroons: changing perspectives in "Bush
Negro" studies. CS 11 (4):82-105.

1024.   1973   Avenging spirits and the structure of Saramaka
lineages. BTLV 129:86-107.

1025.   1973   Maroon societies: rebel slave communities in the
Americas, ed. by Richard Price. Garden City, N.Y.:
Doubleday Anchor. [DLC/KTLV/SM]

1026.   1973   Reply [to Jean Hurault 1973]. CS 12 (4):121-22.

1027.   1973   Review of Charles J. Wooding 1972. AA 75:1884-86.

1027a.   1973   The study of Afro-American aesthetics: a Saramaka
perspective. Paper presented to the 72nd Annual
Meeting of the American Anthropological Association,
New Orleans. MS.

1028.   1975   KiKoongo and Saramaccan: a reappraisal. BTLV
131:461-78. [Commentary on item 346.]

1029.   1975   Saramaka social structure: analysis of a maroon
society in Surinam. Caribbean Monograph Series 12.
Rio Piedras: Institute of Caribbean Studies of the
University of Puerto Rico. [DLC/KTLV/SM]

PRICE, RICHARD and SALLY PRICE

1030.   1972   *Kammbá*: the ethnohistory of an Afro-American art.
Antr 32:3-27.

1031.   1972   Saramaka onomastics: an Afro-American naming
system. Eth 11:341-67.

1032.   1976   Secret play languages in Saramaka: linguistic disguise in a
Caribbean creole. *In* Speech play on display, Barbara
Kirshenblatt-Gimblett (ed.). Philadelphia: University of
Pennsylavnia Press.

1033.   1974   The music and verbal arts of the Saramaka maroons of
Suriname: a field collection on deposit in the Archives
of Traditional Music, The Folklore Institute, Indiana
University, Bloomington, Indiana. [Includes Saramaccan
texts and annotations—1043 pp.—and original field
recordings.]

PRICE, THOMAS J.

1034.   1967   Review of Jean Hurault 1965. CS 6 (3):55-56.

1035.   1968   How three Negro cultures view their African heritage.
TA 5 (8):71-75.

1036.   1970   Ethnohistory and self-image in three New World Negro
societies. *In* Afro-American anthropology, Norman

E. Whitten, Jr. and John F. Szwed (eds.). New York: The Free Press, pp. 63-71. [DLC/KTLV/☐]

PRINCE, JOHN DYNELEY

1037.　1934　Suriname Negro-English. AS 9:181-86.

PRINS, J.

1038.　1952　Vragen inzake Bosneger-volksrecht. WIG 33:53-76.

QUANDT, C.

1039.　1807　Nachricht von Suriname und seinen Einwohnern. Görlitz: J. G. Burghart. [Facsimile reprint with foreword by H. C. van Renselaar, 1968. Amsterdam: S. Emmering.] [Y/KTLV/SM]

QUELLE, O.

1040.　1938　Sprachwissenschaftliche Forschung der Herrnhuter Missionare in Ibero-Amerika bis 1800. IAA 12:266-69.

QUINTUS BOSZ, A. J. A.

1041.　1954　Drie eeuwen grondpolitiek in Suriname. Assen: Van Gorcum. [DLC/KTLV/SM]

1042.　1965　De rechten van de Bosnegers op de ontruimde gronden in het stuwmeergebeid. SJ 5:14-21.

*1043.　1965　De rechten van de bosnegers op de ontruimde gronden in het stuwmeergebied. We 1 oktober.

van RAALTE, J.

1043a.　1973　Secularisatie en zending in Suriname. Wageningen: H. Veenman & Zonen. [JHU/KTLV/SM]

RAATZ-BARTELS, M.

*1044.　1930　Zendingsdienst in Suriname's boschland. OS dec.

RAMOS, ARTHUR

1045.　1937　As culturas negras no Novo Mundo. Bibliotheca de Divulgaçao Scientifica Vol. 12, Rio de Janeiro: Civilizaçao Brasileira, S/A. [DLC/☐/☐]

RATELBAND, K.

1046.　1944/45　Een Boschnegerschrift van Westafrikaanschen oorsprong. WIG 26:193-208.

REGERING VAN SURINAME

1047.　1955　Gids van Suriname, uitgegeven ter gelegenheid van het bezoek van H. M. Koningen Juliana en Z. K. H. Prins Bernhard. Paramaribo: N. V. Drukkerij Eldorado. [O/KTLV/SM]

REGERINGSVOORLICHTINGSDIENST SURINAME

1048.　1965　Gids ter gelegenheid van het Koninklijk bezoek aan Suriname. Oct. 1965. Paramaribo. [O/KITC/SM]

REICHEL, LEVIN THEODOR

1048a.　1860　Missions-Atlas der Brüder-Unität. Herrnhut: Missions-Verwaltung. [JHU/☐/☐]

REICHLEN, H.
1049.   1941   Une mission ethnographique en Guyane Française.
                    JSAP 33:181-83.

REID, GEORGE R.
1050.   1934   A week in Suriname. Ti 1:48-52.

RENAUD, GEORGES
*1051. 1885/6   Review of Prince Roland Bonaparte 1884. RGI
                    10(122): [?]; 11:205-7, 230-31, 253-55.

RENS, LUCIEN L. E.
1052.   1953   The historical and social background of Surinam's
                    Negro-English. Amsterdam: North-Holland
                    Publishing Co. [DLC/KTLV/SM]

van RENSELAAR, H. C.
1053.   1963   Colin, profeet van Coronie. *In* Uit Suriname's historie.
                    Amsterdam: Surinaamse Historische Kring/Sticusa,
                    pp. 20-24. [O/□/SM]
*1054. 1964   De negers van de Nieuwe Wereld. *In* Panorama der
                    volken, P. van Emst (ed.). Roermond en Maaseik:
                    J. J. Romen en Zonen, vol. 1, pp. 325-46.
                    [O/KTLV/□]
1055.   1966   Tembe: Bosnegerkunst in hout. OW 60:16-18.

van RENSELAAR, J. C. and J. D. SPECKMANN
1056.   1969   Social research on Surinam and the Netherlands
                    Antilles. NWIG 47 (1):29-59.

REULE, ANT. S.
1057.   n.d.   Avonturen in oost en west: in het goudland; onder de
        [±1900]   Boschnegers. Almelo: W. Hilarius Wzn. [O/BM/□]

RICHTER, D. JULIUS
1058.   1939   Die Deutsche Evangelische Weltmission in Wort und
                    Bild. Nürnberg: Ludwig Liebel. [Y/□/□]

de RIDDER, J. HERMAN
1059.   1857   Een levensteken op een doodenveld. Over het leven
                    van de negers en over de zending in Suriname.
                    Schoonhoven. [O/UBU/SM]

RIEMER, JOHANN ANDREUS
1060.   1801   Missions-Reise nach Suriname und Barbice zu einer
                    am Surinamflusse im dritten Grad der Linie
                    wohnenden Freinegernation. Zittau und Leipzig.
                    [O/UBL/SM]

RIJNDERS, B. J. C.
1061.   1947   Het werk van de Evangelische Broedergemeente in
                    Suriname. WIG 28:300-311.

RIKKEN, H. F.
1062.   1904   Codjo, de brandstichter: oorspronkelijk
                    historisch-romantisch verhaal uit het jaar 1832.
                    Paramaribo: J. Timmerman. [O/□/SM]

1063.   1973   Kodjo ontwerpt een plan [selection from item 1062].
                    In Kri, kra! proza van Suriname, Thea Doelwijt (ed.).
                    Paramaribo: Bureau Volkslectuur, pp. 48-54.
                    [O/KTLV/SM]

RISLER, JEREMIAS
1064.   1805   Geschichte der Mission in Sud-Amerika, *In* Erzählungen
                    aus der Geschichte der Brüderkirche (1803-5), II (3).
                    Barby: Conrad Schilling. [LTS/RPU/☐]

RIVIÈRE, PETER G.
1065.   1966   A policy for the Trio Indians of Surinam. NWIG
                    45:95-120.
1066.   1969   Marriage among the Trio: a principle of social
                    organisation. London: Oxford University Press.
                    [DLC/KTLV/SM]

RODMAN, SELDEN
1067.   1970   Ten wonders of South America: a quirky list. NYT:
                    September 27, Section X:13.

RODRIGUES BARATA, FRANCISCO JOSÉ
1068.   1944   Diario da viagem au Surinam. Belem. [Y/☐/☐]

RODWAY, JAMES
1069.   1912   Guiana: British, Dutch and French. New York:
                    Charles Scribner's Sons; London: T. Fisher Unwin.
                    [DLC/KTLV/SM]

ROETHOF, H. J.
1070.   1964   Oude en nieuwe wereld. Sc 58:17-21.

ROETHOF-ENSING, D.
1071.   1970   Medische hulp in het binnenland. Sc 75:35-39.

RONMY
1072.   1861   Excursion dans le haut Maroni (Guyane Française).
                    RMC 1:779-96 [plus map].

de ROOY, C. C.
1073.   1960   De ontwikkeling van het toerisme in Suriname. Mar
                    70:1395-1403.

ROUNTREE, S. CATHERINE
1074.   1972   Saramaccan tone in relation to intonation and
                    grammar. L 29:348-69.
1075.   1972   The phonological structure of stems in Saramaccan. *In*
                    Languages of the Guianas, Joseph E. Grimes (ed.).
                    Norman: Summer Institute of Linguistics of the
                    University of Oklahoma, pp. 22-27. [JHU/SOAS/SM]
1075a. n.d.   Saramaccan personal narrative. MS.

ROUX, H. D.
1076.   1935   L'hinterland Guyanais. Ge 64:205-27.

RUFUS
1077.   1914   Djemie; unsre jüngste Niederlassung im aussersten
                    Buschland Surinames. MBB 78:138-40.

RUFUS, J. Z. HERRENBERG, H. CLARE, and J. M. LEERDAM
1078.   1934   Unsre eingeborenen Evangelisten berichten über ihre
               Arbeit im Buschland Surinams. MBB 98:42-47.

von SACK, BARON ALBERT
1079.   1810   A narrative of a voyage to Surinam; of a residence
               there during 1805, 1806, and 1807 . . . [Letters
               translated from the German by the author.] London:
               W. Bulmer. [Y/KTLV/SM]
1080.   1818   Beschreibung einer Reise nach Surinam. Berlin: Haude
               und Spenerschen Buchhandlung. [Second edition
               1821.] [DLC/KTLV/SM]
1081.   1821   Reize naar Surinamen, verblijf aldaar . . . [Uit het
               Hoogduitsch]. Haarlem: Erven F. Bohn.
               [DLC/KTLV/SM]

de SALONTHA
1082.   1778   Précis de deux lettres avec une reflexion générale
               sur l'état présent de la Colonie de Surinam. Nimmegue:
               Isaac van Campen. [DLC/KTLV/□]

SAMSON, PH. A.
1083.   1946   Bijgeloof in de rechtszaal. WIG 27:141-46.
1084.   1964   De collectie Oudschans Dentz van de Centrale Boekerij
               van het Koninklijk Instituut voor de Tropen. De
               geschriften plakboeken en mappen van Fredrik
               Oudschans Dentz (1876-1961) voornamelijk
               betrekking hebbende op Suriname. Amsterdam.
               [DLC/KTLV/SM]

SAMUELS, JACQUES
1085.   1944   Schetsen en typen uit Suriname. Suriname Serie 7.
               Paramaribo: Drukkerij Eben Haëzer. [O/□/□]

SANCHES, DANIËL I.
*1086. 1871   Een bijdrage op bouwkunstig gebied over Suriname.
               BB 18.

van der SAR, INEKE and TON van der VALK
1087.   1969   Etnische groepen. *In* Suriname informatie. Leiden:
               Nesbie Disputorenraad, pp. 13-14. [O/KTLV/□]

SAROTTE-POULIQUEN
*1088. 1954   Documents pour servir à l'histoire des Noirs Réfugiés
               Boni de la Guyane Française. Paris: Archives du
               Ministère de la France d'Outre-Mer, sér. C-14.
               Multigraph. [O/□/□]

SAUSSE, ANDRÉ
1089.   1951   Pathologie comparée des populations primitives noires
               et indiennes de la Guyane Française. BSPE 44 (7-8):
               455-60.
1090.   1951   Populations primitives du Maroni (Guyane Française).
               Paris: Institut Géographique National. [DLC/KTLV/SM]

SAVON, SAMUEL

1091.   1974   Baaa ku baaa: mati ku mati. Paramaribo: Instituut
voor Taalwetenschap/Ministerie van Onderwijs.
[DLC/□/BCC]

1092.   1974   Bakaa kontu 2. Paramaribo: Instituut voor
Taalwetenschap/Ministerie van Onderwijs.
[DLC/□/BCC]

1093.   1974   Saamaka oto 1. Paramaribo: Instituut voor
Taalwetenschap/Ministerie van Onderwijs.
[DLC/□/BCC]

1094.   1974   Saamaka oto 2. Paramaribo: Instituut voor
Taalwetenschap/Ministerie van Onderwijs.
[DLC/□/BCC]

1095.   1974   Takuhatima oto. Paramaribo: Instituut voor
Taalwetenschap/Ministerie van Onderwijs.
[DLC/□/BCC]

1096.   1974   Wanlö bakaa kontu 1. Paramaribo: Instituut voor
Taalwetenschap/Ministerie van Onderwijs.
[DLC/□/BCC]

SCHAAD, J. D. G.

1097.   1960   Epidemiological observations in Bush Negroes and
Amerindians in Surinam. DMGT 12:38-46.

SCHÄRF, A.

1098.   1911   Ein Besuch im Buschland. Corjalfahrt nach der oberen
Suriname. Missionar . . . nacherzählt von M. Wolter.
Vierte Auflage. Kleine Traktate aus der Brüdermission
No. 12, Herrnhut: Missions-Buchhandlung.
[O/KTLV/□]

SCHELTS, M.

1099.   1914   Zu den Papoto! MBB 78:253-61.

SCHILLING, T.

1100.   1956   Musketiers van de West: een verhaal over de grote
Cottica-slavenopstand 1770-1774. Amsterdam:
H. Meulenhoff. [O/KTLV/□]

SCHIPPER, ARY

1101.   1944/45   Enkele opmerkingen over Surinaamsche muziek.
WIG 26:209-21.

SCHMELTZ, J. D. E.

1102.   1910   Die Niederländische Tumac Humac-Expedition in
Surinam. PICA 16:51-54.

SCHMIDT, LODEWIJK

*1103.   1942   Verslag van drie reizen naar de Bovenlandsche Indianen.
Bulletin No. 58, Departement Landbouwproefstation in
Suriname. Paramaribo. [O/KTLV/□]

SCHMIDT, R.

*1104.   1840   Berigt van Br. R. Schmidt, aangaande zijn bezoek bij
de vrije Auka-negers aan de Sara-kreek. BHW (8):113-117.

SCHMIDT, R. M.
*1105. 1930   De taal der Boschnegers. EC 1 juli.
1106. 1952   Strijd tussen Christendom en animisme. Gem no. 2:2-4.

SCHNABEL, HANS
1107. n.d.   Vliegtuig en oerwoud; de moderne verkeerstechniek
       [1935]   in dienst van de Missie. Amsterdam: Diligentia.
                 [DLC/□/□]

SCHNEIDER, H. G.
1108. 1891   Ein Besuch in Paramaribo. Die gute Botschaft:
                 Missionstraktate der Brüdergemeine Nr. 3. Stuttgart:
                 R. Roth. [Y/KTLV/SM]
1109. 1891   Ein Junger, ein Alter; Zwei Sittenbilder von der Mission
                 in Suriname. Nach den Aufzeichnungen zweier
                 Missionare. Die gute Botschaft: Missionstraktate der
                 Brüdergemeine Nr. 2. Stuttgart: Holland & Cie.
                 [Y/RPU/□]
1110. 1893   Die Buschneger Surinames. AMZ 20, Beiblatt (1):
                 1-16;(2): 17-30;(3): 33-48;(4): 49-64;(5): 72-80.
1110a. 1893   "Foto." Een bezoek in Paramaribo. Met een inleidend
                 woord van Ds. P. van Wijk Jr. Nijmegen: P. J. Milborn.
                 [O/KTLV/SM]
1111. 1903(?)   Ihrer Vier: Leben und Inde einiger junger
                 Missionskaufleute. Herrnhut: Verlag der
                 Missionsbuchhandlung. [Y/KTLV/SM]
1112. 1910   Heidnischer Uberglaube: Suriname. Herrnhut: Verlag
                 der Missionsbuchhandlung. [Y/□/□]
1113. 1911   Sie opfern den Teufeln. Aus der Arbeit unter den
                 Buschnegern Surinames. Die gute Botschaft.
                 Missionstraktate der Brüdergemeine No. 13. Herrnhut:
                 Verlag der Missionsbuchhandlung. [O/KTLV/□]
*1114. 1911   Zantigron oder die Schwärzesten unter den Schwarzen
                 Surinames. Herrnhut: Verlag der Missionsbuchhandlung.
                 [O/KTLV/□]

SCHÖFFER, C.
1115. 1922/25   Die Buschneger von Surinam. JMVL 9:133-34.

SCHOLZE, H.
1116. 1914   Der Djuka Wilhelm in Suriname. MBB 78:134-38.

SCHRIEKE, B. J. O., and M. J. van HEEMSTRA (eds.)
1117. 1947   Ons koninkrijk in Amerika: West-Indië. The Hague:
                 W. van Hoeve. [DLC/KTLV/SM]

SCHUCHARDT, HUGO
1118. 1914   Die Sprache der Saramakkaneger in Surinam.
                 Verhandelingen der Koninklijke Akademie van
                 Wetenschappen te Amsterdam 14 (6). Amsterdam:
                 Johannes Müller. [CPL/KTLV/SM]

SCHULER, MONICA
1119.   1970   Ethnic slave rebellions in the Caribbean and the
                    Guianas. JSH 3:374-85.

SCHULZE, ADOLF
1120.   1901   Abriss einer Geschichte der Brüdermission. Herrnhut:
                    Verlag Missionsbuchhandlung. [O/☐/☐]
*1121. 1935   Johannes King, der Buschland-prophet. In Das Buch
                    der deutschen Welt-mission, J. Richter. Gotha: L.
                    Klotz. pp. 290-93, [DLC/☐/☐]

SCHUMANN, C. L.
1122.   1778   Saramaccanisch Deutsches Wörter-Buch. In Die
                    Sprache der Saramakkaneger in Surinam, Hugo
                    Schuchardt. Verhandelingen der Koninklijke Akademie
                    van Wetenschappen te Amsterdam 14 (6), 1914.
                    Amsterdam: Johannes Müller, pp. 46-116.
                    [CPL/KTLV/SM]

SCHÜTZ, HARALD
1123.   1925/26   Schetsjes uit Albina. WIG 7:271-78.

SEDOC-DAHLBERG, BETTY
1124.   1974   Meerjarig sociaalplan: ontwikkelingskernen in de
                    distrikten en het binnenland. Paramaribo: Stichting
                    Planbureau Suriname. Mimeo. [For internal circulation,
                    Stichting Planbureau.]

SEVERO, RICHARD
1125.   1972   For Surinam tribe, city's allure is fatal. NYT
                    November 4:13.

SHAW, JOANN NEGEL
1126.   1973   African art of the two continents selected from the
                    Herskovits collection. Evanston: Northwestern
                    University Library. [NU/☐/☐]

SIBINGA MULDER, J.
*1127. 1931   De marrons van Suriname. OA 4:257-63.

SIBOUR
1128.   1861   Nos relations avec les nègres et les indiens du haut
                    Maroni (Guyane Française). RMC 1:117-29.

SIEBECK, H.
1129.   1908   Buschnegermärchen aus Surinam. HBV 7 (1):10-16.

VAN SIJPESTEIJN, C. A.
1130.   1854   Beschrijving van Suriname; historisch-, geographisch- en
                    statistisch overzigt, uit officiëlle bronnen bijeengebragt.
                    The Hague: De Gebroeders van Cleef. [Y/KTLV/SM]

SILVA NETO, SERAFIM
*1131. 1949   O dialeto crioulo de Surinam. Cu 1 (2):57-70.

SIMONS, R. D.
1132.   1921/22   Brieven uit Suriname. WIG 3:281-87.

1133. 1932/33 De maatschappelijke beteekenis der Surinaamsche
ziekten (van 1919 tot 1931). WIG 14:429-39.
1133a. 1947-55 Bosnegers. *In* E. de Bruyne, G. B. J. Hilterman, and
H. R. Hoetink (eds.), Winkler Prins Encyclopaedie,
6^e geheel nieuwe druk, pp. 624-25. [O/KB/□]
1134. 1949 Een merkwaardige brief. WIG 30:136-38.
*1135. 1959 Bijgeloof en godsziekte. Amsterdam: Uitgeverij De
Brug Djambatan. [DLC/KITC/□]
1136. 1959 Bijgeloof en lepra in de Atlantische negerzônes. VG
3 (5):5-61.
1137. 1960 Boscreool. Dj 2 (4):2-3.
1138. 1960 Bosland-Creolen. Dj 3 (1):6-7.

SMITH, J. ROBERT
1139. 1964 Pity the poor jungle animals: ISPA goes to the aid of
wildlife in Suriname. OF 61 (2):4-7.
1140. 1966 Surinam animal rescue. NH 75:24-29.

SMITH, NICOL
1141. 1941 Bush master; into the jungles of Dutch Guiana.
Indianapolis and New York: Bobbs-Merrill.
[DLC/KTLV/□]

SMITH, NORVAL S. H.
1141a. 1975 Vowel harmony in two languages of Surinam.
S 4-6:315-20.
1141b. 1975 Similarities between the vowel harmony systems of
Saramaccan and Lingala. MS.

SNELLEMAN, JOH. F.
1142. 1928/29 Boeksbespreking: Aan de Marowijne; zeven fraters met
vacantie. [Review of Anon. 1928 (?).] WIG 10:417-24.

SOKOLOV, RAYMOND A.
1142a. 1974 A greenhorn's tour of French Guiana's "green hell."
NYT November 3, XX 1, 15.

SPALBURG, J. G.
1143. 1896- Diarium Drietabbetje. MS. [O/RPU/□]
1900,
1908
1144. 1899 Schets van de Marowijne en hare bewoners. Paramaribo:
H. B. Heyde. [O/KTLV/SM]
1145. 1900 Tijdtafel der Evangelische Broeder-Gemeente in
Suriname. Paramaribo: Kersten. [O/KITC/SM]

SPITZLY, J.
1146. 1889 Ethnographische Gegenstände aus Surinam. VBS
21:212-14.
*1147. 1890 Beschreibung einer kurzen Reise nach dem Marowyne
oder Maroniflusse, dem Grenzflusse von Surinam und
Cayenne, den Wasserfäller von Armina und dem
Meriancreek. [Offprint from Jahresbericht der St.

Gallischen Naturwissenschaftlichen Gesellschaft
1888/89. St. Gallen.] [O/KTLV/□]

SPRANGERS, E. CH.

1148.   1973   Ontwikkeling van de dans. *In* 100 jaar Suriname:
gedenkboek i. v. m. één eeuw immigratie
(1873–5 juni–1973), J. H. Adhin (ed.). Paramaribo:
Nationale Stichting Hindostaanse Immigratie, pp.
181-83. [O/□/SM]

STAAL, G. J.

1149.   1921/22   Het voorspel der installatie van den posthouder bij
de Aucaners. WIG 3:630-36.

1150.   1922/23   Boschneger-herinneringen. WIG 4:42-47.

1151.   1922/23   Overeenkomst met de Aucaner Boschenegers
(geteekend 20 September 1921). WIG 4:48-52.

1152.   1928   Nederlandsch Guyana. Een kort begrip van Suriname.
Bibliotheek voor Cultuur en Wetenschap. Amsterdam:
Groot Nederland. [O/KTLV/SM]

STAEHELIN, F.

1153.   1909   Tiermärchen der Bushneger in Surinam. HBV 8 (3):
173-184.

1154.   1913-19   Die Mission der Brüdergemeine in Suriname und Berbice
im achtzehnten Jahrhundert. Herrnhut: Vereins für
Brüdergeschichte in Kommission der
Unitätsbuchhandlung in Gnadau. [JHU/KTLV/SM]

STAGE, H. H.

1155.   1947   DDT has a namesake in Dutch Guiana (an application
of DDT to cognomination). MN 7:55-57.

STAHEL, G.

1156.   1930   Over de jacht in Suriname. IM 53 (33):708-9.

1157.   1944   Het Boschneger vraagstuk en het Coronieplan.
Departement Landbouwproefstation in Suriname,
Mededeling 9, Paramaribo. [Y/KTLV/SM]

STAHEL, G., *et al.*

1158   1926,   De expeditie naar het Wilhelmina-gebergte (Suriname)
1927   in 1926. TKNAG (2^e serie) 43:545-96, 651-59, 662-68,
757-79; 44:16-65, 209-63, 383-92.

STAMPAERT, GASTON

*1159.   1924/25   Schetsen uit West-Indië: de Boni negers. Z.

STAUDE, A. C.

*1160.   1890   Reise zu den heidnischen Aukanern an der oberen
Cottica, Likanan und Coermotibo vom 5 bis 15.
November 1889, geschrieben 1890. MS. [O/ABU/□]

STEDMAN, CAPTN. J. G.

1161.   1796   Narrative, of a five-years' expedition, against the
revolted Negroes of Surinam, in Guiana, on the Wild
Coast of South America; from the year 1772, to 1777.

London: J. Johnson & J. Edwards. [Reprinted 1971. Barre, Mass.: Imprint Society.] [A portion of Volume 2 is reprinted as Guerilla warfare: a European soldier's view. *In* Maroon societies, Richard Price (ed.). Garden City, N.Y.: Doubleday Anchor, 1973, pp. 305-11.] [DLC/KTLV/SM]

1162. 1799/ Reizen naar Surinamen, en door de binnenste
      1800 gedeelten van Guyana. Amsterdam: Johannes Allart. [Translation of Stedman 1796.] [Facsimile reprint, 1974. Amsterdam: S. Emmering.] [DLC/KTLV/SM]

STEINBERG, H. G.

1163. 1933 Ons Suriname. De zending der Evangelische Broedergemeente in Nederlandsch Guyana. The Hague: N.V. Algemeene Boekhandel voor inwendige en uitwendige Zending. [Y/KTLV/SM]

*1164. 1936 In het boschland aan de Suriname-rivier. NZ juli (no. 7).

van STOCKUM, A. J.

1165. 1904 Verslag van de Saramacca-expeditie. TKNAG (2^e serie) 21:88-122, 227-310, 651-721, 822-78, 1022-58.

1166. 1905 Een ondekkingstocht in de binnenlanden van Suriname. Dagboek van de Saramaka-expeditie. Amsterdam. [O/KTLV/SM]

STRUYCKEN de ROYSANCOUR, C. A. J.

*1167. 1909/10 Expeditie naar de Djoeka-kreek. Handelingen der Staten Generaal. Bijlage C, Koloniaal Verslag: II Suriname supplement. [O/KTLV/□]

STUART of DROMANA, [HENRY WINDSOR] VILLIERS

1168. 1891 Adventures amidst the equatorial forests and rivers of South America; also in the West Indies and the wilds of Florida. London: John Murray. [DLC/KTLV/SM]

SUE, EUGÈNE

1169. 1844 The adventures of Hercules Hardy; or Guiana in 1772. (Translated from the French by Thomas Pooley.) New York: J. Winchester, New World Press. [UV/□/□]

SUMWALT, MARTHA MURRAY

1170. 1971 Surinam in pictures. New York: Sterling. [DLC/KTLV/□]

SURINAMER

*1171. 1927 Jankoesoe en de Volkenbond. HP 30 april.

SWEET, R.

*1172. 1961 Aucaners weren beschaving af. P1 11 (1):6-10, 27-30.

SYNNOTT, ANTHONY

1173. 1971 Slave revolts in Guyana and Trinidad: a history and comparative analysis. MS. Sir George Williams University, Montreal. [O/□/□]

TAMANCO, JULIO [pseud of W. J. van BALEN]

1174.   n.d.   Ons Amerikaansche gebiedsdeelen. Utrecht: Joh.
        [1942?]   de Liefde. [O/KTLV/□]

TAYLOR, DOUGLAS RAE

1175.   1963   The origin of West Indian creole languages: evidence
                  from grammatical categories. AA 65:800-814.
1176.   1964   Review of Donicie and Voorhoeve 1963. IJAL
                  30:434-39.
1177.   1964   Review of Jean Hurault 1961. AA 66:1193-95.
1178.   n.d.   Languages of the Caribbean. Baltimore: Johns Hopkins
                  University Press. In press.

TEENSTRA, M. D.

1179.   1833   Bijzonderheden betrekkelijk den brand te Paramaribo,
                  in den nacht van den 3den op den 4den september
                  1832. Paramaribo: J. J. Englebrecht. [Y/□/SM]
1180.   1835   De landbouw in de kolonie Suriname. Groningen: H.
                  Eekhoff Hz. [CU/KTLV/SM]
1181.   1842   De negerslaven in de kolonie Suriname en de uitbreiding
                  van het Christendom onder de heidensche bevolking.
                  Dordrecht: H. Lagerweij. [DLC/KTLV/SM]

TEX-BOISSEVAIN, A. den

1182.   n.d.   Tora bij de Trio's. Amsterdam: N. V. Drukkerij
        [1923?]   Jacob van Kampen. [O/KTLV/□]

van THIEL, P. H.

*1183. 1961   De malariaproblematiek in verband met de uitvoering
                  van het Brokopondo-project. Mimeo. The Hague:
                  Stichting Surinaams-Nederlands Instituut voor de
                  Volksgezondheid in Suriname [Sunevol]. [O/□/□]
*1184. 1962   De kans op infectie met Filaria en Schistosoma in
                  verband met de uitvoering van het Brokopondo-Project.
                  Mimeo. The Hague: Stichting Surinaams-Nederlands
                  Instituut voor de Volksgezondheid in Suriname.
                  [O/KITC/□]

THODEN van VELZEN, H. U. E.

*1185. 1964   De dood van een granman. VN 11 juli.
1186.   1965   Review of Jean Hurault 1961, Les Noirs Réfugiés
                  Boni de la Guyane Française. Afr 35:333-34.
1187.   1965   Review of Silvia W. de Groot 1963. AA 67:1609-10.
1187a. 1965   Visiting deities. [16 mm. black and white film with
                  sound, 10 min., available through Instituut für den
                  wissenschaftlichen Film, W 870.]
*1188. 1966   De registratie van sociale processen. Ku 7 (2):21-25.
1189.   1966   Het geloof in wraakgeesten: bindmiddel en splijtzwam
                  van de Djuka matri-lineage. NWIG 45:45-51.
1190.   1966   Politieke beheersing in de Djuka maatschappij: een
                  studie van een onvolledig machtsoverwicht. Leiden:
                  Afrika-Studiecentrum. Mimeo. [O/KTLV/SM]

1191.   1973   Robinson Crusoe and Friday: strength and weakness of
                   the Big Man paradigm. Ma (N.S.) 8:592-612.
1192.   1974   Beroering onder de Bosnegers. K no. 5 (mei):2-10.
1192a. 1975   Why disorder? In Rule and reality: essays in honour of
                   André J. F. Köbben, Peter Kloos and Klaas W. van der
                   Veen (eds.). Amsterdam: Universiteit van Amsterdam,
                   Afdeling Culturele Antropologie, Antropologisch-Socio-
                   logisch Centrum Uitgave 8, pp. 134-54. [JHU/KTLV/□]
1192b. n.d.   Power wielding in Tapanahoni Djuka society: a field
                   analysis. MS.
1193.   n.d.   Some aspects of power exertion in Tapanhoni Djuka
                   society: a field analysis. MS. [Y/□/□]

   THODEN van VELZEN, H. U. E. and WILHELMINA van WETERING
1193a. 1975   On the political impact of a prophetic movement in
                   Surinam. In Explorations in the anthropology of
                   religion: essays in honor of Jan van Baal, W. E. A. van
                   Beek and J. H. Scherer (eds.). Verhandelingen van het
                   Koninklijk Instituut voor Taal-, Land- en Volkenkunde
                   74. The Hague: Martinus Nijhoff. [DLC/KTLV/□]
1193b. n.d.   Djuka religious leaders. MS. in preparation.

   THOMPSON, ROBERT FARRIS
1194.   1970   From Africa. YAM 34 (2):16-21.
1195.   1974   African art in motion: icon and act in the Collection of
                   Katherine Coryton White. Berkeley and Los Angeles:
                   University of California Press. [DLC/□/□]
1196.   n.d.   An aesthetic of the cool: the transatlantic tradition.
                   New York: Harper & Row. (In press.)

   THOMPSON, STANBURY
1197.   1962   The journal of John Gabriel Stedman. London: The
                   Mitre Press. [DLC/BM/BCC]
1198.   1966   John Gabriel Stedman: a study of his life and times.
                   Stapleford (Notts.): Thompson and Co. [DLC/BM/□]

   THOMSON, J. R.
1199.   1903   Overzicht der geschiedenis van Suriname. The Hague:
                   Martinus Nijhoff. [Tweede, vermeerderde druk.]
                   [DLC/KTLV/SM]

   van TRAA, A.
1200.   1946   Suriname 1900-1940. Deventer: W. van Hoeve.
                   [Y/KTLV/SM]

   TRIPOT, J.
1201.   1910   La Guyane. Au pays de l'or, des forçats, et des peaux
                   rouges. Paris: Plon-Nourrit. [DLC/BM/SM]

   TROUWBORST, A.
1202.   1964   Review of Jean Hurault 1961, Les Noirs Réfugiés Boni
                   de la Guyane Française. Anth 6:118-20.

   UITTENBOGAARD, LEO
*1203. 1959   Het mirakel van Brokopondo. Wk 5 september.

UITTENBOGAARD, LEO and SIMON CARMIGGELT

*1204.   1959   In de geheimzinnigheid van het achterland. Wk 29
                     augustus.

VALK, W.

1205.   1923   Iets over de Boschnegers. Nat 43:349-51, 355-59.

VANDERCOOK, JOHN WOMACK

1206.   1925   White magic and black, the jungle science of Dutch
                     Guiana. HMa 151:548-54.

1207.   1926   Eternal life in the jungle. HMa 152:510-16.

1208.   1926   Jungle commonwealth and jungle marriage. HMa
                     152:771-79.

1209.   1926   Jungle survival. HMa 152:235-41.

1210.   1926   Tom-tom. New York and London: Harper and Brothers.
                     [DLC/KTLV/SM]

1211.   1926   We find an African tribe in the South American jungle.
                     Me 14 (3):19-22.

1212.   1927   Magic is the jungle science: the black tribes of Guiana do
                     not believe in death. Me 14 (12):18-19.

*1213.   1927   Surinam: South America's melting pot. WoT February.

1214.   1935   Tam-tam, een oerwoudstaat in Suriname. Amsterdam:
                     Wereldbibliotheek. [Translation of item 1210.]
                     [O/KTLV/SM]

VAN DER ELST, DIRK H.

1215.   1970   The Bush Negro tribes of Surinam, South America: a
                     synthesis. Unpublished Ph.D. dissertation,
                     Northwestern University, Evanston, Ill. [NU/□/SM]

1216.   1974   The real Ningre. [Reply to Woodward 1974] New 84
                     (15):17.

1217.   1975   The Coppename Kwinti: notes on an Afro-American
                     tribe in Surinam. Part I: History and development.
                     NWIG 50:7-17.

1218.   1975   The Coppename Kwinti: notes on an Afro-American
                     tribe in Surinam. Part II: Organization and ideology.
                     NWIG 50:107-122.

1219.   1975   The Coppename Kwinti: notes on an Afro-American
                     tribe in Surinam. Part III: Culture change and viability,
                     NWIG 50:200-11.

VATTER, E.

1220.   1925   Ein bemaltes Büffelfell und andere amerikanische
                     Ethnographica im Städt. Völkermuseum zu Frankfurt
                     a. M. AAEU 2:75-112.

van der VEER, JOHAN J.

1221.   1969   De daad bij het woord: zendingswerk in Suriname.
                     Baarn: Bosch en Keuning. [HU/BM/SM]

VEER, W. N.

1222.   1960   Volk en religie. Sc 38:8-11.

VERRILL, A. HYATT
1223.   1925   Indians of Surinam. InNo 2:309-13.

VERSCHUUR, G.
1224.   1894   Voyage aux trois Guyanes et aux Antilles. Paris:
                    Hachette. [DLC/KTLV/SM]

VERSTEEG, G.
1225.   1905   Op expeditie in Suriname. EGM 30:170-84, 249-56,
                    317-28.

VIDAL, G.
1226.   1862   Voyage d'exploration dans le Haut-Maroni, Guyane
                    Française (septembre à novembre 1861). RMC
                    5:512-48, 638-62 [and map facing p. 564].
1227.   1862   Voyage d'exploration dans le haut Maroni, Guyane
                    Française (septembre à novembre, 1861). Paris:
                    Challamel. [DLC/□/□]

VIRCHOW, R.
1228.   1887   Bericht über den Schädel und das Becken eines
                    Buschnegers und den Schädel eines Karburgers von
                    Surinam. ZE 19:615-24.

VLIER, M. L. E.
1229.   1863   Beknopte geschiedenis der kolonie Suriname, voor de
                    meer gevorderde jeugd. Amsterdam: H. de Hoogh.
                    [DLC/KTLV/SM]
1230.   1881   Geschiedenis van Suriname. Voor de hoogste klasse
                    der volkschool. The Hague: C. van Doorn en Zoon.
                    [Revised edition of Vlier 1863.] [O/KTLV/SM]

VOIGT, J. H. P.
1231.   1837   Verhaal van Broeder J. H. P. Voigt, aangaande zijne
                    reize onder de vrije Auka- en Saramakka-negers aan de
                    Boven-Suriname, in September en October 1835. BHW
                    (1):8-16; (2):17-29; (3):33-44.

VOLDERS, J. L.
1232.   1966   Bouwkunst in Suriname: driehonderd jaren nationale
                    architectuur. Hilversum: G. van Saane. [DLC/KTLV/SM]

VOORHOEVE, JAN
1233.   1953   De studie van het Surinaams. WIG 33:175-82.
1234.   1958   Op zoek naar de handschriften van Johannes King.
                    VG 3 (1):34-40.
1235.   1958   Tori vo dem bigin vo Anakee en moro fara. KEB 52:nr.
                    13 (30 maart), 23 (8 juni), 24 (15 juni), 25 (22 juni),
                    27 (6 juli), 37 (14 sept.), 43 (26 okt.), 46 (16 nov.),
                    47 (30 nov.).
1236.   1958,   Johannes King: een mens met groot overtuiging. KEB
        1959   52:nr. 51 (28 dec.); 53:nr. 1 (4 jan.), 2 (11 jan.),
                    3 (18 jan.), 4 (25 jan.).
1237.   1959   An orthography for Saramaccan. Wo 15:436-45.

1238.   1961   A project for the study of creole language history in
                Surinam. *In* Proceedings of the Conference on Creole
                Language Studies. Creole Language Studies II, R. B.
                Le Page (ed.). London: Macmillan, pp. 99-106.
                [DLC/KTLV/□]
1239.   1961   Le ton et la grammaire dans le Saramaccan. Wo
                17:146-63.
1240.   1962   Some problems in writing tone. BT 13 (1):34-38.
                [Reprinted in Orthography studies, William A.
                Smalley (ed.), London, United Bible Societies, 1964,
                pp. 127-131.]
*1241. 1963   Johannes King: een mens met grote overtuiging, Plus
                Minus 1830-1899. We 22 mei, 24 mei.
1242.   1964   Johannes King 1830-1899. *In* Emancipatie 1863/1963.
                Biografieën. Paramaribo: Surinaamse Historische
                Kring, pp. 53-66. [O/KTLV/SM]
1243.   1967   Review of Robert A. Hall, Jr. 1966. L 18:101-5.
1244.   1971   Church creole and pagan cult languages. *In*
                Pidginization and creolization of languages, Dell Hymes
                (ed.). Cambridge: Cambridge University Press, pp.
                305-15. [DLC/KTLV/□]
1245.   1973   Historical and linguistic evidence in favour of the
                relexification theory in the formation of creoles.
                LS 2:133-45.
*1246. n.d.   De heidense obiaman en zijn invloed binnen de
                gemeente. Mimeo.
1247.   n.d.   Swadesh's 200-item list in 3 Creole languages of
        [1973] Surinam. [Prepared for use with Voorhoeve 1973.]
                Mimeo. [Y/KTLV/□]

VOORHOEVE, JAN, and ANTOON DONICIE
1248.   1963   Bibliographie du Négro-Anglais du Surinam, avec
                une appendice sur les langues créoles parlées à l'intérieur
                du pays. Koninklijk Instituut voor Taal-, Land- en
                Volkenkunde. The Hague: Martinus Nijhoff.
                [DLC/KTLV/SM]

VOORHOEVE, JAN and URSY M. LICHTVELD (eds.)
1249.   1975   Creole drum: an anthology of Creole literature in
                Surinam. English translations by Vernie A. February.
                New Haven: Yale University Press. [DLC/KTLV/SM]

VOORHOEVE, JAN and H. C. van RENSELAAR
1250.   1962   Messianism and nationalism in Surinam. BTLV
                118:193-216.

VOULLAIRE, R.
1251.   1907   A journey among the bush men of Surinam. MRW
                20 (11):815-19.
*1252. 1907   Een reis door het land der Boschnegers in Suriname: een
                vergeten zendingsterrein. NeZ 18:457-70.

1253.	1913	De zending der Broedergemeente in Suriname: 1863-1913. BHW (7):98-109.
1254.	1915	Onze Boschnegers in Suriname. Zendingsabstracten der Broedergemeente te Zeist 1. [O/UBL/SM]
*1255.	1915	Unsere Buschlandmission in Suriname. MS. [O/AHZ/☐]
1256.	1916	Onze Boschnegers in Suriname. BHW (7):102-18.
1257.	1919	Jüngste Missionsreise an die obere Saramakka. MBB 83:149-57, 173-78, 200-1, 236-40, 250-52.
1258.	1919-20	Reis naar de Boven-Saramacca. BHW 1919 (juli): 107-12; (oct.):166-68; 1920 (april):49-55; (mei):65-66.
*1259.	1923	Pobosi; uit de Surinaamsche zending. NZ juli.

VOULLAIRE, W. R.

1260.	1925	Land, Leute und Missionsleben in Suriname: eine missionsgeschichtliche Skizze und ein Handbuch für Missions-Studien-Kreise. Herrnhut: Missionsbuchhandlung. [O/KTLV/SM]

de VRIES, ANNE

1261.	1961	Dagoe, de kleine bosneger. Nijkerk; G. F. Callenbach [4^e druk]. [DLC/☐/SM]

de VRIES, JAN

1262.	1967	Het clansysteem bij de Saramaccaner Bosnegers; oorsprong en functie. MS.
1263.	1968	Rapporten betreffende het onderwijs in het binnenland van Suriname en tevens behelsende voorstellen voor planning en organisatie. Paramaribo. Mimeo. [O/☐/☐]
1264.	1969	Personeelsbeleid en culturele anthropologie. SMA 24:759-65.
1265.	1970	Het medisch werk in Suriname's bosland (een socio-pedagogische beschouwing). NWIG 47:139-57.
1266.	1972	Voorlopig verslag van een aantal aspecten van het aanvullend onderzoek naar de funktie van het onderwijs in het binnenland, in het bijzonder bij de Saramaccaners. Mimeo. [O/☐/☐]
1267.	1973	Dienstbaar onderzoek: naar een methodologie voor de agogische wetenschappen. Meppel: Boom. [O/☐/☐]

de VRIES-HAMBURGER, L.

1268.	1959	Over volkskunst in het algemeen en die van Suriname in het bijzonder. Kp 1:106-10.
1269.	1959	Sierkunst. Sc 35:17-20.
1270.	1959	Volkskunst en huisnijverheid. Sc 35:13-16.
1271.	1959	Volkskunst in Suriname. Wi 7:77-79.

de WAAL MALEFIJT, ANNEMARIE

1272.	1963	The Javanese of Suriname: segment of a plural society. Assen: Van Gorcum. [DLC/KTLV/SM]

WAALDIJK, A. L.

*1273.	1930	Moeten ook niet de Boschnegers noordwaarts? EC 1 juli.

WAALDIJK, L. TH.
*1274.   1970   Enige aantekeningen over het bosnegerrecht in
                    Suriname. Paramaribo. [O/KITC/□]
*1274a. 1974   Enige aspecten van het strafrecht der bosnegers in
                    Suriname. SJ.

WACHTER, A.
*1275.   1929   Weinachsabend in einer Buschlandgemeine (aus dem
                    Negerenglischen). MMBS nos. 1, 2.

WALLER, JOHN AUGUSTINE
1276.   1820   A voyage in the West Indies . . . with some notices and
                    illustrations relative to the city of Paramaribo, in
                    Surinam. London: Sir Richard Phillips. [DLC/BM/SM]

WALSH, JOHN with ROBERT GANNON
1277.   1967   Time is short and the water rises. New York: E. P.
                    Dutton. [DLC/KITC/SM]
1278.   1967   Time is short and the water rises. [Condensation of
                    item 1277.] RD 91 (543):213-43.
1279.   1968   De tijd is kort en het water wast. Operatie Gwamba,
                    de redding van 10,000 wilde dieren. Zwolle: La
                    Rivière en Voorhoeve N.V. [Translation of item
                    1277.] [DLC/□/SM]

WARREN, GEORGE
1280.   1667   An impartial description of Surinam upon the
                    continent of Guyana in America, with an history of
                    several strange birds, beasts, fishes, serpents, insects
                    and customs of that colony. London: William Godbid.
                    [DLC/BM/□]
1281.   1670   Een onpartydige beschrijvinge van Surinam, gelen op
                    het vaste landt van Guiana in Amerika . . . Amsterdam:
                    P. Arentsz. [Translation of item 1280.]
                    [DLC/□/SM]

WAYS, P., J. BRYANT, and I. D. GUICHERIT
1282.   1956   Histoplasmin sensitivity among the Bush Negroes of
                    Surinam. DMGT 8 (4):383-91.

WEBBER, ALBERT RAYMOND FORBES
1282a.   1931   Centenary history and handbook of British Guiana.
                    Georgetown: Argosy. [DLC/□/SM]

WEHLE, P.
1283.   1895   Suriname: onder de Aukaners; eene reis naar het
                    heidensche Matuariland; eene reis naar het Matuariland.
                    BHW (3):37-43; (8):121-27, 131-34.

WEISS, H.
1284.   1911   Ons Suriname. The Hague: Boekhandel van den
                    Zendings-studie-raad. [DLC/KTLV/SM]
1285.   1915   Vier maanden in Suriname. Nijkerk: G. F. Callenbach.
                    [Y/KTLV/SM]

1286.　1919　　Het zendingswerk der Herrnhutters in de oerwouden van
de Boven-Suriname. WIG 1:102-10.
1287.　1920　　De Zending der Herrnhutters onder de Indianen in
Berbice en Suriname 1738-1816. WIG 2:36-44, 109-21,
187-97, 249-64.

van WEL, F. J.
1288.　1967　　De zending van de Moravische Broeders. Sc 66:1-8.
1289.　1971　　De Friderici, gouverneur op de grens van twee
tijdperken. Sc 77:34-41.

van WENGEN, G. D.
1290.　1954　　The study of creole folk music in Surinam. IFM
11:45-46.

van WESTERLOO, GERARD
1290a.　1975　　Marowijne, Marowijne, of: het leven langs de rivier.
VN 36, 21 juni: 15, 17.
1290b.　1975　　Toen was er een conflict tussen hun god en mijn god.
VN 36, 28 juni: 17-19.

van WESTERLOO, GERARD and WILLEM DIEPRAM
1290c.　1975　　Frimangron. Amsterdam: Uitgeverij de Arbeiderspers.
[JHU/KTLV/BCC]

WESTERMANN, J. H.
1291.　1971　　Historisch overzicht van de wording en het onderzoek
van het Brokopondo-Stuwmeer. NWIG 48:1-55.

WESTEROÜEN van MEETEREN, F. W.
1292.　1883　　La Guyane Néerlandaise. Leiden: E. J. Brill.
[O/UBL/SM]

van WETERING, WILHELMINA
1293.　1966　　Conflicten tussen co-vrouwen bij de Djuka. NWIG
45:52-59.
1294.　1973　　Hekserij bij de Djuka: een sociologische benadering.
Academisch proefschrift, Amsterdam. Mimeo.
[O/KTLV/SM]
1295.　1973　　Witchcraft among the Tapanhoni Djuka. *In* Maroon
societies: rebel slave communities in the Americas,
Richard Price (ed.). Garden City, N.Y.: Doubleday
Anchor, pp. 370-88. [DLC/KTLV/SM]
*1295a.　1975　　The sociological relevance of a distinction between
sorcery and witchcraft. *In* Rule and reality: essays in
honour of André J. F. Köbben, Peter Kloos and Klaas
W. van der Veen (eds.). Amsterdam: Universiteit van
Amsterdam, Afdeling Culturele Antropologie,
Antropologisch-Sociologisch Centrum, Uitgave 8,
pp. 171-84. [JHU/KTLV/□]
1296.　n.d.　　The dynamics of witchcraft accusations in Djuka
society. MS. [Y/□/□]

WEYNE, J.
*1297.　1924　　De Boschnegers in Suriname. HP 28 februari.

WHITON, LOUIS CLAUDE

1298.   1962   Reconstructed African tribal life in South America.
                    EJ 40:15-20.
1299.   1970   Impact of superstition on social behavior among the
                    Djukas. EJ 48:42-54. [Reprinted in SS 6 (4).]
1300.   1971   Under the power of the Gran Gadu. NH 80 (7):14-16,
                    18, 20, 22.
1301.   1972   Under the power of the Gran Gadu. OP 39 (8):47-48,
                    51, 54, 56, 60, 64, 67, 69. [Reprint, with new photos,
                    of Whiton 1971.]
1302.   1972   Under the power of the Gran Gadu. YAM 36 (2):
                    71-73. [Reprint, with editing, of Whiton 1971.]
*1303. n.d.   Changes in the Djuka Bush Negroes of Surinam since
                    1928. MS.

WIJMANS, R. H.

1304.   1910   De Saramaccaner Boschnegers: woordenlijst, benevens
                    enkele bijzonderheden. TKNAG (2e serie) 27:681-87.

WIJNHOLT, MEINDERT RUTGERT

1305.   1965   Strafrecht in Suriname. Deventer: A. E. Kluwer.
                    [DLC/KTLV/☐]

WILLIAMS, ERIC

1306.   1970   From Columbus to Castro: the history of the
                    Caribbean 1492-1969. London: André Deutsch.
                    [DLC/KTLV/☐]

de WIT, HENDRIK

1307.   1951   Suriname en de Nederlandse Antillen: een kort
                    overzicht van de twee rijksdelen in Amerika. The
                    Hague: W. van Hoeve. [DLC/KTLV/BCC]
1308.   1963   Reizen in het binnenland van Suriname. Sc 53.

WITH, JULIAN S.

1309.   1974   Ja, ik ben een Marron. Paramaribo: H. v. d. Boomen.
                    [JHU/KTLV/☐]

WIVINE, SR. M.

*1310. 1934   Van Langa oekoe en pikien zantie. EM dec. (no. 1).
*1311. 1935   Het rouwfeest by de Aucaners. EM 25 juni (no. 7).
*1312. 1935   Oerwoudstemmen. EM 25 dec (no. 1).

WOLBERS, J.

1313.   1854   De Surinaamsche negerslaaf; verhaal van een bezoek
                    op eenige plantaadjes in Suriname. Amsterdam: H. de
                    Hoogh. [Y/KTLV/SM]
1314.   1861   Geschiedenis van Suriname. Amsterdam: H. de Hoogh.
                    [Facsimile reprint 1970. Amsterdam: S. Emmering.]
                    [DLC/KTLV/SM]

WOLFF, H. J. de

1315.   1934   Historisch overzicht over Suriname: 1613-1934. The
                    Hague: Surinaamsche Handelskantoor. [O/KTLV/SM]

1316.   n.d.   Suriname: het land der behoring, maar toch het land der
                    beproeving. The Hague: Surinaamsch Handelskantoor.
                    [O/KTLV/SM]

WONG, E.
1317.   1938 Hoofdenverkiezing, stamverdeeling en stamverspreiding der
                    Boschnegers van Suriname in de 18e en 19e eeuw.
                    BTLV 97:295-362.

WOODING, CHARLES JOHAN
1318.   1972   Winti: een afroamerikaanse godsdienst in Suriname.
                    Meppel: Krips Repro b. v. [JHU/KTLV/SM]

WOODWARD, KENNETH L.
1319.   1974   The missing link? New 84 (11):3, 51.

WOUTERS, A. E.
1320.   1972   Suriname, historische en toeristische informatie.
                    Amsterdam: Allert de Lange. [DLC/□/BCC]

WULLSCHLAEGEL, H. R.
1321.   1855   Iets over de Neger-Engelsche taal en de bijdragen tot
                    hare ontwikkeling en literatuur, door de zendelingen
                    der Evangelische broedergemeente geleverd. (In het
                    Hoogduitsch ingezonden). WI 1:286-95.

ZAMUEL, H. S.
1321a. 1975   Johannes King, ca. 1830-1899. Profiel van een
                    Surinaamse boslandprofeet. Doctoraal scriptie, Theologie,
                    Utrecht. MS. 81 pp. [O/MI/□]

ZANGEN, H.
*1322. 1922   Granman Staal-Kondre: ons eerste Boschlandstation
                    met ziekenbehandeling. BHW sept.-oct.:73-74.

1323.   1922   Helpt uw naaste! Philantropische hulpactie voor onze
                    Boschnegers aan de Boven-Suriname (boven de
                    Christelijk dorpen). Paramaribo: H. B. Heyde
                    [O/KTLV/□]

ZEEGELAAR, J. F.
1324.   1871   Suriname en de opheffing der slavernij in 1863.
                    Amsterdam: Gebroeders Binger. [O/KTLV/SM]

van ZICHEM en SWEEB
*1325. n.d.   Een reis met Jankoeso. MS. [O/□/LP]

de ZIEL, H. F.
*1326. 1956   De Boslandcreolen in Suriname. The Hague:
                    Koninklijk Bibliotheek. [O/KTLV/□]

ZIMMERMAN, G. P. H.
*1327. 1880   La rivière de Surinam. BSGP 20 (6):97-123.

1328.   1883   De Surinaamsche inboorlingen op de tentoonstelling te
                    Amsterdam in 1883. EH 1883:401-5, 413-15.

ZONNEVELD, J. I. S.
1329.   1952   Luchtfoto-geografie in Suriname. WIG 33:35-48.

ZONNEVELD, J. I. S. and G. J. KRUIJER

1330.   1951   Nederzettings- en occupatie-vormen in Suriname. TKNAG (2^e serie) 68:376-411.

Library of Congress Cataloging in Publication Data

Price, Richard, 1941-
    The Guiana Maroons.

    (Johns Hopkins studies in Atlantic history and culture)
    Includes bibliographical references.
    1. Maroons—Suriname—Bibliography. 2. Maroons—
Suriname.   3. Suriname—History. I. Title. II. Series.
Z1808.N4P74   [F2431.N3]   016.988'3   76-8498
ISBN 0-8018-1840-0